*Arthur Kitson*

# Captain James Cook

*Arthur Kitson*

**Captain James Cook**

ISBN/EAN: 9783954272242
Erscheinungsjahr: 2012
Erscheinungsort: Bremen, Deutschland

© maritimepress in Europäischer Hochschulverlag GmbH & Co. KG, Fahrenheitstr. 1, 28359 Bremen. Alle Rechte beim Verlag und bei den jeweiligen Lizenzgebern.

www.maritimepress.de | office@maritimepress.de

Bei diesem Titel handelt es sich um den Nachdruck eines historischen, lange vergriffenen Buches. Da elektronische Druckvorlagen für diese Titel nicht existieren, musste auf alte Vorlagen zurückgegriffen werden. Hieraus zwangsläufig resultierende Qualitätsverluste bitten wir zu entschuldigen.

TO MY WIFE LINDA DOUGLAS KITSON.

TO MY WIFE LINDA DOUGLAS KITSON.

# PREFACE

In publishing a popular edition of my work, Captain James Cook, R.N., F.R.S., it has, of course, been necessary to condense it, but care has been taken to omit nothing of importance, and at the same time a few slight errors have been corrected, and some new information has been added, chiefly relating to the disposition of documents.

I must not omit this opportunity of thanking the Reviewers for the extremely kind manner in which they all received the original work—a manner, indeed, which far exceeded my highest hopes.

ARTHUR KITSON.                                    LONDON, 1912.

| | |
|---|---|
| PREFACE | 3 |
| EARLY YEARS | 9 |
| 1755 TO 1757: H.M.S. EAGLE | 16 |
| 1757 TO 1759: H.M.S. PEMBROKE | 22 |
| 1759 TO 1762: H.M.S. NORTHUMBERLAND | 35 |
| 1763 TO 1767: NEWFOUNDLAND | 43 |
| 1768: PREPARATIONS FOR FIRST VOYAGE | 54 |
| 1768 TO 1769: PLYMOUTH TO OTAHEITE | 62 |
| 1769: SOCIETY ISLANDS | 71 |
| 1769 TO 1770: NEW ZEALAND | 81 |
| 1770: AUSTRALIA | 97 |
| 1770 TO 1771: NEW GUINEA TO ENGLAND | 110 |
| 1771: PREPARATIONS FOR SECOND VOYAGE | 119 |
| 1772 TO 1774: SECOND VOYAGE | 127 |
| 1774 TO 1775: SECOND VOYAGE CONCLUDED | 159 |
| 1775 TO 1776: ENGLAND | 167 |
| 1776 TO 1777: THIRD VOYAGE | 177 |
| 1777 TO 1779: THIRD VOYAGE CONTINUED | 199 |
| 1779 TO 1780: THIRD VOYAGE CONCLUDED | 217 |
| APPRECIATION AND CHARACTER | 227 |

# EARLY YEARS

James Cook, the Circumnavigator, was a native of the district of Cleveland, Yorkshire, but of his ancestry there is now very little satisfactory information to be obtained. Nichols, in his Topographer and Genealogist, suggests that "James Cooke, the celebrated mariner, was probably of common origin with the Stockton Cookes." His reason for the suggestion being that a branch of the family possessed a crayon portrait of some relation, which was supposed to resemble the great discoverer. He makes no explanation of the difference in spelling of the two names, and admits that the sailor's family was said to come from Scotland.

Dr. George Young, certainly the most reliable authority on Cook's early years, who published a Life in 1836, went to Whitby as Vicar about 1805, and claims to have obtained much information about his subject "through intercourse with his relatives, friends, and acquaintances, including one or two surviving school companions," and appears to be satisfied that Cook was of Scotch extraction. Dr. George Johnston, a very careful writer, states in his Natural History of the Eastern Borders, that in 1692 the father of James Thomson, the author of The Seasons, was minister of Ednam, Roxburghshire, and a man named John Cook was one of the Elders of the Kirk. This John Cook married, on the 19th January 1693, a woman named Jean Duncan, by whom he had a son, James, baptised 4th March 1694, and this child, Johnston positively asserts, was afterwards the father of the future Captain Cook. The dates of the marriage and baptism have been verified by the Reverend John Burleigh, minister of Ednam, and they agree with the probable date of the birth of Cook's father, for he died in 1778 at the age of eighty-five. Owing to the loss of the church records for some years after 1698, Mr. Burleigh is unable to trace when this James Cook left Ednam to "better himself," but he would take with him a "testificate of church membership" which might possibly, but not probably, still exist. Attracted, perhaps, by the number of Scotch people who flocked into the north of Yorkshire to follow the alum trade, then at its height, James Cook settled down and married; and the first positive information to be obtained is that he and his wife Grace (her maiden name has so far escaped identification, though she is known to have been a native of Cleveland) resided for some time at Morton, in the parish of Ormsby, and here their eldest child, John, was born in January 1727. Dr. Young says that James

Cook had a superstition that his mother's farewell was prophetic of his marriage, for her words were "God send you Grace."

## BIRTH-PLACE

Shortly after the birth of John, the Cooks left Morton for Marton, a village a few miles away, and the similarity of the two names has caused some confusion. At Marton the father worked for a Mr. Mewburn, living in a small cottage built of mud, called in the district a clay biggin. This cottage was pulled down in 1786, when Major Rudd erected a mansion near the spot. Afterwards, when the mansion was burned to the ground, the site of the cottage was planted with trees, and was popularly known as Cook's Garth. Dr. Young was shown the spot by an old shoemaker whose wife's mother was present at Captain Cook's birth, and he says there was a willow-tree occupying the site, but no vestige of the walls was left. Mr. Bolckow, the present owner of Marton Hall, says: "The cottage was found destroyed when my uncle bought Marton in 1854, but we came across the foundations of it when the grounds were laid out." A granite vase has been erected on the spot. The pump which Besant says still exists, and was made by Cook's father to supply his house with water, was "put there after Cook's time," and has disappeared.

In this humble clay biggin James Cook, the Circumnavigator, was born on 27th October 1728, and was registered as baptised on 3rd November in the Marton church records, being entered as "ye son of a day labourer." He was one of several children, most of whom died young; John, the eldest, who lived till he was twenty-three, and Margaret, who married a Redcar fisherman named James Fleck, being the only two that came to maturity.

The Cooks remained at Marton for some years, during which time they removed to another cottage, and young James received some instruction from a Mistress Mary Walker, who taught him his letters and a little reading. Dr. Young and Kippis call her the village schoolmistress, but Ord, who was a descendant on his mother's side, says:

"she was the daughter of the wealthiest farmer in the neighbourhood, and wife of William Walker, a respectable yeoman of the first class residing at Marton Grange."

Young James, a lad of less than eight years old, worked for Mr. Walker:

"tended the stock, took the horses to water, and ran errands for the family, and in return for such services the good lady, finding him an intelligent, active youth, was pleased to teach him his alphabet and reading."

In 1736 Cook's father was appointed to the position of hind or bailiff by Mr. Skottowe, and removed with his family to Airy Holme Farm, near Ayton. According to Besant, a hind was one who, residing on a farm, was paid a regular wage for carrying on the work, and handed over the proceeds to the landlord. Young James, now eight years of age, was sent to the school on the High Green kept by a Mr. Pullen, where he was instructed in writing and arithmetic as far as the first few rules—"reading having apparently been acquired before." He is said to have shown a special aptitude for arithmetic, and it is believed that owing to the good reports of his progress, Mr. Skottowe paid for his schooling. According to Dr. Young, his schoolfellows gave him the character of being fond of his own way, and, when any project was on foot for birds-nesting or other boyish amusement, and discussion arose as to the method to be pursued, he would propound his own plans, and insist on their superiority; should his views not meet with approval, he would pertinaciously adhere to them, even at the risk of being abandoned by his companions.

## STAITHES

Most authorities say that Cook was bound apprentice to Mr. Saunderson, a grocer and haberdasher of Staithes, at the age of thirteen; but Mrs. Dodds, Saunderson's daughter, told Dr. Young that, after leaving school, he remained on the farm, helping his father, till 1745, when he was seventeen years old and then went to Staithes to her father on a verbal agreement without indentures, and would thus be free to leave or be discharged at any time.

The shop and house where he was engaged was situated about three hundred yards from the present slipway, and close to the sea, in fact so close that in 1812 it was threatened by the water, and was pulled down by Saunderson's successor, Mr. John Smailey, and the materials, as far as possible, were used in erecting the building in Church Street which is now pointed out as Cook's Shop. The late Mr. Waddington of Grosmont, near Whitby, says he visited Staithes in 1887 and found the original site covered by deep water. He was informed by an old man, who, as a boy, had assisted in removing the stock from the old shop, that not only were the stones used again in Church Street, but also most of the woodwork, including the present door with its iron knocker, at which, probably, Cook himself had knocked many a time.

At Staithes Cook remained as Saunderson's assistant for about eighteen months, and it may easily be imagined how this growing lad listened with all his ears to the tales of the old sailors recalling brave deeds and strange experiences in storm and shine on that element which for so many years was to be his home, and at length, impelled by some instinctive feeling that on it lay the path ready at his feet to lead him on to future distinction, he vowed to himself that he would not bind down his life to the petty round of a country storekeeper.

At length the opportunity came, which is related, in a breezy and life-like manner, by Besant as follows. After painting Saunderson's character in colours of a rather disagreeable hue, as one too fond of his grog for himself and his stick for his apprentices, he says that Cook stole a shilling out of the till, packed up his luggage in a single pocket-handkerchief, ran away across the moors to Whitby, found a ship on the point of sailing, jumped on board, offered his services as cabin boy, was at once accepted, showed himself so smart and attentive that he completely won the heart of the sour-visaged mate, and through his good graces was eventually bound apprentice to the owners of the ship, and thus laid the foundation of his fortunes. This account does not explain how it was that the dishonest runaway apprentice it depicts continued to retain the friendship and esteem of his master and Mrs. Dodds.

## APPRENTICED TO THE SEA

There undoubtedly was a difficulty about a shilling, and Dr. Young's version, gathered from those who knew Cook personally and lived in Staithes and Whitby at the time, is more probable. He says that Cook had noticed a South Sea shilling, and being struck by the unusual design (it was only coined in 1723), changed it for one of his own. Saunderson had also noticed it, and when he missed it, enquired for it perhaps in somewhat unmeasured terms, but, on the matter being explained, was fully satisfied. Afterwards, seeing that the boy was bent upon a sea life, he obtained the father's permission, and took young James to Whitby himself, where he introduced him to Mr. John Walker, a member of a shipping firm of repute, to whom he was bound apprentice (not to the firm), and with whom he never lost touch till the end of his life. The period of apprenticeship was, on the authority of Messrs. John and Henry Walker, three years, and not either seven or nine as is usually stated, and the difficulty about being apprenticed to both Saunderson and Walker is, of course, set at rest by Mrs. Dodd's explanation.

Whitby was at the time a very important centre of the coasting trade, and possessed several shipbuilding yards of good reputation, and it was in a Whitby-built ship, the Freelove, that Cook made his first voyage. She was a vessel of about 450 tons (some 80 tons larger than the celebrated Bark Endeavour), was employed in the coal trade up and down the east coast, and no doubt Cook picked up many a wrinkle of seamanship and many a lesson of the value of promptitude in the time of danger which would prove of service when he came to the days of independent command: for the North Sea has, from time immemorial, been reckoned a grand school from which to obtain true sailormen for the Royal Service.

As usual in those days, Cook stayed in his employer's house in the intervals between his trips, and his time ashore was longer during the winter months as the ships were generally laid up. The house in Grape Street, at present occupied by Mr. Braithwaite, is pointed out as the one where he lived whilst with Mr. Walker; but this is incorrect, for Mr. Waddington ascertained from the rate books that Mr. Walker's mother was living there at that time, and Mr. Walker lived in Haggargate from 1734 to 1751, removing thence to the north side of Bakehouse Yard in that year, and to Grape Street in 1752, after his mother's death. That is, he did not reside in Grape Street till three years after Cook's apprenticeship was ended, when, following the usual custom, he would have to fend for himself. During these periods of leisure between his voyages, Cook endeavoured to improve his store of knowledge, and it is believed he received some instruction in elementary navigation. He made great friends with Mr. Walker's housekeeper, Mary Prowd, from whom he obtained the concession of a table and a light in a quiet corner away from the others, where he might read and write in peace. That he worked hard to improve himself is evident from the fact that Mr. Walker pushed him on at every opportunity, and gave him as varied an experience of things nautical as lay in his power.

After several voyages in the Freelove (which is stated by the Yorkshire Gazette to have been "lost, together with one hundred and fifty passengers and the winter's supply of gingerbread for Whitby, off either the French or Dutch coast" one stormy Christmas, the date not given) Cook was sent to assist in rigging and fitting for sea a vessel, called the Three Brothers, some 600 tons burden, which was still in existence towards the close of last century. When she was completed, Cook made two or three trips in her with coals, and then she was employed for some months as a transport for troops from Middleburg to Dublin and Liverpool. She was paid off by the Government at Deptford in the spring of 1749, and then traded to Norway, during which time Cook completed his apprenticeship, that is, in July 1749. Cook told the naturalist of the second South Sea voyage, Mr. Forster, that on one of his trips to Norway the rigging of the ship was completely covered with birds that had been driven off the land by a heavy gale, and amongst them were several hawks who made the best of their opportunities with the small birds.

### OFFERED COMMAND

When his apprenticeship had expired he went before the mast for about three years. In 1750 he was in the Baltic trade on the Maria, owned by Mr. John Wilkinson of Whitby, and commanded by Mr. Gaskin, a relative of the Walkers. The following year he was in a Stockton ship, and in 1752 he was appointed mate of Messrs. Walker's new vessel, the Friendship, on board of which he continued for three years, and of which, on the authority of Mr. Samwell, the surgeon of the Discovery on the third voyage, who paid a visit to Whitby on his return and received his information from the Walkers, he would have been given the command had he remained longer in the mercantile marine. This was rapid promotion for a youth with nothing to back him up but his own exertions and strict attention to duty, and tends to prove that he had taken full advantage of the opportunities that fell in his way, and had even then displayed a power of acquiring knowledge of his profession beyond the average.

About this time Cook's father seems to have given up his position at Airy Holme Farm and turned his attention to building. A house in Ayton is still pointed out as his work, but has apparently been partially rebuilt, for Dr. Young speaks of it as a stone house, and it is now partly brick, but the stone doorway still remains, with the initials J.G.C., for James and Grace Cook, and the date 1755. The old man has been represented as completely uneducated, but this cannot have been true. Colman in his Random Recollections, writing of a visit he paid to Redcar about 1773, relates how a venerable old man was pointed out who:

"only two or three years previously had learnt to read that he might gratify a parent's pride and love by perusing his son's first voyage round the world. He was the father of Captain Cook."

If it is true that he was the son of an Elder of the Scottish Church, it is extremely improbable that he was entirely uneducated, and the position he held as hind to Mr. Skottowe would necessitate at any rate some knowledge of keeping farming accounts. More convincing information still is to be found in the Leeds Mercury of 27th October 1883, where Mr. George Markham Tweddell, of Stokesley, writes:

"I may mention that Captain Cook's father was not the illiterate man he has been represented; and I have, lying on my study table as I write, a deed bearing his signature, dated 1755; and the father's signature bears a resemblance to that of his distinguished son."

Reading is invariably learnt before writing, and as in 1755 the old man was sixty-one, it is evident he did not wait till he was eighty to learn to read.

## FATHER'S GRAVE

He claimed to have carved the inscription on the family tombstone in Great Ayton churchyard, and after spending the last years of his life under the roof of his son-in-law, James Fleck of Redcar, he died on 1st April 1778, aged eighty-four years. He was buried in Marske churchyard, but there was nothing to mark his grave, and its place has long been forgotten. His death is registered as that of a "day labourer."

# 1755 TO 1757
# H.M.S. EAGLE

Notwithstanding the Treaty of Aix-la-Chapelle, 1748, troubles were constantly arising between the French and English in which the American Colonies of both nations took a conspicuous part, and ultimately led to open war. The first shot was fired on 10th June 1755, although war was not formally declared till May 1756. In June 1755 the Friendship was in the Thames, and it is said that to avoid the hot press which had been ordered Cook first went into hiding for some time and then decided to volunteer. This is untrue, for, as has been shown, he had already made up his mind and had refused Messrs. Walker's offer of the command of one of their ships, the acceptance of which would have saved him from the press as Masters were exempt. He now saw his opportunity had come. He knew that experienced men were difficult to obtain, that men of a certain amount of nautical knowledge and of good character could soon raise themselves above the rank of ordinary seamen, and had doubtless in his mind many cases of those who entering as seamen found their way to the quarterdeck, and knowing he had only to ask the Walkers for letters of recommendation for them to be at his service, he determined to take the important step and volunteer into the Royal Navy. It must be remembered that this act of leaving employment which, to most men of his position, would have seemed most satisfactory, was not the act of hot-headed youth, no step taken in mere spirit of adventure, but the calmly reasoned act of a man of twenty-seven years and some eight or nine years experience of both the rough and smooth sides of maritime life.

Several letters were written to Mr. Walker, one or two of which relating to a later period were seen and copied by Dr. Young, but they fell into the hand of a niece, who unfortunately, not recognising their value, destroyed them shortly before her death, which occurred some years ago. However, it is certain that he wrote one about this time and evidently received a favourable reply, for he shortly afterwards wrote again acknowledging the service done him.

### ENTERS NAVY

Having made up his mind how to proceed, Cook went to a rendezvous at Wapping and volunteered into H.M.S. Eagle, a fourth-rate,

60-gun ship, with a complement of 400 men and 56 marines, at that time moored in Portsmouth Harbour. On the Muster Roll, preserved in the Records Office, the following entry occurs: "161 from London rendezvous, James Cook, A.B., entry, June 17th 1755, first appearance June 25th 1755." On the 24th July, that is, thirty-seven days after the date of entry into the Navy, he is rated as Master's mate, a position he held till 30th June 1757, when he quitted H.M.S. Eagle.

His appointment was facilitated by the difficulty experienced in obtaining men for the Service, as may be gathered from Captain Hamar's letters, who writes applying to the Admiralty for permission to break up his London Rendezvous, as he says it has "procured very few men, and those only landsmen." Again, he complains of the quality of the men he has received, and says he is one hundred and forty short of his complement. In another letter:

"I do not believe there is a worse man'd ship in the Navy. Yesterday I received from the Bristol twenty-five supernumeraries belonging to different ships, but not one seaman among them: but, on the contrary, all very indifferent Landsmen."

These complaints were endorsed by Captain Pallisser, who succeeded Hamar on the Eagle, for he wrote that some of the crew were turned over from ship to ship so often that he was quite unable to make out their original one:

"they being such that none choose to own them. Of forty-four said to belong to the Ramilies, she wanted only six the other day, but her boatswain could find out only those amongst them that he thought worth having." In the face of these deficiencies in quantity and quality of men, and remembering the good character he doubtless obtained from Mr. Walker, there can be no surprise that when Cook sailed out of an English port for the first time as a Royal Navy sailor he held the rating of Master's mate. It is usual to look upon him as an explorer and surveyor only, but a little enquiry shows that he played an active part in some of the most stirring events of the next few years. The records of his personal deeds are wanting, but his ships saw service, and from his character it is certain that when duty called, James Cook would not be found wanting. Many of the men under whom he served have left behind names that will always be associated with the construction of the present British Empire, and with most of them he was in immediate personal contact, and obtained in every case their respect, in some their close personal friendship.

## PALLISSER COMMANDS

On the 1st July the Eagle was ordered to fit and provision for the Leeward Islands, but having received 62 men and 53 marines, the orders were changed to cruise between Scilly and Cape Clear, and she sailed on the 4th August. She was caught in a gale off the old Head of Kinsale and received some damage, and her main mast was reported as sprung, so she returned to Plymouth for survey and repairs. Thinking that the removal of the mast would be a good opportunity to scrape his ship, which was very foul, Captain Hamar had her lightened for that purpose, but on examination the mast was found to be in good order, and the Admiralty was so annoyed at the absence of the ship from her cruising ground that they ordered Captain Pallisser to take over the command and prepare for sea without further loss of time. This he did on the 1st October, and sailed from Plymouth on the 7th, and after cruising about in the Channel and making a few small captures he returned on the 22nd November, remaining till the 13th March; and during this time Cook had a short spell of sickness, but it can hardly be called serious, as he was only in hospital for ten days, being back to his duty on the 17th February. In April, when "off the Isle of Bass, brought to and sent on board the cutter a petty officer and five men with arms, provisions, etc." This extract from the log records Cook's first independent command; the cutter was one of two hired vessels which had joined the squadron the previous day under convoy, and the armed party was probably put on board as a precaution against privateers who were at that time pretty busy on the French coast. Cook took her into Plymouth Sound, and he and his five men went on board the St. Albans, and in her rejoined his own ship on the 2nd May, and then returned to Plymouth on the 4th June. Pallisser, in reporting his arrival to the Secretary of the Admiralty, said that he had:

"put ashore to the hospital 130 sick men, most of which are extremely ill: buried in the last month twenty-two. The surgeon and four men died yesterday, and the surgeon's two mates are extremely ill: have thirty-five men absent in prizes and thirty-five short of complement, so that we are now in a very weak condition."

This sickness and mortality was attributed to the absolute want of proper clothing, many of the men having come on board with only what they stood in and some in rags, so the Captain asked for permission to issue an extra supply of slops, a request that was immediately granted.

## DUC D'AQUITAINE

After another short cruise the Eagle returned to Plymouth with Pallisser very ill with fever. He obtained sick leave, and Captain Proby was ordered to take command, but was detained so long in the Downs by contrary winds that Pallisser, who had heard a rumour of a French squadron having been seen in the Channel, shook off his fever and resumed the command of his ship, which was almost ready for sea. Every part of the Channel mentioned in the rumour was carefully searched, but no signs of the enemy were seen, and the author of the report, a Swede, was detained in Portsmouth for some months.

On the 19th November the Eagle's crew was increased to 420 men, and she was kept cruising throughout the winter, and on the 4th January 1757 she was caught in a heavy gale off the Isle of Wight, where she had most of her sails blown out of her. On 25th May she sailed from Plymouth Sound in company with H.M.S. Medway, and a day or two afterwards they fell in with and chased a French East Indiaman, the Duc d'Aquitaine, in rather heavy weather. The Medway was leading, but when getting close, had to bring to in order to clear for action, as otherwise she would be unable to open her lee ports. Pallisser, on the other hand, was all ready, and pressed on, bringing the chase to action. After a hard set-to, lasting about three-quarters of an hour, the Frenchman struck, having lost 50 men killed and 30 wounded, whilst the Eagle lost 10 killed and 80 wounded; and the list of damages to the ship reported to the Admiralty shows that the action was sharp though short. The Medway was only able to afford assistance by firing a few raking shots, and suffered no damage except having ten men wounded by an accidental explosion of gunpowder. The masts and sails of the prize were so much damaged that she lost them all in the night; one of the masts in falling sank the Medway's cutter. It was found she had a complement of 493 men, and was armed with 50 guns. She had landed her East Indian cargo at Lisbon, and then proceeded to cruise for fourteen days on the look-out for an English convoy sailing in charge of H.M.S. Mermaid. She had succeeded in picking up one prize, an English brig, which was ransomed for 200 pounds. This was Cook's first experience of an important naval action, and Pallisser was complimented by the Lords of the Admiralty for his gallant conduct. The Duc d'Aquitaine was purchased for the Navy, and was entered under her own name as a third-rate, 64 gun ship, with a complement of 500 men.

The Eagle returned with her consort and her prize to Plymouth, and soon afterwards Cook's connection with her came to an end. According to Dr. Kippis, Mr. Walker had interested the Member for Scarborough, Mr. Osbaldiston, on the subject of Cook's promotion, but the rule was that candidates for Lieutenancy must have been employed on board a king's ship for a period of not less than six years, and an order had recently been issued that this regulation was to be strictly adhered to. Captain Pallisser therefore wrote to Mr. Osbaldiston that Cook:

"had been too short a time in the service for a commission, but that a Master's warrant might be given him, by which he would be raised to a station that he was well qualified to discharge with ability and credit. "The result of this correspondence is shown in the Eagle's muster roll, for on 27th June James Cook attended his last muster, and on the 30th he was discharged. The succeeding rolls registering "D. 30th June 1757. Solebay prefmnt."


## THE MERCURY COOK

At this point all the writers on Captain Cook have been led into error by following the lead of Dr. Kippis. Everyone (with the single exception of Lord Brougham, who by an evident slip of the pen puts him on board the Mersey) writes that he was appointed Master of H.M.S. Mercury, and that he joined the fleet of Admiral Saunders in the Gulf of St. Lawrence at the time of the capture of Quebec in that ship. From the Public Records it has been ascertained that the Mercury was not in the Gulf of St. Lawrence with Saunders, but in the latter half of 1759 was sent to New York, thence to Boston, and was at Spithead in April the following year. The same source also shows that not only was the Circumnavigator never on board the Mercury in any capacity, but in all probability he never even saw her. He is also said to have been Master's mate on the Pembroke, and Dr. Kippis has him appointed to three different ships on three consecutive days: the Grampus, but she sailed before Cook could join her; the Garland, but she was found to have a Master when Cook joined; and, lastly, the Mercury.

The explanation of this confusion as far as the Mercury is concerned (the rest was imagination) is that there was a second James Cook in the service, who was appointed Master of the Mercury under a warrant dated 15th May 1759 and entered on his duties immediately. He was with his ship at Sheerness on 12th July, at which time his namesake was before Quebec. On the return of the Mercury from Boston her Master was returned for some time as "sick on shore," and on 11th June 1760 was superseded by one John Emerton. Soon after he was appointed third lieutenant of the Gosport, his commission bearing date 1st April 1760, that is before he left the Mercury. He was with his new ship at the recapture of St. John's, Newfoundland, in 1762, with John Jervis, afterwards Lord St. Vincent, as his Captain. In 1765 he was on the Wolf on the Jamaica station, and was selected by Admiral Burnaby to carry despatches to the Governor of Yucatan. This duty he successfully carried out, and in 1796 published a pamphlet describing his adventures during the journey. On his return to England he applied to the Duke of Newcastle for the command of a cutter, and the letter is now in the British Museum, having been included in a collection in mistake for one written by his celebrated namesake. There is a certain similarity in the writing, but in the signature he writes the Christian name as Jas, whilst Captain Cook usually wrote Jams. The Mercury Cook was lieutenant of the Speedwell in 1773, and having had some property left him in Jersey he received leave of absence in August. He never rose above lieutenant, and disappears from the Navy List after July 1800.

A manuscript log kept by James Cook whilst Master's mate of the Eagle is now in the possession of Mr. Alexander Turnbull of Wellington, New Zealand.

# 1757 TO 1759
# H.M.S. PEMBROKE

Cook joined H.M.S. Solebay on the 30th July 1757 at Leith, where she was then stationed, but the date of his warrant has not been ascertained, although the Public Records and Trinity House have both been searched for the purpose. His stay was not long, for after a cruise of a few days she returned to Leith, and on 17th September Cook was superseded by John Nichols; in fact, his time on board was so short that his signature is not appended to any of the rolls.

In April 1757 Mr. Bissett, who was Master of the Eagle when Cook was Master's mate, and who therefore would have a better chance than any one else to measure his subordinate's character and capabilities, was appointed Master of H.M.S. Pembroke, a new ship, and superintended her fitting for sea. On 26th October he found himself transferred to the Stirling Castle, and it is only reasonable to suppose that, having formed a high opinion of Cook's work, and knowing of his ambition to rise in the service, he would give information of the opportunity and, as far as he could, push forward his friend's interests. At any rate, the Muster Rolls show that in less than six weeks from leaving the Solebay, Cook was established on board the Pembroke as Master, under a warrant bearing date 18th October 1757, and entered upon his duties on 27th October, the twenty-ninth anniversary of his birth; and from that date to his discharge into the Northumberland he signed the usual documents. At the time of his joining, the ship was fitting and victualling for sea at Portsmouth, and on 8th November she sailed for the Bay of Biscay, under the command of Captain Simcoe, returning to Plymouth on 9th February 1758.

## LOUISBERG

The British Government had decided on making a determined effort to wrest the Colony of New France from the hands of the French, and one of the few steps was to attempt the capture of the port of Louisburg, at the entrance to the Gulf of St. Lawrence; a place which the enemy were said to have rendered almost impregnable at an expenditure of some million and a quarter pounds. They looked upon it as second only to Quebec in its importance to the safe keeping of the colony. In order to carry out this design a fleet was prepared under Admiral Boscawen (known to his men as Old Dreadnought, and, from a peculiar carriage of the head, said to have been contracted from a youthful habit of imitating one of his father's old servants, Wry-necked-Dick), to convey a small army under Major-General Amherst to the scene of action. Boscawen sailed with his fleet, one member of which was the Pembroke, for Halifax, where they arrived, via Madeira and the Bermudas, on 8th May.

Having completed his arrangements, Boscawen left Halifax on 28th May with 17 sail of the Royal Navy and 127 transports, picking up 2 more men-of-war and 8 transports just outside, and a couple more of the latter a few hours later. He had to leave behind at Halifax, with orders to rejoin him as soon as they were fit, several ships, the Pembroke being one, as their crews were so weakened by scurvy during the voyage from England. The Pembroke had lost 29 men, but was sufficiently recovered to be able to sail with 3 transports, 2 schooners, and a cattle sloop on 7th June, and arrived off Louisburg on the 12th, four days too late to take part in the landing which had been successfully carried out in the face of great difficulties caused by the roughness of the weather, the rocky coast, and the opposition of the enemy. In fact, James Wolfe, who was a Brigadier throughout the siege, and on whose shoulders a very large portion of the work seems to have fallen, says: "Our landing was next to miraculous." There were 3 officers and 49 men killed; 5 officers and 59 men wounded of the army; 11 men killed, and 4 officers and 29 men wounded of the navy; and 19 men wounded of the transport service. The weather was so bad that no stores or artillery could be landed for several days, the first gun being got ashore on the 16th, so Cook was in plenty of time to take his share in the difficult task of landing supplies; a task so dangerous that the fleet lost one hundred boats in this duty alone. As well as forming the supply base for the army, the fleet also provided 583 men to act as gunners and engineers ashore; but none of these were from the Pembroke. The nature of the ground rendered the work of constructing the approaches and batteries extremely difficult, and it was not till 20th June that the first gun opened fire. Wolfe formed a battery on Lighthouse Point, one side of the entrance to the harbour whilst the town was on the other side, with a fortified island in between; and the harbour held a French fleet which, at the time of the arrival of the British, consisted of nine men-of-war. One escaped on the very day of the landing, and was shortly afterwards followed by two more. One L'Echo, was captured by Sir Charles Hardy, and was taken into the British Navy; whilst the other, though chased for some distance, made good its escape to L'Orient with the first news of the siege. Previously to the coming of the British, two ships had been sunk in the harbour's mouth to render entrance therein difficult; two more were added to these, and then a fifth. One ship was blown up by a British shell, and setting fire to two others that lay alongside her, they also were destroyed.

The fate of the other two is described in the Pembroke's log, kept by Cook, as follows:

"In the night 50 boats man'd and arm'd row'd into the harbour under the command of the Captains La Foure [Laforey] of the Hunter, and Balfour [of the Etna] in order to cut away the 2 men-of-warr and tow them into the North-East Harbour one of which they did viz.: the Ben Fison [Bienfaisant] of 64 guns, the Prudon [Prudent] 74 guns being aground was set on fire. At 11 A.M. the firing ceased on both sides."

The boats concerned in this attack, which Boscawen describes as "a very brilliant affair, well carried out," were a barge and pinnace or cutter from all the ships, except the Northumberland, which was too sickly, commanded by a lieutenant, mate or midshipman, and Dr. Grahame in his History of the United States of North America, says:

"The renowned Captain Cook, then serving as a petty officer on board of a British ship-of-war, co-operated in this exploit, and wrote an account of it to a friend in England. That he had distinguished himself may be inferred from his promotion to the rank of lieutenant in the Royal Navy, which took place immediately after."

This statement that he was in the affair may be true, but there is no evidence on the point, and as he was a warrant and not petty officer, and as his promotion did not take place for several years, Dr. Grahame's story may well be doubted. It is believed that Cook did write to Mr. Walker from Louisburg, but the letter was one of those so unfortunately destroyed.

The loss on this occasion to the British was very slight, there being only 7 killed and 9 wounded. The Bienfaisant having been surveyed, was received into the Navy and given to Captain Balfour whilst the command of L'Echo was conferred on Captain Laforey.

In consequence of this success and the threat of an immediate assault on the town, the French commander, M. Drucour, decided to surrender on the following day. This success was highly esteemed in England, and Admiral Boscawen and General Amherst received the thanks of the Houses of Parliament.

## WOLFE AND HARDY

After the siege Wolfe wrote to Lord George Sackville, speaking in warm terms of Boscawen and his men, and says: "Sir Charles Hardy, too, in particular, and all the officers of the Navy in general have given us their utmost assistance, and with the greatest cheerfulness imaginable. I have often been in pain for Sir Charles's squadron at an anchor off the harbour's mouth. They rid out some very hard gales of wind rather than leave an opening for the French to escape, but, notwithstanding the utmost diligence on his side, a frigate found means to get out and is gone to Europe charge de fanfaronades. I had the satisfaction of putting 2 or 3 hautvizier shells into her stern and to shatter him a little with some of your Lordship's 24 pound shot, before he retreated, and I much question whether he will hold out the voyage."

The Pembroke formed one of this squadron under Sir Charles Hardy, and after the capitulation of the town, was despatched with nine other ships, and a small body of troops under Wolfe to harry the French settlements around Gaspe Bay as a preparation for the attack on Quebec it was intended to make in the following year. Several settlements and magazines were destroyed, four guns and a pair of colours were captured, and then the squadron returned to Halifax for the winter.

Admiral Sir Charles Saunders was selected to command the fleet that was to be employed in this new movement against the capital of New France; a man of whom Horace Walpole wrote:

"The Admiral was a pattern of the most sturdy bravery, united with the most unaffected modesty. No man said less, or deserved more. Simplicity in his manners, generosity, and good-nature adorned his genuine love of his country."

## WITH DURELL'S SQUADRON

He left Spithead on 17th February 1759, with the intention of calling at Louisburg, the appointed rendezvous for the expedition, on his way to Halifax; but the season had been so severe that Louisburg, usually free from ice, was found to be unapproachable, so he went on, arriving at Halifax on 30th April. Admiral Durell had been sent out earlier from England, and was now despatched from Halifax with a squadron, of which the Pembroke was one, to prevent, if possible, the entry into the river of the usual spring fleet from France with supplies and reinforcements for Quebec, and to keep the French from putting up any fortifications on the Ile aux Coudres, thereby adding to the difficulties of the fleet in ascending this dangerous portion of river. The weather was bad, and the trouble caused by fog and ice so great that Durell found the fleet of 18 sail, convoyed by two frigates, had escaped him, but one or two small store ships were captured which proved of service to the British afterwards. On the way up the Gulf, Captain Simcoe of the Pembroke died, and the ship was given temporarily to Lieutenant Collins of Durell's ship, and afterwards to Captain Wheelock, who remained in her till after Cook left.

Durell's squadron arrived off the Ile aux Coudres on the 25th, and on the 28th the Pembroke landed the troops she had on board, "as did ye rest of ye men of warr," and they took possession of the island, which was found to be deserted by its inhabitants. The troops that were on board Durell's ships were under the command of Colonel Carleton, the Quartermaster-General of the force, and Wolfe's great friend, whose services had only been obtained from the king with the greatest difficulty. Whilst awaiting the arrival of Saunders with the remainder of the expeditionary force, every endeavour was made to gain knowledge of the difficulties of the river, and Cook's log notes how the boats were out "sounding ye channel of ye Traverse"; and on the 11th June there is: "Returned satisfied with being acquainted with ye Channel." The Traverse here spoken of is that channel running from a high black-looking cape, known as Cape Torment, across into the south channel, passing between the east end of the Ile d'Orleans and Ile Madame. It is still looked upon as one of the worst pieces of the river navigation.

The British had some charts of the river showing the course taken by the French vessels, for in a note to the orders issued by Saunders on 15th May to the Masters of Transports, special attention is called to "a plan or chart showing the route which His Excellency intends to make from Louisburg Harbour to the Island of Bic"; and this chart was most probably taken from one captured by Boscawen in 1755, and published in September 1759 by T. Kitchen in the London Magazine having the Traverse shown on a larger scale. The soundings taken at the time Durell was waiting would be to verify those shown on this chart.

After a short delay in Halifax, Saunders left for Louisburg to gather up the remainder of the forces and stores, and on his arrival still found the port hampered by ice; in fact, Major Knox, of the 43rd

Regiment, relates that even so late as 1st June men were able to get ashore from their ships, stepping from one piece of ice to another. There was also further cause for dissatisfaction, delay in the arrival of the ships with soldiers and stores. Some of the troops had been directed to other work without any intimation to Wolfe, whilst others were in a very bad state from scurvy and measles; some had lost their entire equipment, and it was with the greatest difficulty replaced; the supply of money was criminally small, and yet it is pleasant to read on the authority of Major Knox that:

"I had the inexpressible pleasure to observe at Louisburg that our whole armament, naval and military, were in high spirits; and though, by all accounts, we shall have a numerous army and a variety of difficulties to cope with, yet, under such Admirals and Generals, among whom we have the happiness to behold the most cordial unanimity, together with so respectable a fleet and a body of well-appointed regular troops, we have every reason to hope for the greatest success."

## ORDERS TO TRANSPORTS

Before leaving, Saunders issued his instructions as to the order of sailing. He divided the transports into two divisions, the Starboard flying a red flag, and the Larboard a white one: he assigned to each vessel its position and duties, and pointed out to each Master of a hired transport that if the orders of his officers were not promptly and exactly carried out they would be fired on, adding with a touch of grim humour that the cost of the powder and shot so expended would be carefully noted and charged against the hire of the offending ship. On the 6th June Saunders was off Newfoundland with 22 men-of-war and 119 transports, and the cold winds blowing off the snow-covered hills of that island were severely felt by the troops. On the 18th, when off the Island of Bic, they were joined by Wolfe in the Richmond, and five days after picked up Durell at the Ile aux Coudres. Here Saunders transferred his flag to the Stirling Castle, which he had selected in England for the purpose, owing to her handiness (Cook's friend, Mr. Bissett, was still on board), and leaving Durell with eleven of the deepest draught to guard against any interference from a French fleet, he proceeded up the river with the remainder. The work was hard, constantly anchoring and weighing to take every advantage of wind and tide, and the progress was slow; but at length the whole of the ships passed the Traverse, and on the

26th the fleet anchored off St. Laurent, on the Ile d'Orleans, and the troops were landed on the following day. Thus the much-dreaded passage up the St. Lawrence had been carried out, and the fact that no loss of any kind had occurred to either man-of-war or transport, reflects the very greatest credit on all engaged in the operation. Knox relates how the Master of the transport he was on, a Brother of Trinity House and Thames pilot, named Killick, refused the services of a French prisoner as pilot, and observing, "Damme, I'll show them an Englishman can go where a Frenchman dar'n't show his nose," took his ship up himself, chaffing the occupants of the mark boats as he passed, and in the end declared that it was no worse than the Thames.

The wonderful success of their passage was emphasised the afternoon after their arrival at St. Laurent when a heavy gale struck the fleet, driving several ships into collision or ashore, and causing considerable loss in anchors and cables. As soon as possible the men-of-war boats were out rendering every assistance, and all the vessels were secured but two, which were too firmly fixed to be towed off shore, and these were soon afterwards burnt by the enemy.

## FIREWORKS

Thinking to profit by the disorder which must necessarily have been caused by the storm, the French made a determined attempt to destroy the fleet by means of eight fireships which were floated down stream on the unsuspecting British. Fortunately they were ignited prematurely, and the boats of the Pembroke and other ships were again out, employed in the hazardous task of towing these undesired visitors into such places as would permit them to burn themselves out without danger to the shipping. Six were quickly got into safety, whilst the other two grounded and burnt out without causing further inconvenience. Captain Knox describes the scene as a display of "the grandest fireworks that can possibly be conceived." The only result was to cause the retirement of a picket at the western end of the Ile d'Orleans, and the officer in command, who thought he was about to be attacked in force, was to have been tried by court-martial, but being advised to throw himself on Wolfe's mercy, was pardoned for his error of judgment. To guard against a repetition of such an attack, a system of guard boats, some moored across the river and some patrolling, was established, entailing considerable extra work on the sailors.

An examination of the position showed Admiral Saunders that the safety of the fleet, and therefore the interests of the army, would be best consulted if he proceeded into the Basin of Quebec, as to remain cooped up in the south channel added to the danger if a further attempt should be made to fire the fleet. He therefore pointed out to Wolfe that the small battery established by the French on Point Levi, which threatened any ship entering into the Basin, should be taken, and the Point occupied. This was at once carried out by Monckton's brigade, and a battery was established which did serious damage to the town. When too late the French sent over three floating batteries to aid in repulsing the English, but they were driven back by one broadside from a frigate Saunders moved up for the purpose.

Montcalm had entrenched his army on the north bank of the St. Lawrence, between the rivers Charles and Montmorenci, and Wolfe determined to seize on a piece of high ground to the east of the Montmorenci, to form a camp there, and endeavour to force on a general action. In pursuance of this design, a body of about 3000 men were landed successfully on 9th July, under the protecting fire of some of the fleet, and a camp was formed, and the next few days provided employment for the boats of the Pembroke and other ships in landing men, stores, and artillery. The bombardment of the town opened on 12th July from the batteries erected at Point Levi and a portion of the fleet, and continued with little intermission till 13th September. When fire was opened on the town other ships in the Basin and guns at the camp at Montmorenci opened on Montcalm's lines at Beauport.

On the 18th two men-of-war, two armed sloops and two transports succeeded in passing the town without loss, but a third ship, the Diana, ran aground in trying to avoid collision with a transport, and was attacked by the enemy's boats, but was brought off by the Pembroke and Richmond. She was so seriously damaged that she had to be sent to Boston for repairs and then returned to England. On the 20th Wolfe joined the up-river squadron in a barge, and in passing the town had his mast carried away by a shot from the Sillery Battery, but no further damage was done. He made a short reconnaissance which led to nothing at the time, but may have had an important influence in the choice of a landing-place afterwards.

## ATTACK ON BEAUPORT

On his return to his camp at Montmorenci he decided to make an attack on the left of the French lines from boats and from his camp over a ford which was available at low tide between the falls of Montmorenci and the St. Lawrence. This attack was to be supported by the Centurion, moored in the north channel, and by two armed cats which were to be run aground as near as possible to some small redoubts, the first object of the attack. Here it is certain that Wolfe and Cook came into personal contact, for on the latter fell the duty of taking the necessary soundings for the position to be occupied by the cats, and Wolfe refers in a despatch to a conversation he had with Cook upon the matter. The attack took place on 31st July, aided by the fire of the Pembroke, Trent, and Richmond, which were "anchored clear over to the north shore before Beauport, a brisk firing on both sides," but the boats were thrown into confusion by a reef (marked on the chart as visible at low water), and were some time before they could effect a landing, then a heavy storm of rain came on, rendering the ground, which was steep, very slippery. The troops occupied one redoubt, but were so dominated by the French musketry that they could get no further, and Wolfe deemed it desirable to recall them and to stop the advance across the ford. The two cats were burnt to prevent them falling into the hands of the enemy, and the losses of the English in killed, wounded, and missing were 443, those of the French being estimated at 200. Cook says the repulse was solely owing to the heavy fire from the entrenchments, "which soon obliged our Troops to retreat back to the Boats and Montmorency"; whilst Wolfe, in a general order, throws the blame on the Louisburg Grenadiers, a picked body of men from several regiments, whom he considers got out of hand. He also, in a despatch submitted to Saunders, threw some amount of blame on the Navy, but to this the Admiral strongly objected, and it was withdrawn, Wolfe saying: "I see clearly wherein I have been deficient; and think a little more or less blame to a man that must necessarily be ruined, of little or no consequence."

It has been asserted that Cook led the boats to the attack, but as this was done by Wolfe himself, according to his own letters, and as Saunders was also out with them, both officers having narrow escapes, it seems more probable that Cook would be on his own ship, where, as she was engaged, his services would be wanted, for it was one of the Master's most important duties to work her under the Captain's orders when in action.

A few days before this attack on Beauport was made, the French again paid the fleet the undesired attention of a large fire raft composed of several small vessels chained together and laden with all sorts of combustibles—shells, guns loaded to the muzzle, tar barrels, etc., and again this was grappled by the boats and towed away to a place of safety; and then Wolfe, sending in a flag of truce the next morning, said that if the performance were repeated he should cause the instrument of destruction to be towed alongside two ships in which he had Canadian prisoners, and there let it do its worst. This somewhat cold-blooded threat was sufficient, and the experiment was not repeated.

## A NARROW ESCAPE

During the time the fleet was occupying the Basin, the Masters of the ships were constantly out making observations and sounding, partly for the necessities of the fleet and partly to throw dust in the eyes of the French; and on one occasion Cook had a narrow escape from capture, his men had to row for it to get away from the enemy, and reaching the Isle of Orleans landed just in time, for as Cook, the last man, sprang ashore from the bows an Indian boarded over the stern. The hospital picket turned out, and the French retreated. His friend, Mr. Bissett, was not so fortunate, being taken prisoner on 7th July whilst sounding in the north channel; but he was either exchanged or escaped, for he was only absent from his ship for a few days.

Wolfe, who was almost always ailing, had an attack of fever, and the worry of the repulse at Beauport rendered him incapable of duty for some days; he therefore laid before his Brigadiers plans of future movements, asking their opinions and advice. These plans were not approved, but it was suggested that an attempt should be made to land on the western side of the town and there bring the enemy to action, and Wolfe writes: "I have acquiesced in their Proposal, and we are preparing to put it into execution."

The up-river detachment had been strengthened by the addition of a few more vessels, and Murray with 1200 men had joined in an unsuccessful attempt to get at the French supply fleet which had retreated to a place of safety. He had outwitted De Bougainville, who was detached to watch him, and succeeded in destroying a magazine containing clothing, powder, and other stores, and intercepted letters which told of the surrender of Niagara and the retirement of Bourlemaque upon the Ile aux Noix, to which place Amherst was preparing to follow.

When Wolfe's resolve was taken to follow the advice of his Brigadiers, Saunders again strengthened the force above the town, placing the squadron under the command of Admiral Holmes, and on 3rd September his boats withdrew the artillery and troops from Montmorenci to Point Levi, and on the night of the 4th all the available boats and small craft were sent up, one of the last to pass being a small schooner armed with a few swivels, and called by the sailors The Terror of France. She sailed by in broad daylight, drawing the fire of every gun that could be brought to bear on her, but was untouched, and, anchoring close alongside the Admiral's ship, gave him a salute from the whole of her armament.

The troops which had been quietly marched some distance up the south bank from Point Levi were taken on board the ships, the last detachment on the night of the 12th; and Admiral Holmes sailed up the river as if to beat up the French communications, but when night fell he returned, and the landing was successfully accomplished, and is described by Saunders in his despatch as follows:

"The night of their landing, Admiral Holmes with the ships and troops was about three leagues above the intended landing-place. General Wolfe with about half his troops set off in the boats, and dropped down with the tide, and were by that means less liable to be discovered by the sentinels posted all along the coast. The ships followed them about three-quarters of an hour afterwards, and got to the landing-place just at the time that had been concerted to cover the landing, and considering the darkness of the night, and the rapidity of the current, this was a very critical operation, and very properly and successfully conducted."

In the meantime the ships in the Basin, some fifteen in number, distracted the attention of the French by a heavy cannonade on the Beauport lines, and the boats made a feint as if an attack were contemplated; buoys had been laid in such a way as to lead to the idea that the ships were going to moor as close in as possible as if to support an assault, and every effort was made to draw attention away from the movement up above.

## THE PLAINS OF ABRAHAM

Lieutenant Norman, of the Pembroke, shortly describes the battle in his log:

"At 4 A.M. General Wolfe landed just below Cape Diamond with the whole army. At 8 the signal of Boats man'd and arm'd to go to Point Levi, weighed and dropped hier up. About 10 the enemy march'd up and attacked General Wolfe, the action lasted not 10 minutes before the Enemy gave way and run in the Greatest Confusion and left us a compleat Victuary. Our Army encamped on the plain a back of the Town and made the necessary disposition for carrying on ye siege. Admiral Holmes hoisted his flag on board the Lowestaff, just off the Landing place. In this action fell General Wolfe, of the enemy General Montcalm and his two seconds."

Cook does not mention the death of Wolfe, but says "the troops continued the pursuit to the very gates of the city, afterward they begun to form the necessary dispositions for carrying on the siege."Cook is said by some writers to have piloted the troops to the landing-place, and has even been set within hearing of the legendary recitation by Wolfe of Gray's Elegy, but as he was out with the Pembroke's boats in the Basin at the time Holmes started up the river, and was probably on his ship, with his hands full driving the bombardment, and the recital of the Elegy at such a time was probably a myth, the traditions may be put down to imagination. The boats were piloted to the landing by Captain Chads of H.M.S. Vesuvius.

The town having surrendered five days after the battle, the movements made by Saunders in the Basin no doubt aiding M. de Ramesay, the Governor, in coming to a decision, General Murray was left with a garrison, and the fleet sailed for England, sending a detachment of the Northumberland and six others to Halifax with orders that Captain Lord Colville was to hoist the Broad Pennant as Commander-in-Chief of the North American Station, and as soon as the season opened he was to return to the St. Lawrence to render support to any further movements made in Canada.

## APPOINTMENT TO H.M.S. NORTHUMBERLAND

Before the fleet left, however, Cook's connection with H.M.S. Pembroke came to an end. Captain King, who was with Cook on his last voyage, writes to Dr. Douglas that he does not know the exact date of Cook's appointment to the Northumberland, but he was certainly

Master of that ship in 1758. Here King is in error, for Lieutenant James Norman, of the Pembroke, has the following entry in his log under date 23rd September 1759: "Mr. Cook, Master, superseded and sent on board the Northumberland, per order of Admiral Saunders." It has been said that Lord Colville made this appointment, but of course he could not do so, though he may perhaps have applied for Cook's services, but it is far more probable that the appointment was made by Saunders for the special purpose of having the survey of the St. Lawrence thoroughly well carried out.

# 1759 TO 1762
# H.M.S. NORTHUMBERLAND

On the way down the river from Quebec, the fleet appears to have found the passage very difficult, the dangers of the Channel being aggravated by the strength of the current and bad weather. The Captain, Vesuvius, and Royal William were aground for some time, but were ultimately got off again without much damage; and the Terrible, which was drifting and in great danger, was only brought up by means of an anchor constructed for the occasion by lashing one of the quarter-deck guns to two small anchors. When her large anchors were hauled up they were found to be broken; and so great was the loss of these articles that Lord Colville was obliged to press the Admiralty for a fresh supply to be sent out immediately, as he found it impossible to replace those lost in the Traverse either at Boston or any other place in America.

## RELIEF OF QUEBEC

Colville's squadron arrived in Halifax on 27th October, Cook's thirty-first birthday, and as soon as the winter was over, and the ships were cleaned and fitted for sea as well as the limited appliances would permit, it left for the St. Lawrence, sailing on 22nd April 1760, but was "so retarded by frozen fogs, seas of compacted ice, and contrary winds," that it did not arrive off the Ile de Bic before 16th May. Here they were met by a sloop with the news that Quebec was in urgent need of help. General Murray, hearing of the approach of General de Levis, with a French force, had left the shelter of the forts, and notwithstanding he was greatly outnumbered, had offered battle in the open. He had at first chosen a strong position, but hearing from spies that the French were busy cleaning their arms after being caught in a heavy storm the night before, he advanced upon them, and owing to the sudden attack and the superiority of his artillery, at first gained a considerable advantage, but afterwards the weight of numbers told, and the British were forced to retire to the town with sadly reduced numbers, and Quebec was again besieged. On receipt of this news Colville pushed on with his squadron, and the arrival of the Vanguard and Diamond on the 17th, followed by the Northumberland and the remainder on the next day, caused the French to retire.

During the next four months the fleet passed an uneventful time in the Canadian waters, the flagship being moored in the Basin, and then on the 12th September they received the acceptable news that Montreal and the rest of the province of New France had surrendered to General Amherst, and on 10th October the squadron again returned to Halifax to winter quarters.

On 19th January 1761, Lord Colville records in his Journal that he had "directed the storekeeper to pay the Master of the Northumberland, fifty pounds in consideration of his indefatigable industry in making himself master of the pilotage of the River St. Lawrence." This is the first official recognition that has been found of the fact that Cook had gone beyond the ordinary duties incumbent on every Master in His Majesty's Service, namely: "To observe all coasts, shoals, and rocks, taking careful notes of the same." There is no record in any of the official documents that Cook was specially engaged in surveying the river, but it is very evident from this entry that he must have done the work during the four months that his ship was moored in the Basin of Quebec. That is to say, his promotion to the Northumberland was previous to, and not a consequence of his survey of the river, and that it was on account of his fitness for the work, and not because it had been done, as is constantly asserted, that he had been selected.

## THE NORTH AMERICAN PILOT

Admiral Saunders had issued orders the previous year, that the general instructions of the Admiralty as to taking observations, soundings, and bearings were to be carefully carried out, and the information obtained was, as opportunity offered, to be forwarded to him "so that all existing charts may be corrected and improved." This information, in the ordinary course, would be handed to Mr. Bissett, the Master of the flagship, for comparison and compilation, and he, knowing Cook's fitness for the work, may have asked for his assistance and thus introduced him to the notice of Saunders, noted for his quick eye for merit, who, seeing his aptitude, selected him for the completion of the task. Saunders, after his return to England, wrote to the Secretary of the Admiralty, on 22nd April 1760, saying that he had, ready for publication, a Draught of the River St. Lawrence with its harbours, bays, and islands, and asked for their Lordships' directions thereon. With their Lordships' approval it was published, and may be found at the end of The North American Pilot, London, 1775, together with other maps, some of which are Cook's work. At the commencement of the book is a letter from Cook to the compiler of the volume, congratulating him on the collection, and referring to the fact that some of the charts contain his work, but he does not lay claim to any special ones. On Saunders' chart there is a long note which concludes:

"The distances between Isle Coudre and Isle of Orleans, the Pillar Rocks and Shoals in the south channel were accurately determined by triangles. The other parts of this chart were taken from the best French Draughts of this River."

It is doubtful if this triangulation could have been carried out by Cook during his passage up and then down the river, the only time he had in 1759, but if it were, it argues much greater knowledge of nautical surveying than he is generally supposed to have had at the time.

During the winters that the Northumberland stayed in Halifax Harbour, Cook employed his spare time in improving his knowledge of all subjects that were likely to be of service to him in his profession. He read Euclid for the first time, and entered upon a study of higher mathematics, especially devoting himself to astronomy. King in his sketch of Cook's life, says, on the authority of the man himself, that these studies were carried on "without any other assistance than what a few books and his own industry afforded him."

At the opening of the season, Lord Colville dispersed his squadron to those stations where their services appeared most necessary, and remained with his ship at Halifax, as it was considered inadvisable to leave such an important naval post open to attack from the French or the Spaniards. He had been advised by despatches, dated 26th December 1761, that war had been declared with the latter nation. During this period of waiting the words "nothing remarkable" are in constant use in Captain Adams's (the second Captain of the Northumberland) Journal. Cook utilised this time to make a thorough survey of Halifax Harbour, the notes of which are now in the United Service Museum, Whitehall.

At length the period of inaction was ended. Captain Charles Douglas, H.M.S. Syren, who was cruising off Cape Race, received information that a squadron of four French ships of the line, having some 1500 picked troops on board, had made a descent on Newfoundland, and had captured St. John's, the capital, which had been most shamefully neglected, and its garrison reduced to 63 men. The Grammont, 22-gun sloop, was unfortunately in harbour at the time, and was also taken. Douglas at once pressed two English merchant vessels into the service, and putting a petty officer in command of one, the William, and his Master in the other, the Bonetta, despatched them to cruise in search of Captain Graves, the reappointed Governor of Newfoundland, who was daily expected from England. The Bonetta soon fell in with the Antelope, Graves's ship, and she immediately joined Douglas, and then proceeded to strengthen the Isle of Boys as far as time would allow. Then going to Placentia, a place of as much importance as St. John's, and more capable of defence, they set about making preparations to beat off any attack, leaving a garrison of 99 men and as many marines as could be spared. Graves then despatched Douglas with the remainder of the Syren's marines to take possession of Ferryland, and sent the ship herself off with letters to Lord Colville, but the William having missed the Antelope, made her way to Halifax with the news of what had occurred.

## RECAPTURE OF ST. JOHN'S

Colville at once sent word to General Amherst, Commander-in-Chief in America, asking him to forward any troops he could spare, and started, accompanied by the Gosport, and an armed colonial vessel, the King George, 20 guns, to cruise off the Newfoundland coast in order to prevent the arrival of French reinforcements or supplies. He met Graves at Placentia on 14th August, and landed all the marines he could, and then continued his cruise. Amherst collected every available man from New York, Halifax, and Louisberg, and putting them under the command of his brother, Colonel William Amherst, ordered him to use every despatch and join Lord Colville without delay. This the Colonel succeeded in doing on 12th September off Cape Spear, and the next day they landed at Torbay, some three leagues north of St. John's. They drove in the French outposts and took possession of a small harbour named Quidi Vidi, which had been blocked at the entrance by the French. Clearing away the obstructions they landed their stores and some artillery, and advancing on St. John's, compelled its surrender on the 17th. Notwithstanding that, as Captain Graves reported, "the French had put St. John's in a better state of defence than ever we had it in."

On the 16th a strong gale blew the English ship some distance off the coast, and was followed by a thick fog, during which the French squadron managed to tow out of the harbour, but were in such a hurry to get away that they did not stop to pick up their boats and immediately made sail, being so far out of reach in the morning, that though some of them were seen by the British, it was not realised that they could be the French escaping from a squadron inferior in strength. Lord Colville, writing to the Admiralty, says:

"At six next morning it being calm with a great swell, we saw from the masthead, but could not bring them down no lower than halfway to topmast shrouds, four sail bearing South-South-East, distance 7 leagues. We lost sight about seven, though very clear, and sometime after a small breeze springing up from the South-West quarter, I stood towards Torbay in order to cover the shallops that might be going from thence to Kitty Vitty. In the afternoon I received a note from Colonel Amherst, acquainting me that the French fleet got out last night. Thus after being blocked up in St. John's Harbour for three weeks by a squadron of equal number, but smaller ships with fewer guns and men, M. de Ternay made his escape in the night by a shameful flight. I beg leave to observe that not a man in the squadron imagined the four sail, when we saw them, were the enemy; and the pilots were of opinion that they must have had the wind much stronger than with us to overcome the easterly swell in the harbour's mouth. I sent the King George as far as Trepassy, to bring me intelligence if the enemy should steer towards Placentia; and I directed Captain Douglas of the Syren to get the transports moved from Torbay, a very unsafe road, to the Bay of Bulls."

As soon as information was received in England that an expedition had been sent from France, the Admiralty despatched a squadron under Captain Pallisser in pursuit, and as it arrived in St. John's only four days after M. de Ternay left, they must have been very close to a meeting.

## COOK MEETS COOK

Whilst the movements leading up to the recapture of St. John's were being carried on, communication between Colville and Amherst was kept up by the boats of the fleet under the charge of the third lieutenant of H.M.S. Gosport, Mr. James Cook, formerly Master of H.M.S. Mercury, who performed this duty to the complete satisfaction of Lord Colville as signified in his despatches to the Admiralty. It is certain, therefore, that the two namesakes must have come face to face here, and most probably previously in Halifax Harbour.

Entering St. John's Harbour on 19th September, the flagship remained till 7th October, during which time Cook was very busily employed in assisting to place the island in a better state of defence. In a despatch of Lord Colville's, dated "Spithead, 25th October 1762," he says:

"I have mentioned in another letter, that the fortifications on the Island of Carbonera were entirely destroyed by the enemy. Colonel Amherst sent thither Mr. Desbarres, an engineer, who surveyed the island and drew a plan for fortifying it with new works: when these are finished the Enterprise's six guns will be ready to mount on them. But I believe nothing will be undertaken this year, as the season is so far advanced, and no kind of materials on the spot for building barracks or sheds for covering the men, should any be sent there. Mr. Cook, Master of the Northumberland, accompanied Mr. Desbarres. He has made a draught of Harbour Grace and the Bay of Carbonera, both of which are in a great measure commanded by the Island, which lies off a point of land between them. Hitherto we have had a very imperfect knowledge of these places, but Mr. Cook, who was particularly careful in sounding them, has discovered that ships of any size may lie in safety both in Harbour Grace and the Bay of Carbonera."

Mr. Desbarres's design for the fortification of Carbonera, drawn by John Chamberlain, dated 7th April 1763, is to be found in the British Museum; he was afterwards Governor of Cape Breton.

On the return of the Northumberland to Spithead, where she arrived on 24th October, her Master, James Cook, was discharged, the Muster Roll merely noting "superseded" on 11th November, and the pay sheet records the deductions from his wages as: "Chest, 2 pounds 1 shilling 0 pence; Hospital, 1 pound 0 shillings 6 pence. Threepence in the pound, 3 pounds 14 shillings 9 pence," leaving a balance due of 291 pounds 19 shillings 3 pence. He also received from Lord Colville for the Secretary to the Admiralty the following letter which shows the estimation he was held in by his immediate superiors, and would doubtless be of weight when the appointment of a man to execute greater undertakings came under the consideration of their Lordships.

*London, 30th December 1762.*
*Sir,*
*Mr. Cook, late Master of the Northumberland, acquaints me that he has laid before their Lordships all his draughts and observations relating to the River St. Lawrence, part of the coast of Nova Scotia, and of Newfoundland. On this occasion I beg to inform their Lordships that from my experience of Mr. Cook's genius and capacity, I think him well qualified for the work he has performed and for greater undertakings of the same kind. These draughts being made under my own eye, I can venture to say they may be the means of directing many in the right way, but cannot mislead any.*
*I am, sir, your most obedient and most humble servant, Colville.*

## MARRIAGE

Before the close of the year Cook took upon himself further responsibilities as set forth in the following extract from the register of St. Margaret's Church, Barking, Essex:

"James Cook of ye Parish of St. Paul, Shadwell, in ye County of Middlesex, Bachelor, and Elizabeth Batts, of ye parish of Barking in ye County of Essex, Spinster, were married in this Church by ye Archbishop of Canterbury's Licence, this 21st day of December, one thousand seven hundred and sixty-two, by George Downing, Vicar of Little Wakering, Essex."

Besant, who obtained his information from Mrs. Cook's second cousin, the late Canon Bennett, who as a boy knew her well, speaks most highly of her mental qualities and personal appearance, and says the union appears to have been a very happy one. It covered a period of about sixteen years; but taking into consideration the times he was away on duty, sometimes for long periods, Cook's home life in reality only extended to a little more than four years, and Mrs. Cook must often have been months, sometimes years, without even hearing of the existence of her husband. Her family were fairly well-to-do; her grandfather, Mr. Charles Smith, was a currier in Bermondsey; her cousin, also Charles Smith, was a clockmaker of repute in Bunhill Row. Her mother, Mary Smith, married first John Batts of Wapping, and secondly, John Blackburn of Shadwell. Miss Batts is described as of Barking in the Marriage Register, so may perhaps have been living with relations there, and may have met Cook when on a visit to her mother in Shadwell, where he was residing. The engagement must have been very short, for from the time of his joining the Navy in 1755 to his return from Newfoundland in 1762, his leave on shore had been very limited, and, with the exception perhaps of a day or two between leaving the Eagle and joining the Solebay, and again when leaving the latter ship for the Pembroke, none of his time was spent in London. There is a story that he was godfather to his wife, and at her baptism vowed to marry her, but as at that time, 1741, Cook was assisting his father on Airy Holme Farm, the tale is too absurd, but has for all that been repeatedly published.

After their marriage Mr. and Mrs. Cook lived for a time in Shadwell, and then removed to Mile End Old Town, where Cook purchased a house, which was their home till after his death. This house, which he left to his wife, has been identified as Number 88 Mile End Road, and a tablet has been placed on the front to mark the fact.

# 1763 TO 1767
# NEWFOUNDLAND

The commission as Governor of Newfoundland, which now included Labrador from Hudson's Straits to the St. John's River, the island of Anticosti, the islands off the Labrador coast, and the Madelines in the Gulf of St. Lawrence, had again been conferred on Captain (afterwards Admiral Lord) Graves. He had early recognised the fact that it was necessary to have a thorough survey of the coasts of his territory, and therefore made an application to the Board of Trade to have the one commenced as far back as 1714 by Captain Taverner, but only carried on in a desultory fashion, put in hand and completed as quickly as possible. This application resulted in a Representation from the Board to His Majesty, dated 29th March 1763, to be found in the Shelbourne manuscripts, asking that an allowance should be made for the purpose.

Graves had seen during the previous year the work done by Cook at Harbour Grace and Carbonera, and had evidently made up his mind that he had found the man for his purpose, in which opinion he would be backed up by Colville and further supported by the favourable knowledge that the Admiralty had of his work. The Representation was immediately acted on, for in the Records Office is a hurried note from Graves to Mr. Stephens, Secretary to the Admiralty, probably written on the 5th April, in which he asks:

"what final answer he shall give to Mr. Cook, late Master of the Northumberland, who is very willing to go out to survey the Harbours and Coasts of Labradore."

A draughtsman is also mentioned, and one is recommended who was on the Bellona and was willing to go out, ranking as schoolmaster; he did join Cook after a time. On 6th April Graves again wrote to Stephens, telling him he had instructed Cook to get ready to start as soon as the Board gave him orders, and that he was to have ten shillings per diem whilst employed on that service. He also says that Cook had been to the Tower to try to secure a draughtsman, and towards the end of the letter applies for the instruments necessary to carry on the operations. Graves was hurriedly called away to his ship, the Antelope, as the spirit of discontent, then very rife in the Navy, was developing itself in a very threatening manner during his absence. However, on his arrival on board, by judicious reforms, which he saw were carried out, and by quietly replacing some few of the most dangerous of the malcontents, he was very shortly able to report himself ready for sea with a complete and fairly contented crew.

On 15th April he writes to Stephens asking if there was "any change of resolution taken about Mr. Cook, the Master, and an assistant for him, and whether they are to go out with me?" On the 18th he writes again, saying that when in London he had been informed that he was to receive orders to purchase two small vessels of about 60 tons each when he arrived in Newfoundland, one of which he was "to send with Mr. Cook upon the surveys of the coast and harbours," but he was afraid the orders had been forgotten, and he again makes suggestions as to instruments, etc., required for the work. Cook had at the same time made application in proper form for the articles he would require, and was informed that some would be supplied to him from the Government Stores, and for the remainder, he was to purchase them and transmit the bills to their Lordships.

## COOK'S SAILING ORDERS

On 19th April Cook received his orders as follows:

*Sir,*
*My Lords Commissioners of the Admiralty, having directed Captain Graves, of His Majesty's Ship, the Antelope, at Portsmouth, to receive you on board and carry you to Newfoundland in order to your taking a Survey of Part of the Coast and Harbours of that Island. I am commanded by their Lordships to acquaint you therewith: that you must repair immediately on board the said ship, she being under sailing orders, that you are to follow such orders as you shall receive from Captain Graves relative to the said service and that you will be allowed ten shillings a day during the time you are employed therein.*
*I am, etc. etc., PHILLIP STEPHENS.*
*Mr. James Cook, – – Town.*
*Mr. William Test, Tower, to be paid 6 shillings per day.*

On 8th May Graves acknowledged the receipt of the orders he had asked for, authorising him to purchase two small vessels, and announced that Mr. Cook had joined the ship, but that the assistant, Mr. Test, had not been heard of; he therefore proposed that he should endeavour to obtain someone else to fill the vacancy. Mr.

Stephens replied that a difficulty had arisen with the Board of Ordnance with regard to Mr. Test's pay; they were not inclined to continue it during his absence as they would have to put some one else in his place, and since hearing this, as the Admiralty had heard nothing further from Mr. Test, Captain Graves was authorised to fill the vacancy at a suitable allowance, and he at once secured the services of Mr. Edward Smart, who sailed from Plymouth in H.M.S. Spy, and joined Cook in Newfoundland.

In this letter Graves also says that he intends to start Cook on the survey of St. Pierre and Miquelon as they had to be handed over to the French under treaty, whilst he should make some stay upon the coast in order to afford proper time for survey before they had to be surrendered. The possession of these islands carried with it certain fishing and curing rights conferred by the Treaty of Utrecht and confirmed by that of Paris, and the possession of the islands and rights have been a continual cause of irritation to the fishermen of both nations till lately, but now the differences have been satisfactorily settled. It is said that the Earl of Bute was the cause of the inclusion of the clause concerning these islands in the Treaty, and that he received the sum of 300,000 pounds for permitting it to stand. It was specially stipulated that the islands were not to be fortified, and the number of the garrison was to be strictly limited to a number sufficient for police duty alone; but from the very commencement of the peace, it was one continual struggle to evade the terms by one side, and to enforce them by the other, without coming to an actual rupture.

## JUDICIOUS PROCRASTINATION

According to his expressed intention, Captain Graves, on arriving at St. John's, despatched Captain Charles Douglas in the Tweed to superintend the removal of the British settlers from the two islands, and Cook accompanied him with orders to press on the survey as rapidly as possible in order that it might be completed before the arrival of the French. Unfortunately, M. d'Anjac, who was charged with the duty of receiving the islands on behalf of the French king, arrived on the same day as the Tweed, off the islands. Captain Douglas refused to permit the French to land until the islands had been formally handed over by his superior officer, and by a little judicious procrastination in communicating with Captain Graves, and persistent energy on the part of Cook in conducting the survey, sufficient time was gained to complete it. Graves writes to the Admiralty on 20th October 1763:

"Meanwhile the survey went on with all possible application on the part of Mr. Cook. At length, Monsieur d'Anjac's patience being quite exhausted, I received a letter from him on the 30th of June, of which I enclose a copy together with my answer returned the same day. This conveyance brought me a letter from Captain Douglas, expressing his uneasiness on the part of Monsieur d'Anjac and pressing to receive his final instructions, and at the same time gave me the satisfaction to learn St. Peter's was completely surveyed, Miquelon begun upon and advanced so as to expect it would be finished before the French could be put in possession: so that any interruption from them was no longer to be apprehended."

In a paper amongst the Shelbourne manuscripts, said to be an extract from a Journal of Cook's, there is a short description of these islands, and it conveys the impression that the writer looked upon them as absolutely worthless as either naval or military stations, but for all that Captain Graves's successor, Pallisser, was kept continually on the alert to defeat the efforts of the French to strengthen their position.

## THE KING'S SURVEYOR

After the official surrender of these islands, Cook was engaged in surveying different places which the Admiralty had specially marked out, and was borne on the books of either the Antelope or Tweed as might be convenient. He is to be found on the latter ship, entered "for victuals only," as "Mr. James Cook, Engineer, and Retinue." As the dates in the two ships often run over each other it is somewhat difficult to place him, but he was certainly in the neighbourhood of St. John's for some two months, and on 5th November he was discharged from the Antelope into the Tweed, together with Mr. Smart, for the passage to England, where he remained till the spring of the following year. On 4th January the Admiralty authorised the payment up to the end of the previous year of the allowances of 10 shillings and 6 shillings per day, respectively, to Mr. Cook and Mr. Smart. This allowance of 10 shillings per day was the same as that made to the Commander of a Squadron, so, from a financial point of view, Cook's position must be considered one of importance. It was apparently superior to that of a Master surveying under the directions of the Governor, for in a report that Captain

Pallisser, when Governor of Newfoundland, gives of an interview between the French Ambassador and himself in London in 1767, on the subject of the fisheries, he says he produced Cook's chart, and decided the question of the rights of France to the use of Belle Isle for fishing purposes against the Ambassador by its means, and he speaks of Cook officially as the King's Surveyor.

Pallisser was appointed to succeed Graves as Governor in 1764, and at once set aside the schooner Grenville, which Graves had used as a despatch boat for the sole use of the survey party. She had been manned from the ships on the station, but Pallisser wrote to the Admiralty on the subject, and the Navy Board were instructed to establish her with a proper person to take command of her, and a complement of men sufficient to navigate her to England when the surveying season was over, in order that she might be refitted and sent out early in the spring, instead of being laid up in St. John's and waiting for stores from England, "whereby a great deal of time is lost." The establishment was to consist of ten men, i.e. a Master, a Master's mate, one Master's servant, and seven men. The Master and mate were to receive the pay of a sixth rate, and the former was "to be charged with the provisions and stores which shall be supplied to the schooner from time to time, and to pass regular accounts for the same." On 2nd May Stephens wrote to Pallisser that Cook was appointed Master of the Grenville, and as soon as the season was over he was to be ordered to Portsmouth, and on arrival to transmit his Charts and Draughts to the Admiralty. On receipt of this letter Pallisser wrote to Cook, and this communication, together with autograph copies of letters written by Cook having reference to the Grenville, a receipt for her husband's pay, signed by Mrs. Cook, and some other papers of interest relating to his voyages, are now in the hands of Mr. Alexander Turnbull, of Wellington, New Zealand.

It would appear that it was at this time that the friendship between Pallisser and Cook really commenced, for previously there can have been no opportunity for the former to have known anything of Cook's personality. A Captain of a man-of-war saw nothing of a Master's mate, and knew nothing of him except whether he did his duty or not, and that only through the Master's report. In this particular case, as soon as his attention was called to him by outside influence, Cook was withdrawn from his knowledge, and when they again came in contact had already made his mark. Had they been on the very friendly terms that Kippis suggests, it is unlikely that he would have made so many incorrect statements as to Cook's early career in the Navy.

On 23rd April Cook received his orders, and was told at the same time that as he had expressed a doubt about being able to get suitable men in Portsmouth, he would be provided with conduct money and free carriage of chests and bedding for those he could raise in London, and they should be transferred to Portsmouth in the Trent. Mr. William Parker was appointed Master's mate, and the whole crew left Portsmouth on 7th May in H.M.S. Lark, arriving in St. John's on the 14th June. They took possession of their ship on the same day, and the first entry in the Grenville's log runs as follows:

"June 14th, 1764, St. John's, Newfoundland. The first and middle parts moderate and hazy Weather, the Later foggy. At 1 P.M. His Majesty's Ship the Lark anchored here from England, on board of which came the Master and the company of this Schooner. Went on board and took possession of Her. Read over to the crew the Master's Warrant, Articles of War, and Abstract of the late Act of Parliament."

## ACCIDENT TO HAND

After getting the guns and stores on board, and fitting the ship for her new duties, they left St. John's on 4th July for the north. A base line was laid out at Noddy's Harbour, and the latitude of Cape Norman was found to be 51 degrees 39 minutes North; soundings were taken every mile. On 3rd August Cook left the ship in the cutter to continue his work, but having met with a nasty accident he had to return on the 6th. It seems he had a large powder horn in his hand, when, by some means not stated, the powder ignited, and the horn "was blown up and burst in his hand, which shattered it in a terrible manner, and one of the people which was hard by suffered greatly by the same accident." The Grenville left at once for Noddy's Harbour, where there was a French ship which had a doctor on board, arriving there at eleven o'clock, was able to secure some sort of medical assistance, though probably in the eye of a modern medical man, of a very rough nature. At that time surgery, especially on board ship, was very heroic; a glass of spirits the only anodyne, and boiling pitch the most reliable styptic. In reference to this accident the Lords of the Admiralty wrote to Lord Halifax, quoting a letter they had received from Captain Pallisser, dated 14th November 1764:

*"Mr. Cook, the surveyor, has returned. The accident to him was not so bad as it was represented. Nor had it interrupted his survey so much as he (Captain Pallisser) expected. He continued on the coast as long as the season would permit, and has executed his survey in a manner which, he has no doubt, will be satisfactory to their Lordships. I have ordered him to proceed to Woolwich to refit his vessel for the next season, and to lay before the Board, Draughts of his surveys with all his remarks and observations that may be useful to Trade and Navigation in those parts."*

Pallisser did not see Cook till some time after the accident, when the worst was over, and it is quite in keeping with Cook's character to minimise his sufferings, and to insist on the work being kept going as far as possible. The surgeon, Mr. Samwell, relates that after the murder at Owhyee they were enabled to identify his hand by the scar which he describes as "dividing the thumb from the fingers the whole length of the metacarpal bones." Whilst Cook was laid up with his hand, and Mr. Parker was engaged with the survey, some of the men were employed brewing, and either the brew was stronger than usual or, the officer's eye being off them, they indulged too freely, for on 20th August it is noted that three men were confined to the deck for drunkenness and mutinous conduct, and the next day the ringleader was punished by being made to "run the Gantelope."

Early in September, being then in the Bay of St. Genevieve, Cook went ashore for six days and ran roughly the course of several small rivers, noting the chief landmarks, and then on their way back to St. John's, off Point Ferrol, their small boat was dashed to pieces on a ledge of rock, and its occupants were saved with great difficulty by the cutter which by great good fortune happened to be near at the time. They returned to England for the winter, and crossing the Banks, a series of soundings were made and the nature of the bottom carefully noted. When Cook arrived at Woolwich, he pointed out to their Lordships that the completion of his charts would entail his being absent from his ship, and he would be unable to supervise everything that had to be done on board, he therefore suggested that she should be sent to Deptford yard. This was at once agreed to, and Cook was able to devote his whole time to his charts. His own work had to be supplemented by the observations made by six men-of-war stationed in Newfoundland waters as their commanding officers had received special instructions to take ample soundings and careful observations, and to make charts which were to be sent to Captain Pallisser, who was informed that he would be held responsible if these orders were not carried out in their entirety. It is very certain that an order so emphatically enforced on his notice would not be permitted to remain a dead letter.

## GRENVILLE'S RIG CHANGED

Whilst at Deptford, the rig of the Grenville was altered from schooner to brig, as Cook thought that her sailing qualities would be improved by the change, and she also received a thorough overhaul. In the previous year her armament had been supplied from the flagship, and of course had to be returned, so now she was established with "6 swivel guns, 12 Musquets, and powder and shot" of her own, and her crew was augmented to twenty, including a midshipman and a carpenter's mate, paid as on board a sixth rate. Isaac Smith, Mrs. Cook's cousin, afterwards Admiral, who lived with her at Clapham, was the midshipman. On 25th March 1765 the Grenville again left for Newfoundland, arriving at St. Lawrence Harbour on 2nd June to recommence her work. On 14th July, whilst "moored in a bay by Great Garnish, we picked up two men who had been lost in the woods for near a month. They came from Barin, intending to go to St. Lawrence Harbour, and were almost perishing for want of subsistence." Going into Long Harbour, 23rd July, the Grenville ran on a rock and remained so fast that she had to be unloaded before she could be floated off the next day, when she was found to have suffered considerable damage to her forefoot.

From the log of the Grenville it appears that the survey was not carried out continuously, and this may be accounted for by the fact that the Governor was being called upon to settle disputes with the French fishermen, who were only too apt to place the broadest construction on the treaty rights accorded to them. It is very possible that Cook, during this year, rendered assistance to Captains Debbieg and Bassett, engineers, who were engaged in surveying important points and harbours with a view to fortification, and Pallisser had been instructed to give them every help. There is no positive record that Cook did assist, but his ship was several times engaged near where they were at work, and it seems very reasonable to suppose that he worked with them, especially as such work might be very important to both parties.

Cook returned to Spithead on 30th November, and from thence to Deptford for the winter, and in February obtained permission from the Admiralty to publish the charts he had completed; Captain Pallisser, who made the application, said he was of opinion that they "would be of great encouragement to new adventurers on the fisheries upon those coasts."

## ECLIPSE OF THE SUN

He again left Deptford on 20th April 1766, and arrived at Bon Bon Bay, 1st June, to survey the south-west and south coasts. At the Burgeo Islands, near Cape Ray, which were reached on 24th July, Cook was able to take an observation of an eclipse of the sun occurring on 5th August. On his return to England at the end of the year, he handed the results of his observations to Dr. Bevis, a prominent Fellow of the Royal Society, who communicated them to that body on 30th April 1767, and the account is to be found in the Philosophical Transactions of that year. Dr. Bevis describes Cook as "a good mathematician, and very expert at his business," and says he was supplied with very good instruments; that there were three observers "with good telescopes, who all agreed as to the moment of beginning and ending"; that he had shown Cook's results to Mr. George Mitchell, who had calculated therefrom the difference of longitude between the Burgeo Islands and Oxford, where another good observation had been taken.

Cook makes no reference to the eclipse in the log of the Grenville, but it appears that he was peculiarly lucky in the weather, for the five days preceding are described as "foggy," and the four or five succeeding are "raining with squalls." This observation was a most fortunate one for Cook, as it brought him to the favourable notice of the Royal Society, a body of eminent men, outside his own profession, which was able, soon after, to advance his interests, and in course of time to admit him into its own ranks as an ornament of which it is still proud.

On 4th November the Grenville left St. John's for winter quarters at Deptford, and the log ends on 24th November, "Dungeness light North-East by East 2 miles." Mr. Parker, his assistant, was promoted to a lieutenancy, and Mr. Michael Lane, who was mentioned for the post by Captain Graves in 1763, and who was now schoolmaster on the Guernsey, was appointed in his place.

On 5th April 1767 the Grenville had completed her refit, warped out of dock, and was at anchor waiting for the tide to turn in order to drop down to Woolwich, when the Three Sisters, a Sunderland collier, Thomas Boyd, Master, "fell athwart her hawse and carried away her bowsprit, cap, and jibboom," which had to be replaced. The story is that this accident happened to the Endeavour, and that Mr. Cook, who was naturally very indignant, sent for the offending Master of the collier to give him a sound rating for running foul of one of His Majesty's ships; but when he found himself face to face with an old schoolfellow of the Ayton days, he took him down into his cabin, treated him to the best he had on board, and spent a good time with him talking over the old days when they were boys together. From Cook's character the story may well be true, excepting it has been applied to the wrong ship.

When the repairs were executed the Grenville sailed for Newfoundland, arriving off Cape Race on 9th May, and Cook at once set to work on the survey of the west coast. He landed in September at the mouth of the Humber, and made a rapid examination of that river, discovering several lakes, and getting a good general idea of that part of the island. He returned to St. John's for the last time on 14th October, having practically completed the survey of the general run of the coast, and added very considerably to the knowledge of some of the interior parts of the island. In 1762 a map was published, compiled from the very latest information, and on it is the note: "The inland parts of this island are entirely unknown." Cook is said to have discovered valuable seams of coal, but there is no note of anything of the kind amongst his records.

## THE GRENVILLE ASHORE

He sailed for England on 23rd October, and anchored off the Nore in very heavy weather on 11th November. It was soon found that the anchors would not hold, and at length one parted and the ship "trailed into shallow water, striking hard." After a while she again struck heavily, and "lay down on her larboard bilge." As there seemed no prospect of the gale moderating, everything was made as snug as time would allow, and, putting his crew into the boats, Cook made for Sheerness. The weather at length improved, so obtaining assistance he returned and found that fortunately his ship had sustained very little damage, and the next day he successfully floated her, and got her up to Deptford yards on the following Sunday, and then Cook was able to set to work on his charts. On 3rd February, Palliser wrote to Mr. Stephens asking him to obtain permission from the Lords to publish, and at once obtained the necessary authority.

Some of these charts had been published in 1766, and now the complete series appeared with sailing directions for the south and east coasts of the islands. Admiral Sir W.J.L. Wharton, the late hydrographer to the Admiralty, says:

"The Charts he made during these years in the schooner Grenville were admirable. The best proof of their excellence is that they are not yet wholly superseded by the more detailed surveys of modern times. Like all first surveys of a practically unknown shore, and especially when that shore abounds in rocks and shoals, and is much indented with bays and creeks, they are imperfect in the sense of having many omissions; but when the amount of the ground covered, and the impediments of fogs and bad weather on that coast is considered, and that Cook had at the most only one assistant, their accuracy is truly astonishing."On the publication of his charts, Cook's connection with Newfoundland was concluded, and on 12th April 1768 Mr. Lane was "appointed to act as Master of the brig Grenville, and surveyor of the coasts of Newfoundland and Labrador in the absence of Mr. Cook, who is to be employed elsewhere." Mr. Lane was to be paid an allowance of five shillings per day over and above his pay as Master of a sixth rate. Cook and he were paid their allowances up to 31st December 1767, and on 17th June the Navy Board were ordered to complete Cook's allowance up to 12th April. From the wording of Mr. Lane's appointment it would appear that the surveyor's position was to be left open for Cook if it was thought desirable for him to resume it.

# 1768
# PREPARATIONS FOR FIRST VOYAGE

Till a few years ago writers on the subject were content to draw their information as to the first voyage of Cook to the South Seas from the so-called history of Dr. Hawkesworth. This gentleman, who posed as a stylist (Boswell calls him a "studious imitator of Dr. Johnson"), was introduced by Dr. Charles Burney to Lord Sandwich for the express purpose of writing an account of the expedition, and was supplied with all the records in the possession of the Admiralty relating to it, he had access to the Journal of Sir Joseph Banks, the Notes of Dr. Solander and others who accompanied Cook, and, more than all, he had the opportunity of personal communication with the leaders of the party. Notwithstanding these advantages he interpolated so much of his own speculations, conclusions, and dissertations, as to render his voluminous work not only extremely unreliable but often extremely ridiculous. Travellers to the South Seas record that the accounts of things and places described as seen by Cook are remarkably correct, but that the inferences drawn are wrong. They do not realise that the statements of fact are Cook's, whilst the deductions and ornamentations are Hawkesworth's, and were strongly resented by Cook. Boswell relates that he told Johnson that he had met Captain Cook at dinner at Sir John Pringle's (then President of the Royal Society), and gave him an account of a conversation they had together. Johnson:

"was much pleased with the conscientious accuracy of that celebrated circumnavigator, who set me right as to many of the exaggerated accounts given by Dr. Hawkesworth of his voyages."

Cook's opinion on the subject may be seen from his determination to prepare his Journals for the press himself in the future.

Within the last few years the Journal of the Endeavour has been published under the able supervision of the late Admiral Sir W.J.L. Wharton, and the Journal of Sir Joseph Banks, which was missing for a long time, has been recovered and published by Sir Joseph Hooker; and these two books may be preferred with safety over all others that have been written on the subject.

MEMORIAL TO THE KING

It had been calculated that a Transit of Venus would occur in 1769, observations of which would be of great importance to astronomical science, and several of the European nations, notably Russia, were intending to establish points of observation. The Royal Society decided that as England had hitherto taken a lead in astronomy, she should not now fall behind, and appointed a committee to report on the places where it would be desirable to take observations, the methods to be pursued, and the persons best fitted to carry out the work. This committee advised that two observers should be sent to Hudson's Bay, two to the South Pacific and, if Sweden did not send there, two to the North Cape. They also advised that the Government should be asked to supply a ship to convey the party to some island to be decided on in the South Seas, and several gentlemen were suggested as observers, Mr. Maskelyne, President of the Society, especially recommending Mr. Dalrymple as "a proper person to send to the South Seas, having a particular turn for discoveries, and being an able navigator and well skilled in observation." Mr. Maskelyne estimated the voyage would take about two years, and that a sum of ten shillings and six pence per day would be a reasonable allowance for expenses, together with a gratuity the amount of which was to be settled hereafter. A Memorial on the subject was prepared and forwarded to the King, setting forth that as a Transit of Venus over the Sun's disc was expected to occur, and that other nations were intending to take observations thereof in the interests of navigation, it would be desirable that as the British Nation had been justly celebrated for its knowledge of Astronomy, and an Englishman, Mr. Jeremiah Horrox, had been the first person who calculated the passage of the planet over the sun, in 1639, the Government should support the Royal Society in its attempt to take a proper position in the matter, by a grant of money and a ship to take a party to the South Seas. Four thousand pounds was the sum named, and on 24th March the President was able to inform the Council that the King had been pleased to order that it should be placed in his hands, "clear of fees," for the purpose of defraying the expenses of the expedition. In the end, after paying all accounts, there was a considerable balance left, which the King placed at the disposal of the Society, and a portion of it was expended on the bust of His Majesty, by Nollekins, now in its possession.

The gentlemen whose names had been suggested as observers were asked to appear before the Council if they were willing to accept the position, and Mr. Dalrymple wrote in reply to say there was only one part of the world where he would go to take observations, that was the South Seas, and he would only go if he had "the management of the ship intended for the service." Mr. Maskelyne told the Council he had recommended Mr. Dalrymple to the Admiralty for the command of the ship, the use of which had been granted, but had been informed that such an appointment would be "entirely repugnant to the regulations of the Navy." It is said that Sir Edward Hawke, having in his mind the disastrous result of giving Halley the command of a King's ship in 1698, when a serious mutiny occurred, positively refused to sign such a commission, saying that he would "rather cut off his right hand than permit any one but a King's officer to command one of the ships of His Majesty's Navy."

Dalrymple, originally a clerk in the East India Company's service, had spent some years trading amongst the islands of the Malay Archipelago and China, returned to England and published a couple of pamphlets on the East Indies, and in 1767 a book on the discoveries in the South Pacific Ocean, which brought him to the notice of the Royal Society. He was afterwards for a time hydrographer to the East India Company, and was then appointed the first hydrographer to the Admiralty. He was dismissed from this position for exceeding his powers, and soon afterwards died. He appears to have been a clever man, but of an extremely overbearing disposition and a very high opinion of himself. In writing to Dr. Hawkesworth on one occasion, he said: "I never write on any subject I do not thoroughly understand." What makes the remark more interesting is that he was quite in the wrong on the subject under discussion. He appears never to have forgiven Cook for having been successful in obtaining the command of the expedition to observe the Transit of Venus, and for completely upsetting his pet theory of a large continent in the Southern Ocean.

## PURCHASE OF THE ENDEAVOUR

The Navy Board, having been ordered by the Admiralty to propose a proper vessel to convey the observers to the South Seas, first suggested the Tryal Sloop, and then the Rose, but both being found unsuitable they were ordered to purchase one. On 29th March the Board wrote to Stephens that they had bought:

"a cat-built Bark, in Burthen 368 Tuns and of the age of three years and nine months, for conveying such persons as shall be thought proper to the Southward..."

At the same time, instructions were sought as to fitting and arming her for the service, and as to the name under with she was to be registered on the list of the Navy. A cat-built ship is described in the Encyclopaedias as one with round bluff bows, a wide deep waist, and tapering towards the stern. The name is derived from the Norwegian kati, a ship.

The cat-built bark, the now immortal Endeavour, was built by Messrs. Fishburn of Whitby, and owned by Mr. William Milner of that port. Dr. Young says that her original name was the Earl of Pembroke, but Sir Evan Macgregor wrote to Mr. Waddington in 1888 that she was purchased "under the name of the Endeavour, and was entered as a barque." The Warrant Entry Book from Board of Trade proves that Dr. Young was right, as the following entries will show:

"Deptford, March 23rd 1768. Two cats called the Valentine and the Earl of Pembroke to be surveyed and report which is the properest to be purchased."

"Deptford, March 28th 1768. Ship Earl of Pembroke to be received."

"Deptford, April 7th 1768. Ship purchased to be sheathed, filled, and fitted for a voyage to the southward. To be called The Endeavour Bark."

From the Records of the Survey Office, List of H.M. Navy, 1771 to 1776, it has been ascertained that her price was 2,800 pounds, and the cost of fitting her for the voyage was 2,294 pounds. The reason she was named officially either the Bark Endeavour or Endeavour Bark, was that there was another Endeavour in the Navy, stationed at that time at the Nore. Kippis says that Pallisser was entrusted with the selection of the ship, and that he called on Cook for assistance in the matter, and the fact that a Whitby-built ship was chosen, of a kind in which Cook had had considerable experience, adds to the probability of his statement. Dalrymple enters a claim, in letters to Dr. Hawkesworth, to having chosen the Endeavour for the voyage, but as she was not ordered to be surveyed, with a view to purchase, till 23rd March, when it was well-known the Admiralty had refused to allow him the command of the expedition, there is little force in his claim.

## COPPER SHEATHING

Admiral Wharton assumes that as Cook expresses himself averse from having exploring ships sheathed in copper, owing to the difficulty of making repairs in case of accident far from proper facilities, and from the frequent mention of "heeling and boot-topping" in the Journal of the Endeavour, it is most probable that she was sheathed in wood. This assumption is correct, for there is no mention of copper sheathing in the Surveyor's books, nor at the time of her being repaired at the Endeavour River, nor at Batavia, when it is impossible that any account of her damaged bottom could be given without the mention of copper if any such sheathing had been used. The Naval Chronicle says the first ship of the Royal Navy to be sheathed with copper was the Alarm frigate in 1758; and it is also said that the Dolphin, the ship in which Captain Wallis sailed round the world, was the only coppered ship in the service at this time, and she remained the only one for some years.

On 5th May, at a Council Meeting of the Royal Society, Captain John Campbell, R.N., proposed that Cook, who was in attendance, and had been appointed by the Admiralty to the command of the Endeavour, was a fit and proper person to be one of the observers for the Society in the Southern Seas. Cook was called in, and accepted the position in consideration of such a gratuity as the Society should think proper, and an allowance of 120 pounds per year "for victualling himself and another observer in every particular." Mr. Green was also called in, and accepted the place as the other observer for the gratuity of 200 guineas for the two years the voyage was expected to take, and at the rate of 100 guineas a year afterwards. A list of the instruments to be supplied by the Society was also prepared at the same meeting, and the workmen engaged on them were ordered to show them to Messrs. Green and Cook, and give any desired information. A portable observatory, said to have been designed by Smeaton, the builder of the Eddystone Lighthouse, framed of wood and covered with canvas, was also prepared. Mr. Maskelyne, knowing the value of a good watch when observing for longitude, lent the Society one of his own, made by Graham, to be entrusted to Mr. Green, and it was signed for with the other instruments supplied. Chronometers, of course, at that time were in process of evolution, several makers were endeavouring to gain the prize which had been offered for a reliable timekeeper. Shortly after, at a second meeting, Cook agreed to accept a gratuity from the Society of

100 guineas for taking the observations, and was paid 120 pounds sustenance money for Mr. Green and himself, with authority to draw on the Society during the voyage for a further amount not exceeding 120 pounds.

In the Commissions and Warrants Book, under date 26th May 1768, appears the following entry: MR. JAMES COOK (2nd) 1st Lieutenant Endeavour Bark. E.H., C.T., C.S.

The initials signify Edward Hawke, Charles Townshend, and Lord Charles Spencer. The "(2nd)" evidently refers to the fact that there was already one James Cook, a lieutenant in the Navy, namely, the former Master of the Mercury, and Third Lieutenant of the Gosport.

## PENDANT HOISTED

Having received his orders Cook proceeded to Deptford and hoisted his pendant on H.M.S. Endeavour on 27th May, and at once started to prepare for sea. A considerable quantity of coal was taken on board to use for drying the ship, as it occupied so much less room than wood.

Captain Wallis returned from his voyage round the world about this time, and in consequence of his report, the Island of Georgeland, afterwards called by Cook Otaheite and now Tahiti, was fixed upon by the Royal Society as the most desirable place for the observations, and the Admiralty were requested to issue the proper orders, notifying at the same time that Mr. Charles Green and Lieutenant James Cook had been appointed observers. They also in the same letter write that:

"Joseph Banks, Esquire, Fellow of this Society, a Gentleman of large fortune, who is well versed in Natural History, being desirous of undertaking the same voyage, the council very earnestly request their Lordships that in regard to Mr. Banks' great personal merit and for the advancement of useful knowledge, he also, together with his suite, being seven persons more (that is eight persons in all) together with their baggage, be received on board of the ship under command of Captain Cook."

They also requested that the expedition might be landed a month or six weeks before the 3rd June in order that the instruments might be got into proper working order, and for fear the ship might not be able to reach Georgeland, a table of the limits within which the observations might be taken, was enclosed. Full instructions were also given to the two observers, and a list of the fixed stars to be observed was drawn up by Mr. Maskelyne.

The order to receive Mr. Green and Mr. Banks and party was issued on 22nd July, "for victuals only"—i.e., they were to be supplied with the same as the rest of the ship's company whilst on board. The members of Banks's party were: Dr. Solander, naturalist; H. Sporing, assistant naturalist; A. Buchan, S. Parkinson, and Jno. Reynolds, artists; James Roberts and Peter Briscoe, white servants; Thomas Richmond and J. Dorlton, coloured servants.

It was owing to the personal friendship between them that Banks was permitted by Lord Sandwich, the First Lord of the Admiralty, to accompany Cook. He had taken up the study of Botany when at Eton, and at an early age had been elected F.R.S. He seems quickly to have formed a just estimate of Cook's worth; indeed, Sir John Barrow says he took a liking to him at the first interview, and a firm friendship sprang up between them which endured to the end. Many instances are to be found of his interest in and his support to Cook after their return home; and this friendship speaks volumes for Cook, for, though Banks was a most kindly natured man, he had at times a very overbearing manner.

Sir Joseph Hooker, in his introduction, quotes a most interesting letter from Mr. John Ellis, F.R.S., to Linnaeus, the great botanist, in which he says that Mr. Banks, a gentleman of 6000 pounds a year, has persuaded Dr. Solander to go out with him to the South Seas to collect "all the natural curiosities of the place," and after the observations are taken, they are "to proceed on further discoveries." He goes on to mention the library of Natural History and splendid outfit Banks is taking, and says, "in short, Solander assured me this expedition would cost Mr. Banks 10,000 pounds."

The Endeavour left Deptford on 21st July, and, calling at Galleons Reach, took in her guns and gunners' stores. Her armament was originally to have been six carriage guns, four pounders, and eight swivels, but they were increased to ten carriage guns and eight swivels, and at Plymouth four more swivels were added for use in the boats. The complement of men was also increased to 85, including 12 marines who were to join at Plymouth, and a third Lieutenant had been appointed in July.

She had dropped down the river and anchored in the Downs on 3rd August, Cook joining her on the 7th and, discharging his pilot, sailed the next day. He had a very tedious passage down the Channel, and did not arrive a Plymouth till the 14th, when he immediately sent word to Messrs. Banks and Solander, who were still in London, that he was ready for sea, and was only waiting for a fair wind to sail. They therefore started at once, their baggage being already on board, and joined Cook on 20th August.

## CREW WELL SATISFIED

Having received his extra guns, marines, twelve barrels of powder, and other stores, Cook mustered his men, paid them two months advance, and explained to them that they were not to expect any additional pay for the intended voyage. He says, "they were well satisfied, and expressed great cheerfulness and readiness to prosecute the voyage."

The orders under which he sailed were secret, and, unfortunately, are not to be found. Admiral Wharton says the covering letter is in existence, but the orders which should be on the next page are missing. Cook writes:

"I was ordered, therefore, to proceed directly to Otaheite; and, after the astronomical observations should be completed, to prosecute the design of making discoveries in the South Pacific Ocean by proceeding to the South as far as the latitude of 40 degrees: then, if I found no land, to proceed to the west between 40 and 35 degrees till I fell in with New Zealand, which I was to explore, and thence return to England by such route as I should think proper."

His last letter to the Admiralty, before leaving England, was written on the day of his arrival at Plymouth, informing them of that fact, and announcing his intention of proceeding to sea with all possible despatch.

# 1768 TO 1769
# PLYMOUTH TO OTAHEITE

After waiting for some days for a fair wind, Cook eventually sailed at 2 P.M. on 26th August, having, as he says in his Journal, "94 persons, including officers, seamen, Gentlemen and their servants; near 18 months' provisions, 10 carriage guns, 12 swivels, with good store of ammunition, and stores of all kinds" on board. On 1st September they had heavy gales lasting for about four-and-twenty hours, and a small boat belonging to the boatswain was washed away, and "between three and four dozen of our poultry, which was worst of all," were drowned. The ship was found to be very leaky in her upper works, and the sails in the store got very wet. Banks notes that they caught two birds in the rigging that had evidently been blown off the coast of Spain. On 13th September they anchored in Funchal Roads, and during the night "the Bend of the Hawser of the stream anchor slip'd owing to the carelessness of the person who made it fast." The anchor was hauled up into a boat in the morning, and carried further out, but, unfortunately, in heaving it into the water, a Master's mate, named Weir, got entangled in the buoy rope, was carried overboard, and drowned before any assistance could be rendered.

Whilst shifting her berth to a more convenient spot, the Endeavour was fired on by one of the forts owing to some misunderstanding, but satisfactory apologies and explanations were made, and it was thought so little of that neither Cook nor Banks mention it in their Journals. This incident is probably the origin of the story told by Forster in his Journal of the Second Voyage. He says:

"Captain Cook in the Endeavour battered the Loo Fort at Madeira in conjunction with an English Frigate, thus resenting an affront which had been offered to the British flag."

When the Endeavour arrived at Funchal, the only British man-of-war there was H.M.S. Rose, which sailed the following day with her convoy, and neither her Captain's Journal nor his ship's log make any reference whatever to a dispute with the Portuguese. No other British man-of-war came into the port whilst the Endeavour was there, and afterwards, at Rio, Cook expressly informed the Viceroy that he had been well received by the Portuguese at Madeira.

Fresh water, meat, vegetables, and wine were taken on board; wine, fruit, and water being good and cheap, but the meat and poultry, obtained as a favour, were dear. Two men, a marine and a sailor, received twelve lashes for refusing to eat their allowance of fresh meat. This appears to be harsh treatment, but it must be remembered that the lash was at that time almost the only recognised method of punishment in the Navy, however trivial the offence might be; and Cook knew from experience how important it was to prevent the scurvy from getting foothold on board, and he already had determined to fight, by every means in his power, this dread scourge, almost his most dangerous foe. He did conquer it even on this first voyage, and, considering his means, in a most marvellous manner. He would have claimed the victory had it not been for an untoward event, which will be told hereafter, leading him to postpone his claim till he could give further proof. It is important to notice how on every possible occasion he obtained, wherever he could, some change of diet and fresh water.

## EDEN BEFORE THE FALL

Whilst they were at Funchal, Banks spent five days with the English Consul, and he describes the place as very pretty, but the people as primitive, idle, and uninformed; all their instruments of the rudest make; and he thought that the appliances used in the manufacture of wine must have been similar to those used by Noah, "although it is not impossible that he might have used better if he remembered the methods he had seen before the flood." One of the Governors left it on record that, so averse from change were the people, he thought it most fortunate the island was not Eden before the fall, as in that case the inhabitants could never have been induced to wear clothes. He explored as much of the island as he could, but says he could never get more than three miles away from the town as his time was so much broken up. The Governor visited them on one of the days he says was so wasted, but relates, with evident glee, how he took his revenge. There was an electrical machine on board, and His Excellency was most curious on the subject; it was sent for and explained to him, and Banks goes on, "they gave him as many shocks as he cared for; perhaps more." A visit was paid to a convent, where the nuns, hearing they were distinguished scientists, plied them with all sorts of questions, and for the half-hour the visit lasted their tongues were going "all the time at an uncommonly nimble rate." At a monastery they visited they were well received, and the monks, regretting they were then unprepared, invited them to come the next day and, though it would be Friday, they would have roast turkey for dinner.

On 19th September, at midnight, they weighed, sighted Teneriffe on the 23rd, and the day following their first flying fish found its way into Mr. Green's cabin. On the 28th they tried steaks for dinner cut from a young shark, which Banks and Solander reported as very good, but the crew refused to taste them. Cape de Verde was seen on the 30th, and about a fortnight afterwards the line was crossed in 29 degrees 24 minutes West longitude, and the following day the event was celebrated. Lieutenant Hicks had crossed before, so a list was given to him of all on board, including the dogs and cats, and all were mustered on deck, those who had already crossed being separated from the others. Any one who wished could purchase immunity for four days' allowance of wine, but the others had to pay the penalty of ducking. Banks compounded for himself and party, and Cook also seems to have got off, but the others were hauled up to the end of the main-yard on a boatswain's chair, and then at the sound of the whistle dropped into the sea, an operation repeated three times. Cook says the "ceremony was performed to about twenty or thirty, to the no small diversion of the rest."

Whilst near the Equator, great inconvenience was felt from the damp heat; everything was mouldy or rusty, and several of the crew were on the sick-list with a sort of bilious complaint; but it fortunately did not grow into a serious matter.

## RECEPTION AT RIO

They struck soundings on 6th November, and on heaving the lead again found a difference of less than a foot in three or four hours. Land was sighted near Cape Frio, Brazil, in latitude 21 degrees 16 minutes South, on the 8th, and they came across a boat manned by eleven blacks who were engaged in catching and salting fish. Banks purchased some fish, and was surprised to find they preferred to be paid in English rather than Spanish coin. On the 13th they arrived off Rio de Janeiro, where they were very ungraciously received by the Viceroy. They were not permitted to land except under a guard; some of the men who had been sent ashore on duty were imprisoned. Mr. Hicks, who had gone to report their arrival and ask for the services of a pilot, was detained for a time, and it was only with difficulty, and at an exorbitant rate, that they obtained fresh food and water. Consequently little was seen of the place, except from the ship, and Cook took all possible observations from thence, and made a sketch map of the harbour, to which he added all the information he was able to pick up from the pilot. Writing to the Royal Society, he says he is quite unable to understand the true reason of his treatment, and contrasts it with that received by a Spanish ship which came in whilst he was there. This Spanish ship willingly undertook to carry to Europe and forward to the Admiralty copies of the correspondence that passed between Cook and the Viceroy, which Cook describes as

"a paper war between me and His Excellency, wherein I had no other advantage than the racking his invention to find reasons for treating us in the manner he did, for he never would relax the least from any one point."

To every remonstrance the Viceroy pleaded his instructions and the custom of the port. He seems to have been quite unable to grasp the object of the expedition, and Cook says his idea of the transit of Venus was, "the North Star passing through the South Pole. His own words." The crew were accused of smuggling, and it was repeatedly asserted that the Endeavour was not a king's ship. Parkinson, one of Mr. Banks's staff, says that frequently some of them let themselves down from the cabin window at midnight into a boat, and driving with the tide till they were out of hearing of the guard boat established over them, rowed ashore and made short excursions into the country, "though not so far as we could have wished to have done."

Banks, speaking of the supplies obtained at Rio, says the beef was cheap but very lean and dry; the bread tasted as if made with sawdust, and justified its name of Farinha de Pao (wooden meal); the fruits, excepting the oranges, were very indifferent, and he takes particular exception to the banana, which he had not tasted before, it was not at all to his liking. The water also was very bad, and the crew preferred what they had brought with them, though it was very stale.

M. de Bougainville reports that when he visited Rio he was at first received in a very friendly manner by this same Viceroy, but after a time the treatment was altered, and he had to put up with even greater insolence than Cook.

## THE SECOND DEATH

When the stores had been received on board, the anchor was weighed in order to take up a more favourable position for making a start, but, unfortunately, shortly after the ship got underway, a man named Peter Flowers fell from the main-shrouds into the sea and was drowned before assistance could be rendered: the second death since leaving England. The next day the wind was contrary, but every one was so anxious to turn their backs on the place that Cook ordered out the boats to tow, but they were immediately brought up by a shot from the fort of Santa Cruz. A remonstrance was sent ashore, and received the lame excuse that the permit for leaving had been signed but had been delayed on its way, and the officer in command could not allow the vessel to leave till it was received. Another attempt to get away was soon after made, but the anchor fouled a rock, and there was again delay; at length, on the 7th December, they were able to make a start, discharge their pilot, and bid farewell to the guard boat which had so constantly kept watch over them. They were informed that an Englishman, named Foster, an officer in the Portuguese service, who had been of great use to them, was imprisoned for his kind attentions.

On 9th December they met with bad weather and lost their foretop-gallant mast, but the rough handling they got was credited with improving the sailing qualities of the ship, as it took some of the stiffness out of her upperworks. A meteor was noted on the 23rd, like a small bright cloud, emitting flames, travelling rapidly westward, and disappearing slowly with two sharp explosions. The same day an eclipse of the sun was observed.

Christmas Day, for which the men had been saving up their allowances of grog, passed in the usual manner, that is, in considerable over-indulgence. Banks speculates as to what might have happened if they had had bad weather, whilst Cook dismisses the occurrence very shortly: "The people none of the soberest." On the 27th they crossed the mouth of the River Plate, the water being very discoloured, and a good many land insects were found in it. On 2nd January 1769, they saw some of the shoals of red lobsters like those mentioned by Dampier and Cowley, but they were not found in such quantities as those navigators reported.

On the 11th the shores of Tierra del Fuego were sighted, and on working in closer, the country was found to be less desolate in appearance than they had expected from Anson's description. Arriving off the entrance of the Straits of Le Maire, between Staten Island and the mainland, they were driven back by the tide and a strong adverse wind, and trying to shelter under Cape Diego they were carried past, and only after three and a half days' hard work were they able to get through the straits. Cook has left sailing directions for this passage which are followed to the present day. Banks and Solander were ashore for a short time on Staten Island, and returned delighted with the addition of some hundred new plants for their collection. Cook, with an eye to the welfare of his crew, remarks: "They returned on board, bringing with them several plants and flowers, etc., most of them unknown in Europe, and in that consisted their whole value." Cook and Green made a series of observations, "the first ever made so far south in America," and fixed the position of Cape Diego at 66 degrees West, 54 degrees 39 South; Wharton places it at 65 degrees eight minutes West, 54 degrees 40 minutes South.

On the 15th they anchored in the Bay of Success, for wood and water, and met with some of the inhabitants, with whom, by means of gifts of beads and other trifles, they established friendly relations, and three of them were persuaded to go on board the ship. Though by no means a small race of men, they were found to be nothing like the giants reported by the early navigators in this part of the world. They had in their possession buttons, glass, canvas, brown cloth, etc., showing conclusively they had previously some communication with Europeans. Their clothing consisted chiefly of skins, roughly cured, and a plentiful covering of paint and dirt. The only personal property on which they appeared to set any store were their bows and arrows, which were carefully made and always in good order. Their food appeared to consist of seal and shell-fish; their houses, merely shelters of boughs covered with grass and leaves built to windward of a small fire.

## A SNOWSTORM

On 16th January, Banks, Solander, Buchan, Green, Monkhouse, two seamen, and Banks's two coloured servants, tried to get up the hills to see something of the surrounding country, but they found their progress hampered by the dwarf vegetation. To add to their discomfort a heavy snowstorm came on. Several of the party experienced that desire to sleep which is produced by cold, and were warned by Solander of the danger of giving way to it, yet he was almost the first one to give in, and was with great difficulty kept awake. Buchan, most unfortunately, had a fit, so a large fire was made at the first convenient spot, but a sailor and the two coloured men lagged behind. During the night the sailor was heard shouting, and was brought in to the fire, but in the morning the two coloured men were found frozen to death. Cook attributed their death to overindulgence in spirits, the supply for the party being left in their charge. Not intending to remain away the night, supplies ran short, so a vulture was shot and carefully divided amongst them, each man cooking his own, which amounted to about three mouthfuls. At length the weather cleared up and a start back was made, and after three hours they struck the beach, only to find they had never been any great distance away but had been describing a circle and came back almost to the place whence they had started. Banks notes the vegetation as more exuberant than he expected; the dominant colour of the flowers, white; and he collected wild celery and scurvy grass in large quantities, which was mixed with the food on board ship as long as it could be preserved in a wholesome condition. Whilst at the Bay of Success the guns were lowered into the hold so as to allow more room on deck for working the ship in the bad weather they expected to encounter when rounding the Horn.

## THE BALANCE OF THE GLOBE

On 27th January Cape Horn was passed, but owing to fog and contrary wind they did not approach very closely, so they were unable to fix its exact position, but the description they were able to give of its appearance (there is a sketch of it by Mr. Pickersgill, Master's mate, in the Records Office), and twenty-four observations taken in the immediate neighbourhood, settled any doubts they may have had, and Cook puts it at 55 degrees 53 minutes South, 68 degrees 13 minutes West, and Wharton gives the corrected position as 55 degrees 58 minutes South, 67 degrees 16 minutes West. Three days after they reached their furthest south, according to Cook 60 degrees 4 minutes South, 74 degrees 10 West, and the course was then altered to West by North. The continuous and careful observations of the state of the sea, and the absence of currents during the following month, caused Cook to come to the conclusion that the vast southern continent so long supposed to exist somewhere in that part of the globe, and by some people esteemed necessary to preserve its balance, was non-existent. Banks expresses his pleasure in having upset this theory, and observes: "Until we know how the globe is fixed in its position, we need not be anxious about its balance."

The weeks following the change of the course to the north were uneventful, only marked by an occasional success of the naturalists in obtaining a fresh specimen, some of which were experimented on by the cook; an albatross, skinned, soaked all night in salt water, was stewed, served with savoury sauce, and was preferred to salt pork; a cuttlefish of large size, freshly killed by the birds, and too much damaged for classification, was made into soup, of which Banks says: "Only this I know that, of it was made one of the best soups I ever ate." The water obtained at Tierra del Fuego turned out very good: a great boon, as one of their great troubles and a source of great anxiety to Cook was the bad quality of the water so often obtained.

Towards the end of March a change was noticed in the kinds of birds flying round the ship, some being recognised as ones that were known to stay near land, and consequently a sharp look-out was kept. On the night of the 24th a tree-trunk was reported, but when morning came nothing further was seen. It has since been ascertained they were then a little to the north of Pitcairn Island, afterwards the home of the mutineers of the Bounty; but Cook did not feel himself at liberty to make any deviation from his course "to look for what he was not sure to find," although he thought he was "not far from those islands discovered by Quiros in 1606."

On 26th march one of the marines committed suicide by drowning. It seems he had misappropriated a piece of sealskin, and his fellow-soldiers, indignant that such a thing should have been done by one of the cloth, made his life uncomfortable and threatened that he should be reported for theft. This was the fifth death since leaving England, and none by disease.

The 4th April, at 10.30 A.M., Banks's servant, Peter Briscoe, sighted land, and the course of the ship was altered to give them a chance of inspecting it. It was found to be one of those peculiar circular reefs surrounding a lagoon, called atolls, which exist in some quantity in the Pacific. There was no anchorage, so they made no attempt to land, but were able to see it was inhabited. Some twenty-four persons were counted through the glasses, and were described as copper-coloured, with black hair; they followed the ship as if prepared to oppose a landing. The reef was covered with trees, amongst which the coconut palm was conspicuous. Cook gave it the name of Lagoon Island; it is now known as Vahitahi, and is one of the Low Archipelago. Being now in Wallis's track, islands were sighted almost every day, and almost all appeared inhabited, but owing to the want of safe anchorage, no communication could be held with the natives.

On 10th April Osnaburg Island was passed, and next day King George Land was sighted; but the wind failed, and they did not get close in till the 12th, when canoes came out to the ship, bringing branches of trees which were handed up the side, with signs directing they should be placed conspicuously in the rigging, as a token of friendship offered and accepted. When this had been done the natives produced a good supply of trade in the shape of vegetables and fruit; amongst the last Banks enumerates bread-fruit, bananas, coconuts, and apples (a species of hog plum). These were very acceptable and beneficial to the crew after such a lapse of time without vegetable food except the wild plants gathered in Tierra del Fuego.

## AT TAHITI

At 7 A.M. on the 13th they anchored in the bay described by Wallis, known as Matavai, in thirteen fathoms, and Cook says of his route from Cape Horn, "I Endeavoured to make a direct course, and in part succeeded."

# 1769
# SOCIETY ISLANDS

## PRODIGIOUS EXPERT THIEVES

Hardly had the anchor reached the bottom, before they were surrounded by canoes, whose occupants were anxious to sell the supplies of fruits, raw and cooked fish, and a pig they had brought. The price asked for the pig was a hatchet, and as these were scarce, it was not purchased. When all was made safe, a party went ashore and was well received by the natives, but those who had previously been there with Wallis reported that those who were at that time said to be chiefs, were keeping in the background. The next day, however, two men, evidently of rank, came on board, and being invited into the cabin, went through a ceremony described by Banks: "Each singled out his friend; one took the captain, and the other chose myself. Each took off a part of his clothes and dressed his friend with what he took off; in return for this we presented them with a hatchet and some beads." They were then invited by their new friends to go ashore. On landing they were escorted to a building and introduced to an old man they had not seen before, and he presented Cook with a cock, and Banks with a hen, and each with a piece of native cloth. Banks gave in return for his share his large laced silk neckcloth and a linen handkerchief. After this they were permitted to stroll about, and received many tokens of amity in the shape of green boughs, and were then entertained at a banquet, the principal dishes being fish and bread-fruit. Whilst at dinner, Solander had his pocket picked of an opera glass, and Monkhouse lost his snuff-box. As soon as this was made known, Lycurgus, as they had named one of their friends, drove off the people, striking them and throwing anything he could lay his hand to, at them. He offered pieces of cloth as compensation, and when these were refused, extended his offer to everything he possessed. He was, at last, made to understand that all that was wanted was the return of the stolen articles, and after a time the snuff-box and the case of the glass were returned, and, by and by, the glass itself. During the whole of the stay at the island they had the greatest difficulties with the natives for stealing, an accomplishment at which, Cook says, they were "prodigious expert."

On the whole, their first visit ashore was satisfactory, and was thought to augur well for the observations of the Transit. A site was selected for a camp on the eastern point of the bay, to which the name of Point Venus was given, the longitude, according to Cook, 149 degrees 31 minutes West, and to Wharton, 149 degrees 29 minutes West. Lines were traced for the boundaries, and Banks's largest tent was pitched and a guard mounted, and then the others went for a walk of inspection. They passed through some woods that Mr. Hicks had been prevented from exploring the day before, and Banks had the luck to bring down three ducks with one shot, a deed thought likely to impress the natives with respect for the white man's weapon. On their road back to camp they were alarmed by a musket shot, and hurrying on, found that one of the sentries had been pushed down and his musket stolen, so the midshipman in command had ordered a shot to be fired at the thief, who was killed, but the musket was not recovered. All the natives ran away but one, whom Cook calls Awhaa, and whom the Master, Mr. Molineaux, who had been out with Wallis, recognised as being a man of some authority. Through Awhaa an attempt was made to arrange matters, but the natives were very shy when the English landed the next day. However, the two chiefs who had first made friends, to whom the names of Lycurgus and Hercules had been given, again came on board, bringing presents of pigs and bread-fruit; they concluded as Hercules's present was the larger, he was the richer and therefore the more important chief. To lessen the chances of disagreements in trading and to keep some control of prices, Cook ordered that only one person should conduct the purchasing for the ship, and as Banks had shown aptitude in dealing with the natives, he was appointed. The natives were to be treated "with every imaginable humanity."

On the 16th Mr. Buchan, the artist, had another epileptic fit, which was unfortunately fatal, and he was buried at sea in order to run no risk of offending against any of the customs or superstitions of the natives. Cook, in referring to his death, says: "He will be greatly missed in the course of this voyage."

In the afternoon the ship was brought into such a position as to command the site of the proposed camp, and as there was to be an eclipse of one of Jupiter's satellites, Cook and Green stayed ashore to get an observation, but the weather was unpropitious.

## COOK SKETCHES

The camp was now got into order; the north and south sides were protected by a bank 4 feet 6 inches high on the inside, having a ditch

10 feet wide and 6 feet deep on the outside. The west side, facing the bay, had a 4 foot bank crowned by a palisade, with no ditch; and the east side, on the bank of the river, was protected by a double row of water casks. The armament consisted of two carriage guns on the weakest or east side, and six swivel guns, two on each of the other sides. The garrison was forty-five men, including civilians, and Cook considered it was practically impregnable. In the manuscripts department of the British Museum is a pen and ink sketch and plan of the fort, drawn by Cook, which agrees much better with the description than the engraving of Parkinson's drawing published in the History of the Voyage. The natives were disturbed by these preparations, some even leaving the bay, but when no dreadful results occurred, they took courage and returned.

The fort completed, the instruments were landed and put into the required positions to be prepared for their work, and the following morning the quadrant, which had not been removed from the case in which it was packed in London, was found to be missing, although a sentry had been stationed within five yards of it the whole night. Enquiries were made, and it was elicited that the thief had been seen making off with it. Banks, his native friend, and one or two of the English at once started, closely followed by Cook and a party of marines. After a long chase the quadrant was recovered, but some of the smaller parts were missing. After a time these also were returned in the case of a horse-pistol which had been stolen from Banks, and soon after the pistol was recovered, and they were able to return to camp. On their arrival they found Cook's friend, Dootahah (Hercules), had been detained as a hostage, so he was at once released, to the great delight of the natives, who had been much alarmed to see the armed party go into the woods. In order to show his gratitude for his release Dootahah sent a present of two hogs to Cook, for which he refused to take any return; but, afterwards, second thoughts proved best, and he sent a man to ask for an axe and a shirt, and to say he was going away, and would not be back for ten days. As the supplies of vegetables and fruit in the market had been decreasing in quantity, it was thought better to refuse the present in hopes he would apply for it in person, and arrangements could then be made for a regular market, but he sent some one else again, and so word was returned that Cook and Banks would bring it to him the following day. For fear this promise should be forgotten, Dootahah again sent his man, and Cook and Banks started off in the pinnace. On their arrival they were received by a large crowd, which was kept in order by a man in an immense turban, armed with a long white stick, "which he applied to the people with great judgment and relish." The party were conducted to a large tree, and very graciously received by Dootahah, who immediately asked for his axe, which was given him, together with a shirt and a piece of broadcloth made into a boat-cloak. He put on the cloak and gave the shirt to the man with the stick, and refreshments were served. They were afterwards entertained with dancing and wrestling, and then Dootahah accompanied them back to the ship, taking his supplies for dinner; and when it became known he was on board, trading was resumed.

A day or two after, Banks received an urgent message from his friend Taburai (Lycurgus), saying he was very ill. He complained of having been poisoned by one of the sailors. It seems he had noticed the sailors chewing, and had ask for a quid, had bitten off a piece and swallowed it. Banks prescribed large draughts of coconut milk, with happy results.

## SURF RIDING

Flies were a terrible pest; they got into everything, and ate off the artist's colours almost as fast as they were laid on. Tar and molasses was tried as a trap for them, but the natives stole it and used it as ointment for sores. The surf-riding struck the visitors with admiration. Swimming out with a piece of board they would mount it, and come in on the crests of the waves; and Banks says he does not believe that any European could have lived amongst the breakers as they did; he especially admired the manner they timed the waves and dived beneath on their way out from shore.

A blacksmith's forge had been set up, and in spare time the smith would fashion old iron into axes or repair old axes for the natives; and it was noticed that some of these old axes were not of English make, and it appeared unlikely they were obtained from the Dolphin. At length it was ascertained that since Wallis's visit in that vessel, two ships had anchored off the east coast, and it was concluded from the description given by the natives of the flags that they were Spanish, but on the arrival of the Endeavour at Batavia they were able to identify them as the French ships commanded by M. de Bougainville, whose crews were suffering very severely from scurvy at the time.

Paying a visit to Dootahah to see if a supply of fresh meat, which was running very short, could be obtained, they were received in a very friendly manner, but being delayed till it was too late to return to the ship by daylight, they remained all night, and as a consequence nearly every one found they had lost some property; Cook's stockings were stolen from under his pillow, where he had placed them for safety. Perhaps as consolation for their losses they were entertained during the night to a concert. Three drums and four flutes, the latter having four holes into one of which the performer blew with his nostrils, were the orchestra, and Cook's criticism is hardly complimentary: "The music and singing were so much of a piece that I was very glad when it was over." They waited till noon the next day in hopes of meat and the return of the stolen articles, but in vain, though Dootahah promised he would bring all to the ship—"a promise we had no reason to expect he would fulfil."

## THE TRANSIT OF VENUS

The important day of the observation was now approaching, and everything was in readiness. In order to diminish the risk of disappointment through local atmospheric disturbance, Cook sent a party to Eimeo (York Island), and a second one to the south-east of Otaheite, as far to the east of Point Venus as possible. The first party consisted of Lieutenant Gore, Banks, Sporing, and Monkhouse, and the second of Lieutenant Hicks, Clerke, Pickersgill, and Saunders, Mr. Green providing the necessary instruments. At Fort Venus everything was in good working order. The astronomical clock was set up in the large tent, being placed in a strong frame made for the purpose at Greenwich, and was then planted in the ground as firmly as possible and fenced round to prevent accidental disturbance. Twelve feet away the observatory was placed, comprising the telescopes on their stands, the quadrant securely fixed on the top of a cask of wet sand firmly set in the ground, and the journeyman clock. The telescopes used by Cook and Green were two reflecting ones made by Mr. J. Short.

"The 3rd of June proved as favourable to our purposes as we could wish. Not a cloud to be seen the whole day and the air was perfectly clear, so that we had every advantage we could desire in observing the whole passage of the Planet Venus over the Sun's Disk. We very distinctly saw the atmosphere or Dusky Shade round the body of the planet, which very much disturbed the time of contact, particularly the two internal ones. Dr. Solander observed as well as Mr. Green and myself, and we differ'd from one another in observing the times of contact much more than could be expected. Mr. Green's telescope and mine were of the same magnifying power, but that of the Doctor was greater than ours. It was nearly calm the whole day, and the thermometer exposed to the sun about the middle of the day rose to a degree of heat we have not before met with."

In the report published in the Philosophical Transactions he also refers to the heat:

"Every wished-for favourable circumstance attended the whole of the day, without one single impediment excepting the heat, which was intolerable; the thermometer which hung by the clock and was exposed to the sun, as we were, was one time as high as 119 degrees."

This report is accompanied by diagrams illustrating the different contacts and the effects of the penumbra, which Cook believed was better seen by Solander than by himself or Green. It was estimated at about seven-eighths of the diameter of the planet, and was visible to Cook throughout the whole Transit.

The times taken by Green were:
The first external contact: 9 hours 25 minutes 42 seconds A.M. The first internal contact: 9 hours 44 minutes 4 seconds A.M. The second internal contact: 3 hours 14 minutes 8 seconds P.M. The second external contact: 3 hours 22 minutes 10 seconds P.M.

The other two parties were equally successful, and at times Banks was able to employ himself in trading with the natives, with whom he soon got on friendly terms; in fact, he had to decline further purchases as he had as much as they could take away with them. He was also successful in his botanical enquiries, obtaining several plants he had not seen in Otaheite.

Whilst the observations were being taken some of the crew broke into the store and stole a quantity of the large nails that were used as a medium of trade with the islanders. One man was found with seven in his possession, and after careful enquiry was sentenced to two dozen lashes, which seems to have been the severest sentence meted out by Cook during the voyage. The sentence was carried out, and though it was well known that more than one was implicated, he refused to name any one else, but suffered in silence.

## A DOG DINNER

The King's Birthday being on 5th June, Cook entertained several of the chiefs at dinner, and the health of Kilnargo was toasted so many times by some of them that the result was disastrous. One of the presents received from a chief was a dog, which they were informed was good to eat. After some discussion it was handed to a native named Tupia, who had made himself very useful, and afterwards accompanied them on the voyage; and he having smothered it with his hands, and drawn it, wrapped it in leaves and baked it in a native oven. With some hesitation it was tasted, and met with general approval. Cook says: "Therefore we resolved for the future never to despise dog flesh"; and in another place he says they put dog's flesh "next only to English lamb." These dogs were bred for eating, and lived entirely on vegetable food.

The main object of their stay at Otaheite having been attained, steps were taken for further prosecution of the voyage; the ship was careened, her bottom scraped and found free from worm, but the boats had suffered, particularly the long-boat, which had to have a new bottom. She had been varnished only; the other boats, painted with white lead, had not suffered so much. The stores were overhauled, and the ship was fitted for sea. Whilst these preparations were being made, Cook and Banks made a circuit of the island in the pinnace to examine the coast. Several good anchorages were found, with from sixteen to twenty-four fathoms and good holding ground. The south-east portion was almost cut off from the mainland by a narrow, marshy isthmus about two miles wide, over which the natives dragged their canoes with little difficulty. On the south coast one of the large burying-places was seen; by far the most extensive one on the island. It is described as:

"a long square of stonework built pyramidically; its base is 267 feet by 87 feet; at the Top it is 250 feet by 8 feet. It is built in the same manner as we do steps leading up to a sun-dial or fountain erected in the middle of a square, where there is a flite of steps on each side. In this building there are 11 of such steps; each step is about 4 feet in height, and the breadth 4 feet 7 inches, but they decreased both in height and breadth from the bottom to the Top. On the middle of the Top stood the image of a Bird carved in wood, near it lay the broken one of a Fish, carved in stone. There was no hollow or cavity in the inside, the whole being filled up with stones. The outside was faced partly with hewn stones, and partly with others, and these were placed in such a manner as to look very agreeable to the eye. Some of the hewn stones were 4 feet 7 inches by 2 feet 4 inches, and 15 inches thick, and had been squared and polished with some sort of an edge tool. On the east side was, enclosed with a stone wall, a piece of ground in form of a square, 360 feet by 354, in this was growing several cypress trees and plantains. Round about this Morie were several smaller ones, all going to decay, and on the Beach, between them and the sea, lay scattered up and down, a great quantity of human bones. Not far from the Great Morie, was 2 or 3 pretty large altars, where lay the scull bones of some Hogs and Dogs. This monument stands on the south side of Opooreanoo, upon a low point of land about 100 yards from the sea. It appeared to have been built many years and was in a state of decay, as most of their Mories are. "

They were quite unable to gain information as to the history of these remains, nor of the religious belief of the islander, though they appeared to have some vague notions of a future life.

## AN EXCURSION INLAND

When the party returned to Point Venus, they found the refitting nearly complete, but the anchor stocks all had to be renewed owing to the ravages of the sea worms, so Banks and Monkhouse made an excursion up the river on which the camp was situated. In about nine miles the precipitous banks had completely closed them in, and further advance was blocked by a cliff, at least 100 feet high, over which the river fell. The natives with them said they had never been further, so the expedition returned. Charles Darwin, in 1835, made an attempt to ascend the same river, and though he penetrated some distance further, he describes the country as extremely difficult; he saw several places where two or three determined men could easily hold at bay many times their own number.

Gardens had been laid out during their stay, and European seeds were planted which were very fairly successful; except some brought out by Cook in carefully sealed bottles, none of which turned out well.

Some of the sailors were either enticed away, or attempted to desert, so Cook seized one or two of the chiefs as hostages, and the runaways were quickly returned. Some of the natives were anxious to go away with them, and Banks persuaded Cook to let him take Tupia, a man supposed to be of priestly rank, who had proved himself very useful on several occasions, and he was allowed to take with him a boy as servant. Cook records, on leaving, that during the three months' stay they had been on very good terms with the natives, and the few misunderstandings that did occur rose either from the difficulty of explaining matters to each other, or else from the inveterate habits of theft on the part of the natives—iron in any shape being simply irresistible.

On 13th July the Endeavour sailed for Huaheine, anchoring inside the reef on the north-west, on the 17th. Banks, Solander, Monkhouse, and Tupia at once accompanied Cook ashore, where a ceremony, presumed to be a sort of treaty of peace, was gone through, and then they were permitted to go where they liked. On this ceremonial Cook says:

"It further appear'd that the things which Tupia gave away, was for the God of this people, as they gave us a hog and some coconuts for our God, and thus they have certainly drawn us in to commit sacrilege, for the Hog hath already received sentence of Death and is to be dissected tomorrow."

## A CAREFUL PILOT

A market was organised by Monkhouse, and as soon as the natives understood that the stay of the ship would be very short, they managed to produce a fairly good supply of fruits and vegetables. The people were found to be rather lighter complexioned, and certainly not so addicted to thieving as the Otaheitans. As a memorial of the visit, Cook gave the chief a plate with the inscription, "His Britannick Majesty's Ship, Endeavour, Lieutenant Cook, Commander, 16th July, 1769, Huaheine." He also added "some medals, or counters of the English coins, struck in 1761, and other presents," and the recipient promised he would never part with them. From this place they went on to Ulietea (Raiatea), landing on the 21st; and after another ceremonial the English "Jack" was hoisted, and possession taken of the whole group in the name of King George. Tupia proved himself an excellent pilot, with great knowledge of the localities, and, having sent down a diver at Huaheine to ascertain the exact draught of the ship, he was very careful she never went into less than five fathoms of water. He had evidently had great experience in navigating these seas in canoes, boats of whose construction and sailing qualities Cook speaks in the highest terms. Banks at this time remarks, "we have now seen 17 islands in these seas, and have landed on five of the most important; the language, manners and customs agreed most exactly."

Detained by adverse wind off Ataha, and finding the water coming badly into the fore sail-room and powder-room, Cook put into the west side to repair and take in ballast, as the ship was getting too light to carry sail on a wind. He took the opportunity to survey to the north with Banks and Solander. Putting into one place, they were well received and entertained with music and dancing, and Cook's verdict was that "neither their Musick or Dancing were at all calculated to please a European." A sort of farce was also acted, but they could make nothing of it, except that it "showed that these people have a notion of Dramatic Performances."

During the whole stay in the Society Group they had been very well off for fresh food, consequently their sea stores had been little called on.

Jarvis, in his History of the Hawaiian or Sandwich Islands, says that with Cook "a silence in regard to the maritime efforts of his predecessors is observable throughout his Journals"; and as a proof that he traded on the knowledge of others, he remarks that at Otaheite he made enquiries if there were any islands to the north; and afterwards evinced no surprise when he discovered them. Now Cook in his Journals constantly shows that he compares his knowledge with that of others, and often regrets he has not further records to consult. As for his enquiries, he would have been grossly neglecting his duty had he not made them, for it was only a commonsense method of procedure, which evidently Mr. Jarvis could not understand. The result of these enquiries can be seen in the British Museum in the shape of a map drawn by Cook from information given by Tupia. On it are some sentences in the Otaheitan language.

# 1769 TO 1770
# NEW ZEALAND

Leaving the Society Islands on 9th August, they were off Ohetiroa (Rurutu), in the Central Group, on the 14th, but the natives were unfriendly, and they did not land. A canoe came out to meet the pinnace which had been sent to obtain information. The occupants, on being presented with gifts, tried to steal the lot, and were fired over, but by some mischance one of the natives was slightly wounded in the head, whereupon they hurriedly retreated, and further attempts at communication were abandoned. From this place the course was laid to the south to strike the much-talked-of Southern Continent. The weather rapidly got colder, and the pigs and fowls began to sicken and die. On 26th August they celebrated the anniversary of leaving England by cutting a Cheshire cheese and tapping a cask of porter, which proved excellent.

On the 28th an unfortunate death occurred; the boatswain's mate, John Reading, was given some rum by his chief, and it is supposed drunk it off at once, for he was shortly afterwards found to be very drunk, and was taken to his berth, but next morning was past recovery.

On 2nd September, in latitude 40 degrees 22 minutes South, the weather was very bad, and "having not the least visible signs of land," Cook again turned northwards, in order to get better weather and then to push west. The continuous swell convinced him there was no large body of land to the south for many leagues. Towards the end of September frequent signs were noted of being near land, floating seaweed, wood, the difference in the birds, etc., so a gallon of rum was offered to the first to sight land, and on 7th October the North Island of New Zealand, never before approached from the east by Europeans, was seen by a boy named Nicholas Young, the servant of Mr. Perry, surgeon's mate. The boy's name is omitted from the early muster sheets of the ship, but appears on 18th April 1769, entered as A.B. in the place of Peter Flower, drowned. Cook named the point seen, the south-west point of Poverty Bay, Young Nick's Head.

Tasman had discovered the west coast in 1642, and had given it the name of Staten Land, but he never set foot on shore. He was driven away by the natives, who killed four of his men, and naming the place Massacre (now Golden) Bay, he sailed along the north-west coast, giving the headlands the names they still bear. Dalrymple held that this land discovered by Tasman was the west coast of the looked-for Terra Australis Incognita, and his theory was now shattered.

## LAND IN NEW ZEALAND

Nearing the coast a bay was discovered into which the ship sailed, and let go her anchor near the mouth of a small river, not far from where the town of Guisborne now stands. Plenty of smoke was seen, showing the country was inhabited, and the pinnace and yawl were manned and armed, and Cook landed on the east side of the river. Some natives were seen on the other side, and, to try to open communications, the yawl, pulled by four boys, entered the river, whilst Cook followed up the natives, who had retreated towards some huts about 300 yards away. Some Maoris, thinking the boys would be an easy prey, tried to steal on the yawl, but the coxswain of the pinnace observing them called the boat back. One of the Maoris raised his spear to throw, and the coxswain fired over his head, causing a moment's pause of surprise; but, seeing nothing further, he again prepared to throw his spear, so the coxswain shot him, and his friends retreated at once, leaving the body behind. Cook at once ordered a return to the ship, as it was now getting dark.

The next morning, seeing some men near the same place, Cook again landed with Banks, Solander, and an armed party; and Solander went forward to the brink of the river to try and speak with the natives, but was received with a threatening waving of spears and a war dance. Cook retired to the boats, and landing the marines, again advanced with Green, Monkhouse, and Tupia. The latter spoke to the natives; and, to the great delight of the party, found he could make himself understood. After a little parley an unarmed native swam across the river, and was then followed by twenty or thirty more with their arms. Presents were given, but they seemed dissatisfied, and wanted arms. At last one stole Green's hanger, and they all became very aggressive and insolent, whilst more were seen to be preparing to cross; so Cook, thinking the position was getting too serious, ordered the one who had taken the hanger, and who was apparently the leader, to be shot, whereon the rest beat a hasty retreat.

The next day the boats tried to find another landing-place, but the surf was too heavy; and when two canoes were seen coming in from the sea, Cook determined to intercept them and try to come to friendly terms. However, they would not stop when called on, and on a musket being fired over them, the occupants seized their weapons and fiercely attacked the nearest boat, its crew being compelled to fire in self-defence, and Cook says two natives were killed. Banks gives the number as four, and the Maori account agrees with him. Three jumped overboard to swim ashore, but were picked up by the boats and taken on board ship. They were at first very depressed, but soon recovered their spirits on finding themselves well treated, and after eating and drinking enormously, entertained the crew with songs and dances. Cook deeply regretted this incident, and candidly confesses that he was not justified in trying to seize the canoes, but having once committed himself, he was obliged for his own safety to go to the bitter end. Banks says the day is "the most disagreeable my life has yet seen; black be the mark for it, and heaven send that such may never return to embitter future reflection."

The next day a party landed to cut wood, and was accompanied by the three captives, whom they tried to persuade to join their friends. The suggestion was declined, as they professed to be afraid of being eaten, and after a time went and hid in some bushes. Cook, noticing several parties of armed natives advancing in a threatening manner, retired his woodcutters across the river. About 150 to 200 Maoris gathered on the opposite bank. Tupia was put forward to parley, and some presents were shown, and at length one man came over who received a present from each of the British and then rejoined his friends. Cook then returned to the ship, taking with him the three youths, who still seemed afraid of their own countrymen. They were again landed the next morning as the ship was about to sail, and though they still professed to be frightened, were soon seen walking away in friendly converse with some who had come to meet them.

## NATIVE ACCOUNT

Mr. Polack, a New Zealand resident, gives an account in his New Zealand, which he gathered from the children of natives who were present at the landing of Cook. The tribe then living in the neighbourhood were recent arrivals, their leader being Te Ratu — the first man killed by the English. The natives were anxious to avenge him, but were afraid of the "thunderbolts which killed at a long distance," some indeed went so far as to say they felt ill if an Englishman looked at them. The idea of revenge was only ended on the vessel leaving. Mr. Polack's chief witness was the son of a man who was wounded by a ball in the shoulder, but survived his wound till within a year or two of 1836, the time the information was obtained. Before the ship left, a sort of peace was patched up by means of presents, and the dead bodies which had been left where they fell, apparently as a protest, were removed.

Cook describes the country as a narrow slip of low sand, backed by well-wooded hills, rising in the interior into high mountains, on which patches of snow could be seen. That it was fairly populated was evident from the smoke rising through the trees, more especially in the valleys leading into Poverty Bay as he named it, because they were unable to get anything but a small quantity of wood.

At Hawke's Bay, whilst trading was going on, a large war canoe came up, and the occupants received some presents. Cook noticed a man wearing a cloak of some black skin, and offered a piece of red cloth for it. The owner took it off, but would not part with it till he received the cloth, and then his boat was pushed off from the ship, and Cook lost both his cloak and his cloth. Soon after a determined attempt was made to steal Tupia's boy, Tayeto, who was handing some things down to a canoe; the Maoris had to be fired on, and in the consequent confusion the boy jumped into the water and swam to the ship. The point off which this occurred was named Cape Kidnapper. As there was no appearance of a harbour, Cook altered his course to the north at Cape Turnagain, 40 degrees 34 minutes South, to see if he could not do better in the other direction.

All the canoes seen along this coast were well made, far in advance of anything they had seen before, and the grotesque carving and ornamental work was admirably executed. The dresses warn were usually two cloak-shaped garments, one warn round the shoulders, the other round the loins, and were made of a substance like hemp, some being very fine. Banks had purchased something like them at Rio de Janeiro, for which he gave thirty-six shillings, thinking it cheap, but these were as fine, if not finer, in texture. Dogs, which were used as food, and rats were the only quadrupeds seen. Whilst Banks and Solander were collecting, they discovered a large natural arch, which the former describes as the most magnificent surprise he had ever met with. It was sketched by Parkinson, and is engraved in the History. Cook also made a pen-and-ink sketch of it, which is in the British Museum.

## COOK'S WASHING STOLEN

On 31st October they rounded East Cape, and following the coast, which trended more to the west, they saw a great number of villages and patches of cultivation, some of the last looking as if freshly ploughed. The whole aspect of the country was changing for the better, but the inhabitants did not seem more peaceably inclined. Five canoes came out to the ship fully armed, and apparently bent on mischief. Cook was very busy, and did not want them on board, so to keep them off ordered a musket to be fired over them; but as it only caused them to stop for a moment, a round shot was sent over them, and they hurriedly turned tail. The place was given the name Cape Runaway. White Island was named, but it must have been quiescent as there is no note of its being a volcano. As they sailed along the coast they met with canoes from which fish, lobsters, and mussels were purchased, and trading seemed well established, when one gentleman took a fancy to Cook's sheets, which were trailing overboard (they were in the wash), and refused to give them up. Muskets were fired over them and they fled, and Cook lost his sheets. From near White Island, Mount Edgecombe was seen, named after the sergeant of marines. It is a high round mountain, and forms a conspicuous landmark on both sides of the North Island. During this day they had noticed several small villages perched on difficult eminences and surrounded by palisades, which Tupia declared were "Mories or places of worship," but, says Cook:

"I rather think they are places of retreat or strongholds, where they defend themselves against the attack of an enemy, as some of them seem'd not ill design'd for that purpose."

British soldiers have since discovered that a Maori Pah is "not ill designed for that purpose." Cook most unfortunately missed the Harbour of Tauranga, the only safe port on the east coast between Auckland and Wellington for ships of any size.

## NATIVE ACCOUNT

In what is now known as Cook's Bay, they managed to induce the natives to trade, and purchased crayfish, over which Parkinson waxes enthusiastic, and "Mackerell as good as ever was eat," the latter in such large quantities that they were able to salt a considerable number, thus saving their sea stores. After an observation of a transit of Mercury, in which they were not very successful (Wharton thinks they were taken by surprise, the transit occurring somewhat earlier than expected; Green says: "Unfortunately for the seamen, their look-out was on the wrong side of the sun. The end was likewise as grossly mistaken"), they returned to the ship and found that there had been a difficulty with the natives, who had assumed a very threatening manner, and one attempted to run off with a piece of calico which was at that time a subject of barter. Mr. Gore seized a musket and fired, killing his man. Colonel Mundy, in Our Antipodes, says he saw a man named Taniwha, in 1848, who remembered Cook's visit, and imitated his walk, with the peculiar manner he had of waving his right hand, and also told of the kindly way Cook had with the children. Taniwha told Mundy that after the man was shot, the Maoris landed, consulted over the body, and decided that as the corpse "commenced the quarrel by the theft of the calico, his death should not be revenged, but that he should be buried in the cloth which he had paid for with his life." Colonel Wynyard took down the same story from Taniwha's lips in 1852, when he was supposed to be about ninety-three, and says: "His faculties were little impaired, and his great age perceptible more from a stoop and grey hairs than any other infirmity." Cook expressed very strong disapproval of Mr. Gore's conduct.

Next day Cook and Banks explored a river that entered near where they were anchored, the east side of which was very barren, but the west was much better, no signs of cultivation showing on either. Wild fowl were plentiful, and oysters, "as good as ever came from Colchester," and of about the same size, says Banks, were taken on board in large quantities:

"laid down under the booms, and employed the ship's company very well, who, I sincerely believe, did nothing but eat them from the time they came on board till night, by which time a large part were expended. But this gave us no kind of uneasiness, since we well knew that not the boat only, but the ship might be loaded in one tide almost, as they are dry at half ebb."

Cook thinks the inhabitants lived on fish, and shell-fish, with fern roots for bread, for very large heaps of shells were found, but no signs of cultivation.

A fortified village was visited, the inhabitants good-naturedly conducting them all over, and showing whatever they expressed a wish to see. It was built on a high promontory, whose sides were in some places quite inaccessible, in others very difficult, except where it faced the narrow edge of the hill. Here it was defended by a double ditch and bank, with two rows of pickets, the inner row being on the bank, leaving standing-room for the defenders. The inner ditch was 24 feet from bottom to top of the bank. A stage about 30 feet high, 40 feet long, and 6 feet wide, was erected inside the fence, with a second, a few paces from it, placed at right angles; from these the garrison were able to throw their spears and stones on to the heads of their enemies. The whole village was surrounded by a strong picket fence, running close to the edge of the hill. The entire surface of the top of the hill was cut up into small squares, each surrounded by its own fence, and communicating by narrow lanes, with little gateways, so that if the outer defences were forced each square could be defended in turn. Cook says:

"I look upon it to be a very strong and well choose Post, and where a small number of resolute men might defend themselves a long time against a vast superior force, armed in the manner as these people are."

He noticed, with quick eye, the great failing in these native fortresses, that is, the want of storage for water. In these Maori villages it was remarked that sanitary arrangements were provided, such as, says Beckmann in his History of Inventions, did not exist in the palace of the King of Spain at that time.

Large quantities of iron sand were noted here, but the use was quite unknown to the natives, who were indifferent to the iron tools or spikes which had hitherto been such a valuable medium of exchange elsewhere. A large supply of wild celery and a fresh boatload of oysters were put on board; a tree was marked with the name of the ship, the date, and one or two other particulars, the flag was hoisted, saluted, and possession taken of the country, and the ship sailed again on her journey.

### AT THE THAMES

Running closely along the coast, they hauled round Cape Colville into "the Entrance of a Straight, Bay or River," and anchored for the night, and in the morning they stood on along the east side. Canoes came off, and from the behaviour of the occupants, some of whom came on board at the first invitation, it was judged that favourable accounts had been heard of the ship. After running about 5 leagues the water shoaled to about 6 fathoms, and the ship anchored, and boats were sent out to sound. No great increase of depth being found, the pinnace and long-boat went up a river about 9 miles away, and on account of a fancied resemblance named it the Thames. They landed at a village near the mouth, being well received, but desiring to take advantage of the flood-tide which ran "as strong as it does in the River Thames below bridge," they made no stay; they went up about 14 miles, and then, finding little alteration in the appearance of the country, landed to inspect some large trees of a kind they had previously noticed. One was carefully measured, and was found to be 19 feet 6 inches girth at 6 feet from the ground, and, by means of Cook's quadrant, 89 feet to the lowest branch. It was perfectly straight, and tapered very slightly, and some were seen that were even larger. This was the Black Pine; to the Maoris, Matoi, and to the naturalist, Podocarpus.

On the way down the river their friends of the morning came out and "traffick'd with us in the most friendly manner imaginable, until they had disposed of the few trifles they had." When the boats got outside they had to anchor, as a strong tide and breeze were against them, and they did not reach the ship till next morning, when the breeze had increased to a gale, and topgallant yards had to be struck. When the wind dropped, what was left was against them, and the Endeavour would only go with the tide, so Cook took a run ashore to the west side of the bay, but saw nothing of interest, and concluded it was but sparsely inhabited. Whilst he was away natives went off to trade and behaved remarkably well, with the exception of one man who was caught making off with the half-hour glass, so Mr. Hicks had him triced up, and he was given a dozen lashes. When it was explained to his friends why this was done, they expressed their approval, and on his release an old man gave him another thrashing.

The weather now became very unsettled, and they were not able to keep as near the coast as they desired, but on 26th November some cultivated spots were seen, and several canoes came off.

"Some of the natives ventur'd on board; to two, who appeared to be chiefs, I gave presents. After these were gone out of the ship, the others became so Troublesome that in order to get rid of them, we were at the expense of two or three Musquet Balls and one 4 pound shott, but as no harm was intended them, none they received, unless they happened to overheat themselves in pulling ashore."

A STAMPEDE

To the west side of Cape Brett is a deep bay which was seen but not named, and here the town of Russell is now established, said to possess one of the finest harbours in the world, into which vessels of any draught can enter in all weathers and at any state of the tide. The natives were found difficult to deal with, and "would cheat whenever they had an opportunity." The ship left its anchorage, but was after a time driven back again, and Cook, with a party, took the opportunity to land. They were followed up by the Maoris, and were soon surrounded by about two hundred of them, some of whom tried to seize the boats, but being driven off tried to break in on the party. Several charges of small shot, which did no serious damage, were fired into them, and then the ship fired a 4 pounder over them, which caused a stampede, and during the rest of the stay there was no further trouble, but Cook had to punish three of his own men for stealing potatoes from one of the plantations. He invariably tried to hold the balance fairly between his men and the natives.

The country is described as very similar to that seen before, but the number of inhabitants was greater, and though apparently not under the same chiefs, they were on good terms with each other, and inclined to be civil to their visitors. A good deal of the ground was under cultivation, producing good sweet-potatoes. A few trees of the paper-mulberry were seen, from which the natives made a cloth in a similar manner to the Otaheitans, but the quantity was so small that it was only used for ornament. Tupia, who had been instructed to gain as much information about the people as he could, was informed that some of their ancestors once went off in large canoes and discovered a country to the north-west after a passage of about a month, only a small number returning. These reported they had been to a place where the people ate hogs, using the same word for the animal as the Otaheitans, Tupia asked if they had any in New Zealand, and the reply was "no." He asked if their ancestors brought any back, again the answer was "no"; whereon he told them their story must be a lie, for their ancestors could never have been such fools as to come back without some. The land said to have been discovered may have been New Caledonia.

One of the men who had been wounded at the first coming of the ship was seen by Banks. A ball had gone through his arm and grazed his chest. He did not seem to have any pain, and the wound though exposed to the air, was perfectly healthy, and he was greatly pleased to receive a musket ball like the one which had wounded him.

When leaving the bay they nearly grounded, being set by the current towards a small island, but the boats towed them clear. Very soon after they struck on an unseen rock, which was named Whale Rock, but almost immediately got clear, with no "perceptible damage," into twenty fathoms.

## BLOWN OFF THE LAND

Progress was now very slow, owing either to want of, or adverse wind. On 10th December they discovered two bays separated by a low neck of land, Knuckle Point; one bay was named Doubtless Bay and the other Sandy Bay; the country is described as nothing but irregular white sandhills, and Cook concluded from its appearance that the island was here very narrow and exposed to the open sea on the west. This he soon proved to be correct. Foster, in his account of the Second Voyage, says that when the Endeavour was passing Doubtless Bay, M. de Surville was anchored under the land, in the Saint Jean Baptiste, and saw Cook's ship, though himself unseen. In the account of De Surville's voyage, published by the Academie Francaise, it is stated that New Zealand was not sighted till 12th December 1769, and owing to bad weather no anchorage was gained till 17th. No mention whatever is made of the Endeavour being sighted, and M. l'Abbe Rochon, the editor, thinks it most probable that neither navigator knew anything of the movements of the other. De Surville mentions having lost anchors in a place he calls Double Bay, during a storm "ABOUT 22nd December," and it may possibly have been the one Cook encountered on the 28th off the north end of the island. They were blown out of sight of land on the 13th, the main topsail being split, and next day both fore and mizzen topsails were lost, but they managed to bring up under shelter of a small island off Knuckle Point. On the 15th the latitude was found to be 34 degrees 6 minutes South, with land visible to the south-west, and a large swell was coming from the west, so Cook concluded this was the most northerly point of the island, and named it North Cape.

After beating about for some days against westerly winds, they ran up north, returning southwards 23rd December, and the following day sighted land to the south-east, which proved to be Tasman's Three Kings. Here Banks provided the Christmas dinner, shooting several solan geese, which were made into a pie, and were "eaten with great approbation; and in the evening all hands were as drunk as our forefathers used to be upon like occasions."

On the 27th, when about thirty leagues west of North Cape, and about the same latitude as the Bay of Islands, no land in sight, the wind rose so that they had to bring to, under the mainsail, but moderated a little the next day so that they could run in towards the land. Again it freshened up and blew a perfect hurricane, accompanied by heavy rain, and a "prodidgeous high sea," which caused the ship to go greatly to leeward. On the 30th, Cape Maria van Diemen was seen about six leagues off, the land extending east and south. On the last day of the year their position was given as "34 degrees 42 minutes South, Cape Maria van Diemen North-East by North about 5 leagues." Cook says:

"I cannot help thinking but what it will appear a little strange that, at this season of the year, we should be three weeks in getting fifty leagues, for so long is it since we pass'd Cape Brett; but it will hardly be credited that in the midst of summer and in the latitude of 35 degrees South such a gale of wind as we have had could have happened, which for its strength and continuance was such as I hardly was ever in before. Fortunately at this time we were a good distance from land, otherwise it would have proved fatal to us."

## VEGETABLE SHEEP

On 2nd January 1770 Cook fixed the position of Cape Maria van Diemen, giving it as 34 degrees 30 minutes South, 187 degrees 18 minutes West of Greenwich. Admiral Wharton remarks that this is extraordinarily correct, seeing that the ship was never close to the Cape, and the observations were all taken in very bad weather. The latitude is exact, and the longitude only three miles out. He missed seeing Kaipara Harbour, one of the few good ones on the west coast, and describes the land as having a most desolate and inhospitable appearance, nothing but sandhills with hardly a sign of vegetation on them, and says: "If we was once clear of it, I am determined not to come so near again if I can avoid it, unless we have a very favourable wind indeed." On the 11th, a high mountain, its summit covered with snow, was seen, and named Mount Egmont; Wharton gives its height as 8,300 feet, and describes it as a magnificent conical mountain surrounded on three sides by the sea. Banks notes on the sides of the hill "many white lumps in companies which bore much resemblance to flocks of sheep." These were a peculiar plant, Raoulia mammillaris (Hooker), known in New Zealand as vegetable sheep. Fires were seen, the first sign of inhabitants on the west coast.

On the 14th, thinking he was in the entrance of a large bay, Cook ran in under the southern coast, and finding it broken into promising-looking bays, determined to run into one and careen the ship, as she was very foul; it is now called Ship Cove, in Queen Charlotte's Sound. Here they were at once visited by canoes, whose fully armed occupants commenced acquaintance by "heaving a few stones against the ship." Tupia opened a conversation, and a few ventured on board, but did not make a long stay. Cook then landed to look for water, and soon found an excellent supply, and "as to wood the land is here an entire forest." Whilst he was away, the crew got out the nets, and caught about 300 pounds of fish. Some natives also came off with fish, and though it was not good, Cook ordered it to be bought, in order to open up trade with them. However, they soon found these people were inclined to be quarrelsome and threatening, and as the ship was in an awkward position, being already hove down for cleaning, a charge of small shot was fired at the worst offender, which quickly taught them to behave better in future.

They had long suspected the natives were addicted to cannibalism, and now they proved it, as they purchased the bone of a forearm of a man, from which the flesh had been recently picked, and were given to understand that a few days before a strange canoe had arrived, and its occupants had been killed and eaten. They only ate their enemies, but held all strangers to be such. The place where the ship was careened was, according to Wharton, about 70 miles from Massacre Bay, where Tasman's men were killed, and Cook endeavoured to find out if there were any traditions of visits from ships to the neighbourhood, but could gain no information. The natives became friendly as time went on, and brought good fish which they sold for nails, cloth, paper (a great favourite at first, but when they found it would not stand water, worthless), and Cook says: "In this Traffic they never once attempted to defraud us of any one thing, but dealt as fair as people could do."

The surrounding country was too thickly timbered for them to see much, but one day, being out in a boat trying to find the end of the inlet, Cook took the opportunity of climbing a thickly timbered hill, and from there saw, far away to the eastward, that the seas which washed both west and eastern coasts were united, and that one part of New Zealand, at any rate, was an island, and he had thus solved one of the problems he had given him in England. They also saw that much of their immediate neighbourhood was not mainland as they had thought, but consisted of a number of small islands.

## A MORE SENSIBLE PEOPLE

The population of the district was estimated at only some three or four hundred, and appeared to subsist on fish and fern roots. They were evidently poorer than those seen previously, and their canoes are described as "mean and almost without ornament." They soon understood the value of iron, and readily took spike nails when trading, and greatly preferred "Kersey and Broadcloth to the Otaheite cloth, which show'd them to be a more sensible people than many of their neighbours," says Cook.

An old man, who had previously paid several visits, complained that one of the ships boats had fired on and wounded two Maoris, one of whom was since dead. On enquiry, Cook found that the Master and five petty officers, fishing beyond the usual limits, were approached by two canoes in what they thought was a threatening manner and had fired to keep them off. A second native assured Cook no death had occurred, and enquiry failed to discover one; but Cook very severely condemned the action of his men as totally unjustifiable. The ship had, by this time, been brought into fairly good trim, being clean, freshly caulked and tarred, and broken ironwork all repaired, so preparations were made to push through the straits; but, before leaving, two posts were set up, one near the watering place, and the other on the island, Motuara, on which the name of the ship and the date of the visit had been cut, and possession was taken of this land, the king's health being drunk, and the empty bottle presented to the old man who had complained about the shooting, and who was greatly delighted with his present; he also was given some silver threepenny pieces, dated 1763, and spike nails marked with the broad arrow.

On getting out into the strait a very strong current nearly drove them on to a small island, the anchor would not hold, and only a change in the current, probably caused by the tide, saved them. The southern point of the North Island was named "Cape Palliser, in honour of my worthy friend, Captain Palliser," and the north point of the South Island was called Cape Campbell, after Captain John Campbell, F.R.S., who had been one of Cook's strongest supporters as Observer for the Royal Society.

When through the straits Cook was turning south, but finding some of his people were not quite satisfied as to the part they had passed being an island, he took a northerly course till Cape Turnagain was recognised, when he at once went about for the south. Banks says:

"At this time there were two parties on board, one who wished that the land in sight might, and the others that it might not, prove to be a continent. I myself have always been most firm in the former wish, though sorry I am to say that my party is so small that there are none heartily of it than myself, and one poor midshipman, the rest begin to sigh for roast beef."

The east coast was followed down to Banks Peninsula, which was at first thought might be an island, and is marked by dotted lines as doubtful in Cook's chart, when Gore thought he had seen land to the east, and Cook, though convinced it was a mistake, ran out to make sure. On returning the winds proved contrary, and their progress was very slow, but they several times succeeded in running close in to the land, and from what they could see concluded it was very barren, with high ranges in the interior and with very few evidences of inhabitants. A favourable breeze springing up from the north, they tried to make the most of it, "and by that means carried away the main topgallant mast and fore topmast steering-sail boom, but these were soon replaced by others." A high bluff was named after Admiral Saunders, and near were several bays, "wherein there appear'd to be anchorage and shelter from South-West, Westerly, and North-West winds." One of these is now Otago Harbour, the port of Dunedin.

## THE TRAPS

On 26th February it blew hard from west-south-west, so they stood southward. They lost the fore-sail, and then the wind moderated, only to come on with increased fury about daylight, when their main topsail went. The storm continued for forty-eight hours, and half that time they lay to, heading south. After being lost for seven days the land was again sighted near Cape Saunders, and at night a large fire was seen on shore. On 6th March, being satisfied that he had passed the south point of the island, Cook altered his course to the west, and nearly ran on some partially submerged rocks a few miles to the south-east of Stewart Island, to which he gave the suggestive name of the Traps. They were again blown off, but picked up the land again at the western end of Foveaux Straits. Again they had to run off, returning to near Dusky Bay, which he wished to enter as he thought it looked a likely harbour, but the difficulty of getting out again and consequent waste of time prevented him. Off Cape Foulwind—suggestive name—they were again blown out to sea, but soon recovered their position, and Cook describes the land:

"No country upon earth can appear with a more rugged and barren aspect than this does from the sea, for as far inland as the eye can reach nothing is to be seen but the summits of these rocky mountains, which seem to lay so near one another as not to admit any vallies between them."

On the 24th they rounded the north point of the South Island, and on the 27th Cook writes: "As we have now circumnavigated the whole of this country, it is time for me to think of quitting it." He had thus carried out to the fullest extent the instructions to determine the situation and nature of the land seen by Tasman in 1642, and had done it in the most conclusive manner possible—by sailing round it—and thus upset Mr. Dalrymple's favourite theory that it formed part of a continent.

In Admiralty Bay, which he entered to refit for the homeward voyage, the sails were found to require a thorough overhaul, for, as Banks says, they:

"were ill-provided from the first, and were now worn and damaged by the rough work they had gone through, particularly on the New Zealand coast, and they gave no little trouble to get into order again."

The two points forming the bay were appropriately named after the Secretaries of the Admiralty, Stephens and Jackson.

The opinion was expressed that European fruits, grain, etc., would grow well in New Zealand, and an agricultural population would be successful. Timber of excellent quality was plentiful, and it was believed that New Zealand flax promised to be of considerable commercial value. Fish was found in great quantities, the lobsters and oysters being specially remarkable for quality and quantity. No quadrupeds except dogs and rats were seen, and birds did not seem very plentiful. The minerals, in Cook's opinion, did not appear of much value, but he admitted that he was not an authority on the subject. Banks notes the southern islanders appeared to be an inferior race to those of the north, the latter probably more closely allied to the Otaheitan type; many of their customs were similar, and their language practically identical. Tupia had no difficulty in making himself understood.

It would seem that even at this time founding a colony in the southern hemisphere had been under discussion, for Cook says that if a settlement were decided on in New Zealand, he would recommend the Estuary of the Thames and the Bay of Islands as most suitable for the purpose.

Speaking of his chart of New Zealand, Cook points out frankly the places where he thinks he may have fallen into error, and gives his reasons for so thinking, and the opinions of others are worth recording.

## A DULL SAILOR

Admiral Wharton says:

"Never has a coast been as well laid down by a first explorer, and it must have required unceasing vigilance and continual observation in fair weather and foul, to arrive at such a satisfactory conclusion, and with such a dull sailor as the Endeavour was, the six and a half months occupied in the work (2,400 miles of coast) must be counted as a short interval in which to do it."

M. Crozet, second to M. Marion du Fresne in command of the French expedition that was out in the following year, says:

"As soon as I obtained information of the voyage of Cook, I carefully compared the chart I had prepared of that part of the coast of New Zealand along which we had coasted, with that prepared by Captain Cook and his officers. I found it of an exactitude and of a thoroughness of detail which astonished me beyond all power of expression. I doubt whether our own coasts of France have been delineated with more precision. I think therefore that I cannot do better than to lay down our track of New Zealand on the chart prepared by the celebrated English navigator."

# 1770
# AUSTRALIA

The next thing to be done was to decide the course to be taken towards England. Cook would have liked to have returned by the Horn and thus settle the existence or non-existence of a large body of land in the South Pacific, but the time of year and the condition of his ship suggested that would be to court disaster. The same reasons held good against a direct course to the Cape of Good Hope, with the added disadvantage of there being no probability of any fresh discoveries, as that part of the Ocean had been frequently traversed.

"It was therefore resolved to return by way of the East Indies by the following route. Upon leaving this coast to the Westward until we fall in with the East coast of New Holland, and then to follow the direction of that coast to the Northward or what other direction it might take us, until we arrive at its Northern extremity; and if it should be found impracticable then to Endeavour to fall in with the Land or Islands discovered by Quiros."

This extract from Cook's Journal shows that he made no claim to the discovery of Australia, and settles the stupid story that his connection with the discovery of the east coast was an accident. It was a course laid down after thorough consideration of the best charts, very poor at best, in his possession.

## BOTANY BAY

The good ship Endeavour got under way on 31st March 1770, with a favourable wind and clear sky, heading a little north of west. On the 16th a change in the birds denoted the neighbourhood of land, and after a touch of contrary wind, on 19th April 1770 Lieutenant Hicks sighted land extending from north-east to west, distant five or six leagues. This was the looked-for east coast of New Holland, and the ship was at the entrance of Bass Straits, but on his chart Cook shows by a dotted line that he felt uncertain whether van Diemen's Land was joined to New Holland or no. The low hill which was first seen was named Point Hicks after its discoverer, and its position is given as 38 degrees 0 minutes South, 211 degrees 7 minutes West. Three waterspouts were seen a short distance from the ship, and are remarkable as being the first ones mentioned in the log. The course was altered to the north, and the country is described as rather low, not very hilly, covered with green woods, and the shore of white sand. Cape Howe was named the following day, and the position fixed as 37 degrees 28 minutes South, 210 degrees 3 minutes West, which Wharton says is almost exact. The country now appeared to be improving in character, and smoke proved the existence of inhabitants, but none were visible till Cape Dromedary and Bateman's Bay were passed, when some were seen on the shore, but too far away for observation. Cook wished to land at Jervis Bay, but the wind was against him, and he could not afford time to beat in. An attempt was unsuccessfully made at a place that has been identified a little north of Five Islands, near Illawarra, but the surf was too heavy. At daylight on Sunday, 29th April, a bay was discovered, and the Master was sent in to sound the entrance, the ship following closely, and soon the Endeavour anchored for the first time in Australian waters, about two miles within the entrance of Sting Ray, now Botany, Bay. (For note see below.) The time when the name of the Bay was changed has been much disputed, but it is probable it was done some time after leaving the place. It was called Sting Ray on account of the big haul of that fish made soon after their arrival and the name stands in all the logs; Banks refers to it under that name in a general description of the country, written when leaving Cape York. Cook is however, decisive, for under date 6th May he says: "The great quantity of plants Mr. Banks and Dr. Solander found in this place occasioned my giving it the name of Botany Bay."

On coming to an anchor, Cook, Banks, and Tupia went on shore, and Canon Bennett, a second cousin of Mrs. Cook's, and one who knew her personally, relates that the family legend was that on reaching the shore Cook ordered the midshipman to "Jump out, Isaac," and Isaac Smith (afterwards Admiral) also a cousin of Mrs. Cook's, was the first Englishman to set his foot on the soil of New South Wales. The few natives who were near ran away, excepting two, who came forward to oppose any landing. A musket was fired over them, and they retired to where they had left their spears, and then one threw a stone at the boat, and as they were too far away for any serious damage to be done, Cook fired a charge of small shot at him. He then ran off to a small hut near, picked up a wooden shield, and returned to take up his position alongside his comrade, and they threw a couple of spears, receiving a second discharge of small shot in return, which caused them to retire slowly. As Banks, suspicious of some gummy substance on the points of the spears, suggested poison, they were not followed up. The huts, found near the landing-place, were constructed of sticks covered with pieces of bark somewhat similar to those seen in Tierra del Fuego. Some children found carefully covered up were left undisturbed, but forty or fifty spears were taken, and payment in the shape of beads, cloth, nails, etc., was left, but still untouched, on visiting the camp the next morning. The canoes from which the natives were seen fishing are described by Cook as the worst he ever saw, being merely sheets of bark tied with withies at the end and kept open in the middle by a stick.

Considerable difficulty was experienced in obtaining water, and whilst the crew were procuring it, Cook made a survey of the harbour. He describes the country as lightly timbered, with a sandy soil growing a plentiful crop of coarse grass, of which a quantity was cut for the sheep. The soil was interspersed with rocks and swamps, but at the head of the bay appeared richer. A few natives were seen, who ran away when observed, and though one or two spears were thrown no damage was done to any one. Large heaps of oyster, mussel, and cockle shells were found, amongst them, says Cook, "being some of the largest oyster shells I ever saw." An account, said to have been obtained from the blacks, published in a work on Australian discovery (anonymous, Sydney), agrees as far as it goes with those of Cook and Banks, and it is almost unnecessary to say the ship was at first taken for a large bird.

## SUTHERLAND'S DEATH

Whilst here, a seaman named Forbes (Forby, in the Muster Roll) Sutherland, died of consumption, from which he had suffered throughout the voyage, was buried on shore, and the point named Point Sutherland in his memory. The anonymous pamphlet referred to above, says that Cook does not give the cause of Sutherland's death, and that he had been fatally wounded by the blacks whilst trying to secure a metal plate he had found affixed to a tree, recording that the Dutch had previously been on the spot. The pamphlet goes on to say that Cook suppressed these facts in order to have the credit of being the first discoverer, but that the plate had been secured by some one and deposited in the British Museum. Unfortunately, Cook does give the cause of Sutherland's death, and the plate is not in the British Museum, nor has it ever been heard of there. Before leaving, an inscription was cut on a tree near the watering place, giving the ship's name and date; the English colours were displayed on shore every day during their stay, but they could not establish any friendly intercourse with the blacks. A plate has since been attached to the rocks about fifteen feet above high water, and as near as possible to the supposed place of landing.

After leaving Botany Bay the coast was followed up to the north, and Cook noted an "entrance" which he thought might prove a safe anchorage, to which he gave the name of Port Jackson, after Mr. George Jackson, one of the Secretaries to the Admiralty. Within this entrance is now the city of Sydney, and it was to this place that Captain Phillip removed his headquarters when he had discovered the unsuitability of Botany Bay for settlement. Broken Bay, named from the number of small islands therein, was passed, and the voyage was rendered very slow by the light northerly winds, and passing Cape Hawke, he found the set of the current had placed him twelve miles in advance, when reckoned by the log, of his real position given by observation.

Almost the only thing to be seen beyond the outline of the coast was the constantly recurring smoke; one point received the name of Smoky Cape on account of the great quantity seen in its vicinity. Cook, of course, was unaware that these "smokes" were probably, many of them, signals from one party of blacks to another of the arrival of something strange on the coast. That these "smokes" are used by the blacks as a means of communication is a well recognised fact, and the news they can convey by this means is perfectly astonishing to a white man.

The country appeared to increase in height with:

"an agreeable variety of Hills, Ridges, and Valleys, and large plains all clothed with wood, which to all appearance is the same as I have before mentioned as we could discover no visible difference in the soil."

After escaping a reef off Point Danger they discovered a bay, which Cook called Morton Bay after the Earl of Morton, P.R.S.; now wrongly spelt as Moreton Bay. Here, from the colour of the water, they supposed a river emptied into the sea; the surmise was correct, for they were at the mouth of the Brisbane River. At the same time some curiously-shaped hills were given the name of the Glasshouses, from their resemblance to the buildings in which glass is manufactured, and the resemblance is most striking.

After rounding Breaksea Spit, Cook found himself in a large bay, and conjectured, from the birds and the direction of their flight, that there was fresh water to the south-west; and rightly, for here the Mary River enters Hervey's Bay. On 23rd May they landed for the second time, and Cook says this was "visibly worse than the last place," that is Botany Bay. They managed to shoot a bustard of 17 1/2 pounds, and Banks says it was "as large as a good turkey, and far the best we had eaten since we left England." It was so much appreciated that its name was conferred on Bustard Head and Bustard Bay. This bird is known in Australia as the Plain Turkey. Oysters of good quality were also obtained, and Banks made the personal acquaintance of the green tree ant and the Australian mosquito, neither of which were appreciated.

## CAPE CAPRICORN

On 24th May a moderately high, white, barren-looking point was passed, which being found by observation to be directly under the tropic was named Cape Capricorn, and soon after the mouth of the Fitzroy was crossed, with the remark from Cook that from general appearances he believed there was a river in the immediate vicinity. Soundings becoming very irregular, he ran out between the Keppel Islands, on one of which natives were seen. Cape Townshend was named after Charles Townshend, one of the Lords of the Admiralty when the Endeavour left England, and not the Chancellor of the Exchequer, as stated by Wharton.

Rounding the point into Shoalwater Bay they had to haul sharp up to the west to get within the Northumberland Islands, and the water was found to be so shallow that they anchored and sounded from the boats, gradually working nearer in, as Cook was anxious to clean the ship's bottom, which was very foul; and he desired to take advantage of the full moon in these dangerous waters. They landed to take some observations and look for water. The observations were unsatisfactory, for the compass was unreliable, a fault attributed to the ironstone in the neighbourhood, of which signs were very evident, and water was not to be found. The country is reported on as follows: "No signs of fertility is to be seen upon the Land; the soil of the uplands is mostly a hard, reddish clay." Passing Cape Hillsborough, they entered Whitsunday Passage, described by Cook as "one continued safe harbour, besides a number of small bays and coves on each side, where ships might lay as it were in a Basin." The land on both sides was green and pleasant-looking, but on account of the moonlight Cook could not waste any time in landing.

Entering Cleveland Bay, the compass was again very much disturbed; the cause was found to be Magnetical, now Magnetic, Island, lying just off the present Port of Townsville. Blacks were seen, near Rockingham Bay, through the glasses; they were said to be very dark and destitute of clothing, but no communication with them was possible.

## ON THE ROCKS

On 10th June, after leaving a small bay north of Cape Grafton, where they had searched in vain for a watering place, the watch had just turned in, the lead had been cast and given seventeen fathoms, when the unfortunate ship brought all hands on deck, with a crash on a sunken rock. Soundings taken all round showed her to be on the very edge of a coral reef. Making but little water, an attempt was made to warp her off, but unsuccessfully. Steps were then taken to lighten her; decayed stores, oil jars, staves, casks, ballast, and her six quarter-deck guns were thrown overboard, some forty to fifty tons, but with no effect. The tide now rising, the leaks increased rapidly, two pumps being kept constantly at work. Thinking things could only go from bad to worse, Cook determined to heave her off at all hazards, and every one who could be spared from the pumps was sent to the capstan or windlass, and at length, after a stay of twenty-three hours on the rocks, she was hove into deep water. Now, however, it was a case of all hands to the pumps, and for a time it seemed as if they were slowly gaining on the in-rushing water, but suddenly there was an increase reported in the well, casting a shadow of gloom over all, but not for an instant staying the steady beat of the pumps. Shortly it was discovered that a fresh hand had been sent to the well and had sounded from a different mark than his predecessor, accounting for the sixteen to eighteen inches difference in the depth of water reported. This discovery acted like a charm: each one redoubled his exertions, and by morning they had gained considerably on the leak, so sail was made, and they slowly crawled in towards the land.

Midshipman Monkhouse had been on a ship which was leaking at the rate of forty-eight inches per hour, and had seen the operation called "fothering" so successfully performed on her, that, without further repair, she had sailed from Virginia to London. This being brought to Cook's ear, he gave Monkhouse the charge of carrying out a similar experiment. A studding sail was taken, on which oakum and wool was lightly sewn and smothered with dirt; it was then lowered over the bows and dragged by ropes over the place where the worst of the leak was situated, and there secured, with the result, according to Banks, that in a quarter of an hour after it was in position they were able to pump the ship clear, and Cook says one pump was sufficient to keep her free.

Of the conduct of the crew, Cook says:

"In justice to the ship's company, I must say that no men ever behaved better than they have done on this occasion; animated by the behaviour of every Gentleman on board, every man seem'd to have a just sense of the Danger we were in, and exerted himself to the very utmost."

Banks adds his testimony:

"Every man exerts his utmost for the preservation of the ship. The officers during the whole time never gave an order that did not show them to be perfectly composed and unmoved by the circumstances, however dreadful they might appear."

A point off which the reef was situated was given the suggestive name of Cape Tribulation, and some small islands near, Hope Islands, because, as Cook says, he hoped, at the time of their greatest danger, they might be able to reach them. What a prospect to hope for! No possibility of ever seeing a friendly sail, and but little probability of ever being able to reach a civilised port.

## THE ENDEAVOUR RIVER

A boat sent off to search for some spot where temporary repairs could be executed, soon returned and reported a small river had been found which appeared suitable. This was the Endeavour River, and into it the ship was safely taken, and deep water being found close to the bank, a stage was rigged, and most of the stores and ballast were taken on shore; a hospital was erected for the sick, "which amounted at this time to some eight or nine afflicted with different disorders, but none very dangerously ill." Green and Tupia were showing symptoms of scurvy, but the remainder appear to have been free from it.

As soon as the ship was sufficiently lightened she was warped a little further up the river, and at the top of the tide her bows were hauled well into the bank, so that when the tide fell they were able to examine the leak. The damage was found to be very serious; the rock had cut through four planks into the timbers, and three other planks had been badly injured. The manner in which the ship had been injured was "hardy credible, scarce a splinter was to be seen, but the whole was cut away as if done with a blunt-edged tool." A piece of the rock was found wedged in the hole, and had greatly assisted in arresting the influx of water. The sheathing and false keel were very badly damaged, but it was believed that she was not much injured aft, as she made but little water when once the main wound was dry.

At what is believed to be the exact spot at which the Endeavour was beached, a monument has been erected by the inhabitants of Cooktown, a seaport now at the mouth of the river.

There being no danger from the natives the crew were allowed as much liberty as possible, and a good supply of fish, a few pigeons and a small quantity of vegetables, in the shape of yam tops, cabbage palm, and wild plantains, had a very beneficial effect on their health. The longitude was calculated from an observation of "the Emersion of Jupiter's First Satelite," as 214 degrees 42 minutes 30 seconds West, which Wharton remarks on as being an excellent observation, the true longitude being 214 degrees 45 minutes West.

INCENDIARISM BY BLACKS

On 4th July the good ship was afloat again, so well repaired that only about an inch of water per hour was taken in, easily kept under by the pumps. She was laid over on a sandbank on the opposite side of the river and more carefully examined, the sheathing being found to be very badly damaged. The carpenter, in whom Cook had every confidence, reported that, with the means at his disposal, he could not make a satisfactory job, but he thought they might push on to some place where greater facilities could be obtained. She was therefore taken alongside the staging, the stores and ballast replaced, everything got ready for the prosecution of the voyage, and the Master sent off in the pinnace to look for a passage to the north-east; but was unsuccessful. He was again sent out, but again reported badly; the shoals appeared to get worse the further he went. He, however, brought back with him three turtles weighing about 800 pounds, which were most welcome as the crew had now been some months without fresh meat; a second trip to where these were caught resulted in getting three or four more, and a large supply of shell-fish. They had made several attempts to get on good terms with the few natives they had seen, and on one occasion two or three who were fishing had a long and animated conversation with Tupia, in which neither party could understand the other, though one or two were persuaded to visit the camp. Shortly before the last of the stores were taken in, Cook and Banks received friendly overtures from a small party, and ten of them visited the ship. They were offered various gifts, but seemed to set little value on anything except the turtles. They made signs they wanted them, and when they found these signs ignored, attempted to carry off two, and when their aim was frustrated, went ashore to where some of the crew were at work. One of them took a lighted stick from under the pitch kettle, and, making a wide circuit round the place, fired the grass as he ran. Fortunately there were not many things left ashore, and the powder had just been safely got on board, so the most serious damage appears to have been the premature roasting of a young pig. They then went off to where others of the crew were washing, and drying the fishing nets, and another attempt was made to burn the grass; but a charge of small shot caused a retreat, and on their way they set fire to the undergrowth to cover their repulse. Banks was greatly impressed with the manner in which the grass and undergrowth burnt, and declared he would never pitch tents again without first burning the grass for some distance round.

Gore, Banks, and three men made a few days' excursion up the river, but, with the exception of a kangaroo being shot by Gore, the first ever killed by a European, they met with nothing worth noting. On 18th July Cook, Banks, and Solander went up a hill some six or eight miles along the coast to see if they could form any idea of the general run of the coast and the surrounding reefs, and Cook says: "In whatever direction we looked, it [the sea] was covered with shoals as far as the eye could see."

Before leaving the river, Banks gives some notes as to the country, and puts it down as "in every respect the most barren country we have yet seen." The animals were not numerous; he gives kangaroo, wolf (the dingo or native dog), bats (flying foxes), wild cats (dasyurus), and opossums. Amongst the birds, several kinds of duck, shags, pelicans, crows, and flock pigeons, all, with the exception of the last, difficult to shoot. Of the crow he says: "A crow in England though in general sufficiently wary is, I must say, a fool to a New Holland crow." None of the beasts or birds seem to have come amiss to the pot; all that was necessary was the meat should not be salt, "that alone was sufficient to make it a delicacy." He quotes the description given by a sailor of an animal he saw:

"It was as black as the devil and had wings, indeed I took it for the devil, or I might have catched it, for it crawled away very slowly through the grass."

After some little trouble Banks discovered this to have been a large bat (flying fox). Of the insect life seen, he was particularly struck by the white ants and their nests, and formed a very respectful opinion of the mosquito.

Cook's opinion agrees fairly well with that of Banks, but on the whole he thought the east coast was not so barren and desolate as Dampier had described the west coast, and adds: "We are to consider that we see this country in the pure state of nature; the Industry of Man has had nothing to do with any part of it, and yet we find all such things as Nature hath bestowed upon it, in a flourishing state. In this Extensive Country, it can never be doubted, but what most sorts of grain, Fruit, roots, etc., of every kind would flourish here were they once brought hither, planted and cultivated by the hands of Industry; and here are provender for more cattle, at all seasons of the year, than ever can be brought into the country."

This is a fair example of the observations and deductions to be found scattered through Cook's Journals, and an improvement on the would-be scientific and classical rubbish put into his mouth by his editors.

## A MASTHEAD WATCH

At last, on 4th August, they got away from the Endeavour River, only to find themselves surrounded by difficulties. Cook or one of the other officers was continually at the masthead on the look-out, and at length, by keeping very close in shore, they managed to creep past Cape Flattery, and thought the worst was over, but a landing at Point Lookout showed a very unsatisfactory prospect. In hopes of getting a better view Cook went out to Lizard Island, and from there could see, far away to the east, the white breakers on the Great Barrier Reef. This island, on which the only living things to be seen were lizards, they found, from the large piles of shells and remains of fires, was visited periodically by the blacks; a remarkable voyage for their miserable canoes.

Having only three months' supplies at short allowance left, Cook, after a consultation with his officers, made out through an opening in the Barrier Reef that he had seen from Lizard Island, and observes:

"Having been entangled among Islands and Shoals more or less ever since the 26th May, in which time we have sailed 360 leagues by the Lead, without ever having a Leadsman out of the chains, when the ship was under sail, a Circumstance that perhaps never happened to any ship before, and yet it was here absolutely necessary." But their satisfaction in getting outside was diminished when it was found that the increased working of the ship's timbers necessitated the continual use of one pump.

Cook was afraid that being forced outside the Barrier Reef he would be unable to put to the proof the opinion he had formed that New Guinea and New Holland were not joined. He did not know till after his return to England, that the point had already been settled in 1606, by Louis Vaez de Torres, and he readily yields the honour of the discovery in the Introduction to his Second Voyage. The log of Torres's voyage was lost for many years, and was found at Manilla, when that place was taken by Admiral Cornish in 1762. Cook had with him a copy of De Brye's Voyages, published in 1756, which contained three charts that he found to be "tolerably good" with regard to New Guinea, and he evidently formed the opinion that both the Spaniards and the Dutch had circumnavigated that island.

"I always understood, before I had a sight of these maps, that it was unknown whether or no New Holland and New Guinea was one continued land, and so it is said in the very History of Voyages these maps are bound up in. However, we have now put this wholly out of dispute; but as I believe it was known before, but not publickly, I claim no other merit than the clearing up of a doubtful point."

With this question of New Guinea and New Holland in view, he again made to the west, sighting the Barrier again on 15th August, and on the following morning, the wind having changed in the night, the breakers were heard very distinctly. The lead gave no bottom at 140 fathoms, but at daybreak the reef was not a mile away, and they found themselves in a dead calm, rapidly drifting with the current towards the breakers. The yawl and long-boat were got out, the pinnace being under repair, and the sweeps were used from the gun-room ports. By six o'clock she was heading north again, but:

"not above 80 or 100 yards from the breakers. The same sea that washed the side of the ship rose in a breaker prodigiously high the very next time it did rise, so that between us and destruction was only a dismal valley, the breadth of one wave, and even now no ground could be felt with 120 fathoms."

A PERILOUS POSITION

The carpenter had by this time fastened a temporary streak on the pinnace, and it was sent off to assist in towing. Cook had almost given up hope, but he says:

"In this truly terrible situation, not one man ceased to do his utmost, and that with as much calmness as if no danger had been near."

Admiral Wharton draws special attention to the fact that in the very height of the danger, Green, Charles Clerke, and Forwood, the gunner, were engaged in taking a Lunar for the longitude. Green notes:

"These observations were very good, the limbs of the sun and moon very distinct, and a good horizon. We were about 100 yards from the reef, where we expected the ship to strike every minute, it being calm, no soundings, and the swell heaving us right on."

When things seemed perfectly hopeless, a small breath of air, "so small that at any other time in a calm we should not have observed it," came, and every advantage being taken, the distance from the reef was slightly increased, but then again it fell calm. A small opening of the reef was seen and an attempt was made to push through, but the ebb tide was found to be "gushing out like a mill stream." Advantage was taken of this, and they succeeded in getting about a quarter of a mile away, but the current was so narrow they soon lost it. A second opening was seen, and, the tide having changed, they were carried rapidly through Providential Channel and safely anchored in nineteen fathoms of water. Cook says:

"It is but a few days ago that I rejoiced at having got without the Reef, but that joy was nothing when compared to what I now felt at being safe at an anchor within it." Having arrived at a place of safety, Cook resolved to remain till he had his boats in thorough repair and had made a complete study of his difficulties. From the masthead it appeared as if the shoals and reefs offered less obstruction than he had previously towards the north, and he hoped, by keeping as close to the shore as possible, to be able to solve the problem of the passage between New Guinea and New Holland. At this place, boats that had been out fishing brought back a sort of cockle, some requiring two men to lift them, and containing "as much as twenty pounds of good wholesome meat."

## TAKE POSSESSION

Proceeding slowly through a network of reefs, shoals, and islands, the boats always sounding ahead, he had the satisfaction of passing the straits between Cape York and New Guinea, leaving Torres's track considerably to the north. On getting clear of the straits, they landed for the last time in Australian waters, and hoisting the English flag:

"took possession of the whole Eastern Coast from the above latitude (38 degrees 0 minutes South) down to this place by the name of New Wales. We fired three volleys of small arms, which were answer'd by the like number from the ship."

Admiral Wharton says that in the King's and the Admiralty's copies of Cook's Journal the name is given as New South Wales, and in a letter written to Mr. John Walker, of Whitby, dated 13th September 1771, Cook says: "The East coast of New Holland, or what I call New South Wales."

After a narrow escape of running on a reef near Booby Island, from which they were only saved by letting go the anchors with all sails set, they left the difficulties of the New Holland coast behind and sighted New Guinea on 29th August.

FOOTNOTE: STING RAY BAY
"The great number of New Plants, etc., our Gentlemen Botanists have collected in this place occasion'd my giving in [sic] the Name of Botanist Bay."
Extract from the only page known to exist of the Journal of the first voyage written by Cook, and dated 6th May, 1770. It was, July 1911, purchased by Mr. F.T. Sabin for 451 pounds.

# 1770 TO 1771
# NEW GUINEA TO ENGLAND

The water on the New Guinea coast was very shallow, and kept them far out in running westward, but on 3rd September they got a little nearer in, so Cook decided to attempt a landing, and then to leave, as he considered it was only wasting valuable time to go over ground that had already been explored by the Dutch. Banks says the crew were rather sickly, they:
"were pretty far gone with the longing for home, which the physicians have gone so far as to esteem a disease under the name of Nostalgia. Indeed, I can find hardly anybody in the ship clear of its effects, but the Captain, Dr. Solander, and myself, and we three have ample constant employment for our minds, which I believe to be the best if not the only remedy for it."

They were also on short allowance of food, which would necessarily have a depressing effect, and when they learnt that Cook would return to civilisation where fresh supplies could be obtained, there was a marked improvement in the general health.

Calling in at the island of Savu, some supplies were obtained, and the country is described as very lovely, although there had been no rain for seven months; the contrast with the monotonous and barren-looking country of New Holland was very marked.

## AT BATAVIA

According to strict orders from the Admiralty, Cook on 30th September collected all logs and journals that had been kept on board the ship, and enjoined every one that they were on no account to divulge where they had been on their arrival at Batavia. Off Java Head the main topsail was split in a squall, and Cook remarks that all his sails are now in such a condition that "they will hardly stand the least puff of wind." No observations had been possible since leaving Savu, and the strong western current had thrown out their dead reckoning, causing them to run past the Straits of Sunda; but, picking themselves up on 1st October, they got into the straits, and after a wearisome beat up arrived in Batavia on the 10th; and Hicks was sent on shore to announce their arrival, and offer an apology for failing to salute the Dutch flag in a proper manner—the reason being that they had only three guns available.

The ship was thoroughly surveyed, and on the carpenter's report, Cook applied to the Governor for a convenient place in which to heave down and repair, and for permission to purchase such stores as might be necessary. Every assistance was promised, and on Cook's finding a difficulty in getting any private person to cash the bills he would have to draw for his expenses, the Governor ordered the officer in charge of the port to supply whatever amount might be necessary.

During a heavy thunderstorm on the 12th, a Dutch East Indiaman, about two cables away from the Endeavour, had mainmast "split all to shivers." The Endeavour was also struck:

"and in all probability we should have shared the same fate as the Dutchman, had it not been for the electric chain which we had but just before got up; this carried the Lightning or Electrical matter over the side clear of the ship."

On 25th October Cook reopened communication with the Admiralty, forwarding to Mr. Stephens, by the Dutch East Indiaman Kronenberg, Captain F. Kelgar, a packet containing a copy of his Journal (sold to Mr. John Corner in 1890), charts of the South Seas, New Zealand, and the East Coast of Australia. He also wrote a letter giving an outline of his voyage up to date, and concludes:

"In this Journal, I have with undisguised Truth and without gloss, inserted the whole transactions of the Voyage, and made such remarks and have given such descriptions of things as I thought was necessary, in the best manner I was capable of. Although the discoverys made in the Voyage are not great, yet I flatter myself they are such as may merit the Attention of their Lordships, and altho' I have failed in discovering the so much talked of Southern Continent (which perhaps do not exist), and which I myself had much at heart, yet I am confident that no part of the failure of such discovery can be laid to my charge. Had we been so fortunate not to have run ashore, much more would have been done in the latter part of the Voyage than what was, but as it is, I presume this Voyage will be found as compleat as any before made to the South Seas on the same account.

### PRAISES HIS CREW

"The plans I have drawn of the places I have been at, were made with all the care and accuracy that Time and Circumstances would admit of. Thus far I am certain that the Latitude and Longitude of few parts of the World are better settled than these, in this I was very much assisted by Mr. Green, who let slip no one opportunity for making observations for settling the Longitude during the whole course of the Voyage, and the many valuable discoverys made by Mr. Banks and Dr. Solander in Natural History and other things useful to the learned World, cannot fail of contributing very much to the success of the Voyage. In justice to the officers and the whole of the crew, I must say, they have gone through the fatigues and dangers of the Whole Voyage with that cheerfulness and alertness that will always do honour to the British Seamen, and I have the satisfaction to say that I have not lost one man by Sickness during the whole Voyage. I hope that the repairs wanting to the Ship will not be so great as to detain us any length of time; You may be assured that I shall make no unnecessary delay either here or at any other place, but shall make the best of my way home."

Banks, too, notes that there were no sick on board, and contrasts the rosy, healthy appearance of the crew with the pallid faces of the Europeans of Batavia. But on 26th October a series of disastrous entries commence in the Journal.

"Set up the ship's tents for the reception of the ship's company, several of them begin to be taken ill, owing as I suppose to the extream hot weather."

Batavia had an ill-omened reputation, and it has been estimated that from 1735 to 1755 no less than 1,000,000 deaths took place, chiefly from malarial fever and dysentery, and Cook had soon cause to regret that the Dutch had undertaken the repairs of the ship, leaving his men to look on. He knew well the evil effects of want of occupation in such a climate, though he could not guess what it was to cost him. Up to this time he had only seven deaths to record since leaving Plymouth; three from drowning, two frozen (Mr. Banks's servants), one consumption, and one alcoholic poisoning: probably a record never equalled in the history of navigation. On 5th November Mr. Monkhouse, the surgeon, died, and Cook, Banks, and Solander were very ill. The two last went up into the hills, but Cook would not leave his ship.

Meanwhile the repairs went on; the ship was found to be worse than had been expected; two planks and a half had been rasped by the rocks to the thickness of one eighth of an inch for a distance of six feet:

"and here the worms had made their way quite into the timbers, so that it was a matter of surprise to every one who saw her bottom, how we had kept her above water, and yet in this condition we had sailed some hundreds of leagues in as dangerous a navigation as in any part of the world, happy in being ignorant of the continual danger we were in."

By the 14th her bottom was thoroughly repaired, and Cook speaks highly of the Dutch workmen:

"I do not believe there is a Marine Yard in the World where work is done with more alertness than here, or where there are better conveniences for heaving ships down, both in point of safety and Despatch." The water, a perquisite of the Commodore of the Dutch East Indian fleet, was very unsatisfactory, and was found to keep very badly at sea, although its keeping properties had been loudly vaunted by the Commodore. Cook was present at his appointment:

"one of the grandest sights Batavia afforded; that may be too, and yet it did not recompense us for our trouble. I thought that the whole was but ill conducted, and the fleet appeared to be very badly mann'd."

A seaman who had run from a Dutch ship entered on the Endeavour, was claimed by the Dutch on the grounds that he was a Dane from Elsinore. Cook promised he should be given up if he proved not to be a British subject, and enquiry by Mr. Hicks resulted in a report to the Governor that he was an Irishman, so the matter dropped. His name was James Marra, and he will be again met with as gunner's mate on the Resolution.

## DEATH OF TUPIA

Before leaving Batavia there had been seven deaths, including Mr. Reynolds, artist, and Tupia and his boy servant, and Cook gives the number of sick as "forty or more." Hoping the sea breezes might have a beneficial effect, preparations were hurried forward, and they managed to leave the day after Christmas Day, being duly saluted by the garrison with fourteen guns, and the Earl of Elgin with thirteen guns and three cheers, "all of which we return'd."

Calling at Prince's Island in the straits of Sunda, where some of the Batavian water was replaced by better, the sailors were allowed to purchase whatever they fancied in hopes of diminishing the dysentery which was rampant. Every precaution that could be thought of was tried, but in vain. Mr. Banks lost Messrs. Sporing and Parkinson, and on 29th January Mr. Green died; he had been long ill, but Cook says he would not take proper care of himself. To judge from his own Journal, he must have been rather a difficult man to get on with, but his services as observer were invaluable, and he at all times and seasons was devoted to his special duty: indeed, at times he appears to have thought that every other work should give way to his. It is a somewhat suggestive fact that Banks hardly makes any reference to Mr. Green throughout his Journal. On 27th February the terrible list of losses was closed by the deaths of three of the crew, making in all thirty deaths since their arrival at Batavia.

It was afterwards discovered that the season in Batavia had been unusually unhealthy, and several ships that had called in there had to report heavy losses. Cook says:

"Thus we find that ships which have been little more than twelve months from England have suffer'd as much or more by sickness than we have done, who have been out near three times as long. Yet their sufferings will hardly, if at all, be mentioned or known in England; when, on the other hand, those of the Endeavour, because her voyage is uncommon, will very probably be mentioned in every News Paper, and, what is not unlikely, with Additional hardships we never Experienced; for such are the dispositions of men in general in these Voyages, that they are seldom content with the Hardships and Dangers which will naturally occur, but they must add others which hardly ever had existence but in their imaginations, by magnifying the most Trifling accidents and Circumstances to the greatest Hardships, and unsurmountable Dangers without the immediate interposition of Providence, as if the whole merit of the Voyages consisted in the real dangers and Hardships they underwent, or that the real ones did not happen often enough to give the mind sufficient anxiety. Thus Posterity are taught to look upon these Voyages as hazardous to the highest degree."

## AT THE CAPE

On 6th March land was sighted at daylight, about two leagues away, near Cape Natal, and on the 15th the Cape of Good Hope was seen. The first thing to be done was to provide shelter ashore for his sick, of whom he landed twenty-eight, and during the stay the remainder of the crew were given every possible opportunity of being on land, as Cook recognised the value of an entire change of life in shaking off the remnants of sickness. He lost three more of his men here, and hearing from a Dutch ship just in from Europe that war was threatening between England and Spain, he hurried up his preparations for departure and got all his men on board, though some were still very ill. In addition he managed to enter some half-dozen men for the voyage home.

In writing of the Cape, Cook draws attention to the fact: "that a stranger is at once struck with surprise and disappointment, for no country we have seen this voyage affords so barren a prospect as this, and not only so in appearance but in reality."

Then further on he says: "Notwithstanding the many disadvantages this country labours under, such is the industry, economy, and good management of the Dutch, that not only the necessary, but all the Luxuries of Life are raised here in great abundance, and are sold as cheap, if not cheaper, than in any part of Europe, some few articles excepted."

On the other hand, he complains of the exorbitant charges made by the Dutch East India Company for naval stores. As at Batavia, they were sold at a certain fixed price from which there was no deviation.

Calling in at St. Helena, they found H.M.Ss. Portland and Swallow, with a convoy, in the roads, and received some few much-needed stores from them, together with the information that all danger of war between Spain and England was over. They all sailed in company on 5th May, but after a few days Cook explained to Captain Elliott, of the Portland, who had come on board the Endeavour, that his ship, sails, and rigging were naturally not in very good order after his lengthy voyage, and therefore he should probably be unable to keep up with the other ships. He requested the Portland to take charge of letters, charts, and journals for the Admiralty. These papers only arrived in England three days in advance of the Endeavour. For some days the good Bark kept within easy reach of the fleet, and was able to obtain extra medical advice for Mr. Hicks, who was suffering from consumption when he left England, but had held out well till stricken with the Batavian fever, when he gradually sank and died on 25th May; Mr. Charles Clerke was appointed third lieutenant, in place of Mr. Gore, promoted. Since leaving the Cape they had also lost their Master, Mr. Molineaux, of whose intelligence Cook speaks very highly, but deplores his want of steadiness, the true cause of his early death. Mr. Pickersgill was appointed to the vacancy.

## ANCHOR IN THE DOWNS

On the 21st June they were still in sight of some of the convoy, but during the night they had their main topgallant sail split, and the topmast sprung, in a heavy squall; in fact, their gear was in such a bad state that something gave way daily. On 7th July they spoke a brig from London, three days out from Scilly, and learnt that no account of their proceedings had yet been made public, and that wagers were being laid that the Endeavour was lost. On 10th July Nicholas Young, who had sighted New Zealand, sighted the Land's End, and the Lizard was seen the next day. On Saturday, 13th July 1771, "at 3 o'clock in the P.M. anchor'd in the Downs and soon after I landed in order to repair to London."

Before leaving, Cook wrote to Mr. Stephens informing him of his arrival, and announcing that he was coming up to the Admiralty to lay before their Lordships a full account of the whole voyage, and that the ship was to await further orders. He hopes that the appointments that he has made will meet with approval, and requests that his charts, plans, and drawings may be laid before the authorities.

On 2nd August, Stephens wrote to him at Mile End, saying he had received the papers sent from Batavia, those by the Portland and those from the Downs, and that they had been laid before their Lordships. He goes on:

"I have the pleasure to acquaint you that their Lordships extremely well approve of the whole of your proceedings and that they have great satisfaction in the account you have given them of the good behaviour of your officers and men and of the cheerfulness and alertness with which they went through the fatigues and dangers of their late Voyage."

He also notifies at the same time that the appointments made have all been confirmed.

Cook himself was appointed Commander of the Scorpion on 29th August, but owing to other arrangements being made did not put in an appearance on his new ship. Isaac Smith and Isaac Manly were appointed respectively Master's mate and midshipman, taking part in the Second Voyage, being too young for further promotion.

The newspapers, of course, blossomed out into paragraphs on the subject of the voyage, more or less correct, and Bingley's Journal on 23rd July stated:

"In consequence of this discovery, more ships will be destined in search of this new terrestrial acquisition."

Evidently it was quickly decided that Cook's rest was to be short. On 27th the same Journal says:

"His Majesty's Ship, the Endeavour, which is lately arrived in the River from the East Indies, lost by the unhealthiness of the climate, 70 of her hands, tho' they were picked men, and had been several times in the Indies. However, those who survive will have made their fortunes by traffic, having brought home some of the richest goods made in the east, which they are suffered to dispose of without the inspection of the Custom House officers. This, our correspondent says, is allowed them by the Government as a reward for their hard and dangerous service during a voyage of three years."

The amount of the "richest goods made in the East" obtained from New Zealand, Australia, and Otaheite would be but a poor reward for three years' strenuous service; and Cook here finds his premonition as to his losses being exaggerated, only too true.

It is worthy of note that the number of punishments throughout the voyage was remarkably small, those entered in the ship's log being twenty-one, and the heaviest sentence, two dozen lashes for theft. In one case, that of Mathew Cox, A.B., for disobedience and mutinous conduct, the culprit proceeded civilly against Cook, on arrival in England, and the Admiralty solicitors were instructed to defend. The case was probably allowed to drop, as no result can be found.

## LAST OF THE ENDEAVOUR

The good ship which had so bravely borne her part, was not given much rest; but after being paid off at Woolwich, was despatched, under lieutenant James Gordon, to the Falkland Islands on 16th October, and returned with "perishable and unserviceable" stores; in 1772 and 1773 she again made voyages to the same destination, the last one to bring away the garrison and stores, as those islands were to be handed over to Spain. She was paid off at Woolwich in September 1774, and shortly afterwards was sold out of the Navy for the sum of 645 pounds. She is then believed to have been employed as a collier in the North Seas. Mr. Gibbs, of the firm of Gibbs and Canning of Newport, Rhode Island, one day pointed out to the English Consul the remains of an old vessel falling into decay, and informed him that it was Captain Cook's ship, the Endeavour. His story was that the French Government being anxious to compete with England in the whale fishery, offered a bounty to the ships in that trade sailing under the French flag. A Mr. Hayden purchased the old ship from a Dunkirk firm and re-christened her La Liberte, loaded her with oil and consigned her, under French colours, to Gibbs and Canning at Newport. She was chased by an English ship, but escaped, and after laying alongside a wharf for some months received a cargo, but running aground in trying to leave the harbour, she was found in such a bad condition that she was allowed to remain to drop to pieces. Enquiries into this story gave satisfactory results, and a box made from her timbers was presented to J. Fennimore Cooper, the American author, with letters authenticating, as far as possible, the vessel from which the wood had been taken. Miss Cooper mentions this box in her preface to her father's Red Rover, and several other relics of the old ship are still to be found in the neighbourhood of Newport.

# 1771
# PREPARATIONS FOR SECOND VOYAGE

After reporting himself to the Admiralty on his arrival in England, Cook proceeded to his home at Mile End Old Town, where he was for some time employed in completing his Charts and Journals, and on 14th August, the Annual Register announces, he was introduced to His Majesty at St. James's, when he:

"presented his Journal of his Voyage, with some curious maps and charts of different places that he had drawn during the voyage; he was presented with a captain's commission."

He also found time to write two long and instructive letters to his old master and good friend, Mr. John Walker of Whitby, which are to be found in Dr. Young's work. They give a rapid glance at the different places visited, with a few pithy remarks as to their peoples and productions; mention the pleasing reception he had from the king, and he alludes to the probability of being despatched on a second voyage with two ships.

Edgeworth, in his Memoirs, states that about this time Cook was a frequent visitor at Denham Place, the home of Mr. Louis Way, F.R.S., but as that gentleman died in this year, and Edgeworth also refers to events of a later date as occurring at the same time, it is more probable that these visits were paid after the Second Voyage to Mr. Benjamin Way, also F.R.S., and a Director of the South Sea Company. In another place Edgeworth infers that Banks, Solander, and Cook were members of a club which met at Slaughter's Coffee House in 1765. Of course, this is an error, for Cook was then engaged in Newfoundland, and unknown to the Royal Society, whose members composed the club spoken of; in fact, Cook, though a frequent guest in after times, was never a member of the Royal Societies Club.

Fanny Burney (Madame d'Arblay) says that in September her father, Dr. Charles Burney, spent a few days at Hinchinbroke, Lord Sandwich's place, in order to meet Cook, Banks, and Solander, and it is evident that the second voyage had been resolved on, for Dr. Burney's son, James, was introduced to Cook by Lord Sandwich, with a view to going on the expedition. Shortly after this, Sandwich met Dr. Burney at Lord Oxford's, Houghton, and asked him if he could recommend any one capable of writing the history of the voyage of the Endeavour; he gave Dr. Hawkesworth's name, and was requested to introduce him to Lord Sandwich on his return to town.

The object of the Second Voyage was, to use Cook's own words: "To put an end to all diversity of opinion about a matter so curious and important, was His Majesty's principal motive in directing this voyage to be undertaken, the history of which is now submitted to the public, i.e., the existence of another continent in the South."

The discussion on the subject had been resumed with renewed vigour after the return of the Endeavour, and Dalrymple led one party, who held that Cook had not set the matter at rest as he had left far too much space untraversed.

## WHITBY SHIPS AGAIN

The two ships that were to be employed were probably selected in the Thames by Cook himself, and, like the good ship Endeavour, were built by Fishburn of Whitby, and purchased from Captain W. Hammond of Hull. The reasoning which guided Cook in his selection is thus laid down by him in his introduction to the account of the Second Voyage:

"The success of such undertakings as making discoveries in distant parts of the world, will principally depend on the preparations being well adapted to what ought to be the first consideration, namely, the preservation of the adventurers and ships; and this will chiefly depend on the kind, the size, and the properties of the ships chosen for the service. These primary considerations will not admit of any other, that may interfere with the necessary properties of the ships. Therefore, in chusing the ships, should any of the most advantageous properties be wanting, and the necessary room in them be, in any degree, diminished for less important purposes, such a step would be laying a foundation for rendering the undertaking abortive in the first instance. The ship must not be of great draught, but of sufficient capacity to carry a proper quantity of provisions and stores for the crew, and of such construction that she will bear to take the ground, and of such a size that she can be conveniently laid on shore if necessary for repairing any damages or defects, and these qualities are to be found in North Country built ships, such as are built for the coal trade, and in none other."

The larger of the two chosen was 462 tons, purchased for 4,151 pounds, and received into the Royal Navy under the name of the Drake. She was fitted as a sloop at Deptford, at a cost of 6,568 pounds (this sum, probably, covering both the original alterations which proved unsatisfactory and those made immediately before sailing), and at the time of her purchase was about fourteen months old. The second ship was of 336 tons, also fitted at Deptford as a sloop, was eighteen months old at time of purchase, cost 2,103 pounds, and was received under the name of Raleigh.

The complement of the Raleigh was eighty, but two additional carpenters' mates were added to each ship later on. Cook was also instructed not to bear, as was then usual, any servants on the books, but to enter A.B.s instead, and each officer who was entitled to a servant was "to be paid an allowance by Bill equal to the wages of the number of servants respectively allowed them."

On 25th December the names of the two ships were changed, the Drake becoming the Resolution, and the Raleigh the Adventure. The lieutenants appointed to the Resolution were Robert Pallisser Cooper, Charles Clerke, and Richard Pickersgill, and Mr. Tobias Furneaux, Commander, and Joseph Shank first lieutenant, of the Adventure. Of these officers Cook writes:

"I had all the reason in the World to be perfectly satisfied with the choice of the officers. The Second and Third Lieutenants, the Lieutenant of Marines, two of the Warrant officers, and several of the Petty officers had been with me during the former voyage. The others were men of known abilities, and all of them on every occasion showed their zeal for the service in which they were employed during the whole voyage."

## ALTERATIONS TO THE RESOLUTION

Two days after receiving his orders, Cook hoisted his pendant and superintended the alterations that were to be made for the accommodation of Mr. Banks and his party of scientists. These comprised Dr. Solander, Zoffani, the portrait painter, Dr. Lynd of Edinburgh, to secure whose services Parliament had made a special grant of 4000 pounds (though "what discoveries they expected him to make I could not understand," says Cook), and nine others, draughtsmen and servants; at least three more than had been thought necessary when the vessel was purchased. These alterations were:

"to raise her upper works about a foot, to lay a spar deck upon her from the quarter-deck to the forecastle (she having at this time a low waist), and to build a round house or coach for my accommodation, so that the great cabin might be appropriated to the use of Mr. Banks alone."

The Comptroller of the Navy, Captain Pallisser, was strongly opposed to these alterations as likely to be detrimental to the ship's sailing qualities, and though his opinions were overborne, they in the end proved to be correct.

When he had seen the alterations fairly on the way, Cook applied for three weeks' leave of absence, on the plea that he had "some business to transact in Yorkshire, as well as to see an aged father," and his application was at once granted. He therefore went to Ayton, where for the first time for seventeen years he was again amongst his own people. From Ayton he went on to Whitby, and was met some miles out from that town by many of the leading men of the place. From the Walkers he received the heartiest of welcomes, and it is related that the old housekeeper, Mary Prowd, had been carefully instructed that a Commander in His Majesty's Navy was a very different person from one of her master's apprentices, and must be received with all the marks of respect due to his rank. She promised obedience, but, alas, when the time came her memory fled, and opening wide her arms, she exclaimed: "O honey James! How glad I is to see thee!" A welcome, probably, more dear to Cook than any other could have been, and a proof of the affectionate regard he could inspire.

In February he was back in London, and Dr. Burney says in his Memoirs:

"I had the honour of receiving the illustrious Captain Cook to dine with me in Queen's Square [Bloomsbury] previously to his second voyage round the world. Observing upon a table, Bougainville's Voyage Autour du Monde, he turned it over, and made some curious remarks on the illiberal conduct of that circumnavigator towards himself when they met and crossed each other; which made me desirous to know, in examining the chart of M. de Bougainville, the several tracks of the two navigators, and exactly where they had crossed or approached each other.

"Captain Cook instantly took a pencil from his pocket book and said he would trace the route; which he did in so clear and scientific a manner that I would not take fifty pounds for my book. The pencil marks, having been fixed by skim milk, will always be visible."

This volume is now in the British Museum, and the pencil marks on the chart are as distinct as on the day they were made.

The alterations to the ship were completed early in February, and on the 6th she was hauled out of dock, and rigging, ballasting, and storing commenced. Cook says:

"Every department seemed to vie with the other in equiping these two ships, every standing rule and order in the Navy was dispensed with, every alteration, every necessary and useful article, was granted as soon as asked for."

## SUPPLIES INCREASED

In another passage he again refers to the anxiety of the Navy Board to see that the quality of the stores was everything that could be wished, and the quantity was increased from one to two and a half years' supply.

On the 22nd April the two sloops were at Longreach to take in their guns and gunners' stores; twelve carriage guns and twelve swivel musketoons for the Resolution, and ten carriage guns and ten swivels for the Adventure. These should have been taken on board at Galleon's Reach, but the Resolution was drawing too much water—seventeen feet. When here Cook showed that he thought she was rather over-weighted with her new upper works, and might prove crank, but:

"as the Gentlemen's apartments were full of heavy baggage and the sloop a good deal lumbered aloft with heavy and some useless articles, which we might soon get rid of or get into the hold after we had consumed some of our provisions, I still entertained hopes that she would bear all her additional works, and suspended giving any other opinion until a full trial had been made of her, foreseeing what would be the consequence in case she did not answer in the manner she was now fitted."

On 29th April, Mr. Banks gave an entertainment on board to Lord Sandwich, the French Ambassador, and other distinguished personages, and Cook notes that the first named had been on board several times, "a laudable tho ' rare thing in a First Lord of the Admiralty."

Cook obtained a few days' leave to make his final arrangements, and the Resolution was ordered to the Downs under the first lieutenant, whilst the Adventure proceeded to Plymouth; both vessels sailing from Longreach on 10th May. The Resolution, contending against adverse winds, made a very slow trip down to the Nore, being four days on the journey, and Mr. Cooper reported to Cook that she was very crank. The latter at once wrote to the Admiralty that he considered it unsafe to proceed any further with her in that condition, and proposed that her poop should be cut down, her masts shortened, and her guns exchanged to four-pounders. The

123

Navy Board, however, decided that she should be restored to her original state as far as it was possible to do so; she was therefore ordered to Sheerness, and her Captain was instructed to join his ship and see the alterations were properly carried out.

Before leaving London Cook, who had heard it was said that he was not satisfied with the vessels chosen for the voyage, wrote to Mr. Stephens on the subject, giving his opinion that the crankness of the Resolution "was owing to the additional works that have been built upon her in order to make large accommodation for the several gentlemen passengers intended to embark in her." He added that the proposed alterations of the Navy Board would "render her as fit to perform the voyage as any ship whatever"; and, referring to the report that he did not approve of the type of ship, he says, "from the knowledge and experience I have had of these sort of vessels, I shall always be of opinion that only such are proper to be sent on Discoveries to very distant parts." On the 21st he again wrote Stephens that the alterations were making satisfactory progress, and that a man had been in the yard who had known the ship before her purchase, and he had "with some warmth asserted that at that time she was not only a stiff ship, but had as many good qualities as any ship ever built in Whitby." In reply to a rumour that the men were afraid to sail in her, he points out that she is moored alongside a wharf, and the men could go ashore whenever they pleased, yet he had not lost a single man.

## BANKS WITHDRAWS

Mr. Banks did not approve of the reduction in his accommodation necessitated by these alterations, and tried to get a 40-gun ship in place of the Resolution, and he and his friends succeeded in raising a very acrimonious discussion on the subject; but the admiralty stood firm, and the alterations went on under the superintendence of Cook. On 24th May Banks and Solander went to inspect her, and on their return to town Banks wrote to the Admiralty that he should not go the voyage as "the ship was neither roomy nor convenient enough for my purpose, nor no ways proper for the voyage." Cook, who says the preparations had cost Banks "about five Thousand Pounds," does not think that the reasons given by Banks were the only ones he had for not taking part in the voyage, and then continues, "their baggage, etc., were got out of the sloop and sent to London, after which no more complaints were heard of want of room, etc."

Lieutenant Clerke, who was very friendly with Banks, wrote to him on 31st May:

"Indeed I am sorry I'm not to have the honour of attending you the other bout...They are going to stow the major part of the cables in the hold to make room for the people now. I asked Gilbert [the Master], if such was the present case, what the devil should we have done if we had all gone? 'Oh, by God, that was impossible,' was his answer."

Marra (the gunner's mate), in a Journal of the voyage, published by Newberry, 1775, says the success of the voyage was due to their having shaken off:

"the train of gentlemen, who with their attendants occupied the chief accommodations of the ship," and whose presence would have rendered it "out of the power of the most determined officer to have carried such a princely retinue through the icy regions which they were to pass, without murmurs, or perhaps mutiny."

Some of the newspapers tried to make political matter out of the affair, and one at any rate roundly declared that "the true reason" of Banks's withdrawal was on account of a remonstrance from the Spanish Ambassador against any further exploration of the South Seas.

The withdrawal of Banks made no difference to his friendship with Cook, and in the future he was always ready to afford his support whenever it could be of any service either to his friend or family.

## JOHN REINHOLD FORSTER

As soon as it was known that Mr. Banks had withdrawn, Mr. John Reinhold Forster, a German of some scientific reputation, applied for the position of naturalist for the voyage, and, through the interest of Lord Sandwich, was successful. He was to receive the 4000 pounds granted by Parliament for Dr. Lynd, and was to pay all expenses, except ship's allowance of food, and provide all necessary instruments. He was accompanied by his son as assistant, a youth of about twenty years, who afterwards attained some note by his writings and translations. Messrs. Wales and Bayley were appointed astronomers by the Board of Longitude, with instructions to take and compare observations at every possible opportunity, and to take under their special charge the timepieces which were being carried on the two ships for the purpose of testing their accuracy and capabilities in assisting in ascertaining the longitude. Two of these instruments, made by Arnold, were placed in Mr. Bayley's charge on the Adventure, and two, one by Arnold, and the other by Kendal on Harrison's principle, under the care of Mr. Wales on the Resolution. Great precautions were taken to prevent any accident or tampering with these instruments; they were kept in boxes having three locks, the keys were held one by the Captain, one by the first lieutenant, and the third by the astronomer, so they could not even be wound up except in the presence of all three. William Hodges, a painter of repute, was appointed as artist, and his pictures were to become the property of the Admiralty.

The celebrated Dr. Joseph Priestley, at that time minister at Mill Hill Chapel, Leeds, had been invited by Mr. Banks to accompany him as astronomer, and his congregation had undertaken to guarantee his position on his return; but the Board of Longitude took objection to his religious views, and so his application was withdrawn.

# 1772 TO 1774
# SECOND VOYAGE

Saying goodbye to his family on 21st June, Cook, accompanied by Mr. Wales, left London for Sheerness, and the next day dropped down to the Nore. The Resolution was now drawing only fifteen feet ten inches of water instead of seventeen, a very satisfactory improvement. She was given a good trial on a wind, and was found "to answer exceeding well." On 3rd July they arrived at Plymouth, having been boarded the day before by Lord Sandwich and Captain Pallisser, who were on a tour of inspection, and Cook had the pleasure of giving them a satisfactory account of his ship: "I had not one fault to allege."

On arrival at Plymouth, Cook found that orders had been given to the stores that he was to be supplied with whatever he thought necessary, but the only things required were larger coppers for the distilling apparatus, the ones they had on board having proved far too small. The officers and crew were paid up to 28th May, and the petty officers and men also received two months' advance to enable them to provide necessaries and extras for the voyage. Cook remarks:

"The payment of six months' wages to the officers, and crews of these two sloops, being nearly all they had due, was an indulgence never before granted to any of His Majesty's Ships."

Cook now received his final orders, which he had assisted to draw up—in fact, "nothing was inserted that I did not fully comprehend and approve of." He was to call at Madeira for a supply of wine; to sail for the Cape of Good Hope and there refresh his men; then to look for Cape Circumcision, placed by M. Bouvet in 54 degrees South, 11 degrees 20 minutes East, to determine if it formed part of a continent, and if so to explore it, following the coast and endeavouring to get as near to the South Pole as he could without endangering his ships or crews. Should Cape Circumcision prove to be an island, or should he be unable to find it, he was to proceed as far south as he thought there was a probability of meeting with land, and then steering east, circumnavigate the world in as high a latitude as he could. In case of meeting with land he was to explore as far as time would permit. When the season rendered it unsafe to remain in high latitudes he was to retire to the north to refit and recruit, and at a proper season to return to the south. In any unforeseen circumstances he was to use his own discretion, and if the Resolution should be lost, he was to prosecute his voyage in the Adventure. A copy of these orders was given to Captain Furneaux, and in case of separation the following rendezvous were named: Madeira, Port Praya in the island of St. Iago, the Cape of Good Hope, and New Zealand.

## FORSTER SAVES SHIP!

The Forsters evidently were far from pleasant travelling companions, and at one time or another seem to have quarrelled with every one on board the ship. At the very first the father was dissatisfied with the accommodation allotted to him, and offered Mr. Cooper 100 pounds to turn out of his cabin; when this offer was declined, he tried to force Mr. Gilbert, the Master, to give up his, threatening if he refused he should be reported to the king and turned out of the Navy; this threat appears to have been a favourite one, and soon became a by-word with the seamen, who, according to Mr. Wales, would use it to each other on every possible occasion. But, according to his own account, Mr. Forster was able to save the expedition from a very great disaster on 12th July. He says he came on deck and noticed the ship was adrift from her moorings; neither the officer of the watch nor the look-out had seen it till he called attention, and then, after a scene of the greatest confusion, the ship was fortunately brought up within a few feet of the rocks. On the other hand, the Master's log admits the Resolution got adrift, but before Mr. Forster reached the deck the fact had been reported to the Captain, all hands turned up, the jib and forestay sail set, and the ship quietly dropped down into the Sound and anchored, never having been in the slightest danger. The only other one to notice the affair was Midshipman Willis, who simply states, "dropped from the Buoy and anchored in the Sound."

Having received the private signals of the East India Company's Navy, and letters of introduction from the Prince of Orange to all the principal officers of the Dutch East India Company, instructing them to afford every assistance that might be required, Cook hoisted the signal to the Adventure to weigh anchor at 5 A.M. on 13th July, and with a north-west breeze the two ships sailed for Madeira. When well out in the Channel the Resolution's crew was mustered, and it was found that, owing to a mistake of the clerk, there was one man more than the complement, so John Coghlan was entered on the Supernumerary List for Wages and Victuals.

On the 23rd they were able to relieve a small French boat, from Ferrol to Corunna, which had been blown far off her course, and had been short of water for a fortnight. The day following they fell in with three Spanish men-o'-war; Cook says: "The sternmost hoisted English colours and fired a gun to leeward, and soon after hoisted his own proper colours, and spoke with the Adventure." It appears she enquired who they were, and where they were going, and finally wished them a good voyage. This account did not satisfy Mr. Forster, who waxes eloquent and describes the event as "a scene so humiliating to the masters of the sea." He must have formed a strange opinion of Cook if he thought for a moment he was one to put up silently with anything humiliating to the British flag. Marra, in his Journal, points out that the build and rig of the ships were unusual for men-o'-war, and that when the Spaniards found they had stopped king's ships, they "made a proper apology, and very politely took leave, wishing them a good voyage."

## THE FIRST LOSS

At Madeira, where they arrived on 29th July, they were kindly received by Mr. Loughnan, a merchant of Funchal, who entertained some of the party at his house throughout the stay, obtained permission for the Forsters to explore the island, and procured for the ships the stores that were required. Here Cook, with his eye on the scurvy, purchased as many onions as he thought would keep good, and ordered them to be served out regularly to the crews as long as they lasted. A further stock of fresh food in the shape of fowls, pigs, goats, and fruits—chiefly oranges and bananas—was laid in at Port Praya, where they had called for water. On the 19th the first death occurred; one of the carpenter's mates, Henry Smook, was at work on one of the scuttles and, falling overboard, was seen under the stern; every effort was made to save him, but it was too late. Cook says he was a good, steady man, whose loss was often felt during the voyage.

On 27th August Cook learnt that the Adventure had also had her losses. Two midshipman, Lambrecht and Kemp, had died of fever, brought on, Captain Furneaux believed, by bathing and drinking too much water under the hot sun of Port Praya. At this time the Resolution had a clean bill of health, but for fear lest the heavy rains, to which they were continually subjected, might cause sickness, the ship was constantly fumigated, washed down, and thoroughly dried by means of stoves, as advised by Captains Pallisser and Campbell, with satisfactory results. On nearing the Cape a sharp but unavailing look-out was kept for a bank which had been reported, and on 30th October they arrived in Table Bay. The run from home was considered to have been good, as they had in great measure escaped the calms they had been told to expect at that season of the year, and the currents, though very strong, had only caused a difference between the longitude obtained by observation and that by dead reckoning of three-quarters of a degree, so Cook concluded that those north of the Equator in the one direction were balanced by those to the south in the contrary one.

On landing they were received by the Governor, Baron Plattenberg, who told Cook he had received orders from Holland that the two sloops were to have every assistance that the place afforded. He also said that two French ships, commanded by M. de Kerguelen, had discovered land in 48 degrees South, near the meridian of Mauritius, but after sailing along the coast for about forty miles, he had been blown off by a heavy gale, in which he had lost both boats and men. Two other French ships had also called in March, which were on their way to explore the South Pacific under M. Marion.

Wales and Bayley got their instruments ashore in order to make observations for the purpose of correcting the watch machines. That made by Kendal was found to be working well, and gave the longitude within one minute of time when compared with that fixed by Messrs. Mason and Dixon in 1761. The first lieutenant of the Adventure, Mr. Shank, who had been ill almost from the day of leaving England, applied for leave to return home, as he felt unfit to proceed, and Mr. Arthur Kemp was made first lieutenant, his place being taken by Mr. James Burney. Mr. Sparrman, a former pupil of Linnaeus, was engaged by Mr. Forster as an assistant, and makes his appearance on the rolls as servant. The crews were well looked after, as much time granted on shore as possible, and fresh meat, fresh vegetables, and fresh baked bread were served out daily in ample quantity, so that when the ships sailed to the southward they were all "in as good a condition as when they left England." Cook found time to write a letter of farewell to Mr. Walker, as it was: "customary for men to take leave of their friends before they go out of the world; for I can hardly think myself in it, so long as I am deprived of having any connection with the civilised part of it, and this will soon be my case for two years at least."

He at the end speaks of his ships, both "well provided and well mann'd," and of the Resolution he says: "I can assure you I never set foot in a finer ship."

## THE FIRST ICE

On 22nd November they sailed for the south, and soon began to feel the colder climate; the warm jackets and trousers provided by the Admiralty were served out, extra cuffs to protect the hands being sewn on, and warmly-lined canvas capes being made. From the 29th till 6th December they were involved in such a heavy gale that the ships were unable to carry any sail, and a large quantity of the live stock bought at the Cape perished from the effects of wet and cold. A scuttle which had been insecurely fastened was burst open by the sea, and a considerable quantity of water was taken on board, but beyond necessitating some work at the pumps and rendering things unpleasantly damp for a time, no damage was done. It, however, gave Mr. Forster an opportunity for an account of the terrible danger they were in, and, most wonderful to relate, to speak well of the conduct of the crew. The ships were carried so far to the east by the gale, that Cook gave up the idea of searching for Cape Circumcision for the present. On the 10th the first ice was encountered in latitude 50 degrees 40 minutes South, and a little higher they were stopped by a large field, to which they "could see no end, either to the east, west, or south." This field was followed along to the south-east for some days, but no opening was found, so being in constant danger from detached pieces, Cook reluctantly gave orders to change the course to the northward. About the middle of December signs of scurvy began to show, and extra precautions were at once taken; fresh wort was served out regularly to all hands and the worst case received considerable benefit from the treatment, although "Rob of Lemons and Oranges" (a sort of jelly made from the fruits) had had no effect. Furneaux reported at this time that he had cured two very bad cases with the Rob.

## SHIPS PARTED

When they had got thoroughly clear of all signs of ice, Cook once again turned south, and by 26th December had worked down as far as 50 degrees 31 minutes South, 26 degrees 57 minutes East, where, though surrounded by large masses of floating ice, they steered to the west, leaving the main ice field to the north of them. Gradually working down to 60 degrees South in the longitude given for Cape Circumcision, and being some ninety-five leagues further south, with no signs of land, Cook concluded that M. Bouvet must have been deceived by the ice. (Bouvet Island was discovered by the German Deep Sea Discovery ship Valdivia on 25th November 1898. The position was fixed as 54 degrees 26.4 minutes South, 3 degrees 24.2 minutes ??South, and not 54 degrees South, 11 degrees 20 East, as given to Cook, which will account for his want of success in his search for it.) Here Mr. Wales was enabled to get a sight of the moon for the second time since leaving the Cape of Good Hope, and, taking several observations, fixed the position of the ship with tolerable accuracy. Changing the course to East-South-East, very foggy weather was encountered, accompanied by great cold, which coated the rigging with ice, rendering it very pretty to the eye but difficult and unpleasant to work. Cook says that, though this suggested very intense cold to the mind, in reality the thermometer was rather higher than it had been, and the sea was far less encumbered with ice. Taking large blocks of ice on board it was found that, when the sea water was drained off, they provided perfectly fresh water on melting, thus removing a great weight from Cook's shoulders, and he determined on venturing further to the southward. On 17th January 1773 they crossed the Antarctic Circle in longitude 39 degrees 35 minutes East, and at noon their latitude, by observation, was 66 degrees 36 minutes 30 seconds South, the sea being free from ice. However, in the evening they found themselves completely blocked by an enormous field, extending, as far as the eye could reach, from the south-east round to the west; and as the summer was nearly over, Cook decided it was unwise to attempt anything further southwards, and ordered a retreat to the north. Again making for the land claimed to have been discovered by the French, he spent some days searching for it, but nothing was seen except some floating weed and a few birds that are supposed never to get far away from land. On 8th February a brisk gale sprang up, accompanied by very hazy weather, thickening into fog, and the two vessels separated. The Resolution cruised about, firing guns and burning flares, but no response was heard, and when the weather cleared up, the Adventure was not to be seen. Poor Mr. Forster was dreadfully scared when he realised the two ships had parted company; he says that none of the crew "ever looked around the ocean without expressing concern on seeing our ship alone on this vast and unexplored expanse." He seems to have been thoroughly unhappy, for he describes the whole voyage, from the Cape to New Zealand, as a series of hardships such as had never before been experienced by mortal man. Cook conjectured, rightly as it proved, that being a little to the south of Tasman's track, Furneaux would make for the rendezvous he had been given at New Zealand, and therefore felt himself free to push on to the south-east, as he judged that if any large body of land was in the vicinity, it must lie in that direction, for the swell coming from the south-west precluded the possibility of any mass of land being in that quarter.

On 17th February a display of the Aurora Australis was reported to Cook, who speaks of it as something quite new to him, although Banks noted a display during the voyage of the Endeavour between Timor and Batavia. The present one is described as having a spiral motion, the direction not strongly defined, and at times strong flashes of light. A second display was seen on the 25th, but not so marked. On this day, too, some of the ship's boats engaged in watering from a small iceberg, had a narrow escape from destruction as the berg turned completely over whilst they were at work.

The weather becoming very unsettled the Resolution was obliged to make to the north, and on 8th March, the finest day they had experienced since leaving the Cape, they were able to fix their position by observation as 59 degrees 44 minutes South, 121 degrees 9 minutes East, the thermometer registering 40 degrees. Of course this pleasant break was followed by a heavy gale, with a tremendously heavy sea, and the ship ran before it for New Zealand. Cook's wish was to touch at Van Diemen's Land, so as to satisfy himself as to its forming a part of New Holland, but the wind kept obstinately between west and north, having shifted after the gale, and he thought it would occupy a longer time than he could spare, so he bore up for the South Island. It was soon found that a few degrees of latitude made a great difference in the temperature, "which we felt with an agreeable satisfaction."

On 25th March at 10 A.M., New Zealand was sighted, and Cook steered in to the land with the intention of putting in to the first port that appeared suitable, but as the weather became very hazy, he thought it safer to stand off again. He had picked up the land at a point which he had only seen from a distance on his previous visit, and "now saw it under so many disadvantageous circumstances, that the less I say about it, the fewer mistakes I shall make."

## DUSKY BAY

The following day they got safely into Dusky Bay, finding forty-four fathoms at the entrance and a sandy bottom. In about a couple of leagues they found a good anchorage in fifty fathoms, a hawser's length or so from the shore. This was found to be rather inconvenient, but another one was soon found by Lieutenant Pickersgill, and received in consequence the name Pickersgill Harbour. Here the observatory, forge, and tents were set up. Spruce beer was brewed, to which molasses and some of their inspissated malt juice was added, fish caught, and, in fact, everything possible for the comfort of the crew for a short time, was done. They had been a hundred and seventeen days at sea, had sailed 3,600 leagues without a sight of land, and had arrived with only one man sick with the scurvy, "occasioned, chiefly, by a bad habit of body and a complication of other disorders."

One day, passing an island whilst out surveying, Cook was called by a Maori and landed to meet him. The native was accompanied by two women, and after an attempt at conversation, presented Cook with a piece of native cloth, asking, as far as could be understood, for a boat-cloak in return. One was made for him out of red baize, and gave so much satisfaction that he presented Cook with his pattou, a sort of short flat club made of stone. He visited the ship, and took great interest in all that was going on, particularly with the saw pit. After watching the men some time, he intimated his desire to try his hand in the pit, but found the work not quite so easy as it looked, and soon required very little persuasion to relinquish his task.

Cook speaks very favourably of Dusky Bay, a good anchorage, plenty of good water, game, fish, and easy to enter. The timber he describes as the best he had seen in New Zealand, with the exception of that at the Thames. There was but little edible herbage, but he tried to remedy this by planting a quantity of European seeds, and he also left, in a place where he hoped they might be undisturbed, a pair of geese. Whilst here Cook was for a time confined to his cabin by what he describes as a slight cold, but Mr. Forster says was a severe attack of rheumatism. After several unsuccessful attempts, owing to contrary winds, they left Dusky Bay on 11th May, and on the 17th, when near Cape Stephens, fell in with six water-spouts, one of which came within fifty yards of the ship, and Cook regretted he had not fired a gun at it, as he had heard that course recommended. He says he had one ready, but was so busy noting the phenomena that he did not think of it in time. On the other hand, Forster says that one "was ordered to be got ready, but our people being, as usual, very desultory about it, the danger was passed before we could try the experiment."

## FURNEAUX REPORTS

On 18th May they arrived in Queen Charlotte's Sound, finding, as Cook had expected, the Adventure there before them. Furneaux immediately reported himself to his commanding officer, and said they had been there for six weeks. After they had lost sight of the Resolution on 8th February, they heard a gun and bore up for it, firing every half-hour, but heard no reply. They then cruised about for three days as near the spot as the weather would permit, and then, following Tasman's track, as Cook had surmised, made for New Zealand, sighting Van Diemen's Land on 9th March, near Tasman's South Cape. He sent a boat ashore at the first opportunity, and a few traces of natives were seen, but the weather was so threatening that the boat had to return to the ship. They then put in to Adventure Bay, and staying five days took in wood and water; they had been reduced to a quart per day of the last for some time. A few deserted huts and occasional smokes were seen, but no other signs of the inhabitants. They then continued up the coast till it trended away to the west, forming, Furneaux thought, a deep bay. Passing the islands which now bear Furneaux's name, bad weather came on, and he judged it wise to make for his rendezvous, firmly convinced that Van Diemen's Land was joined to New Holland. On 30th March they sighted the South Island, and were greatly retarded in their run up the coast by the heavy swell from the north. On their arrival in Queen Charlotte's Sound, they found the pole erected on Motuara, with the name of the Endeavour and date on it, and several of the inhabitants came forward to trade and enquire after Cook and Tupia. On 11th May they experienced the shock of an earthquake, but no damage was done.

Finding that several of the Adventure's crew were very sick, Cook immediately sent out boats for a supply of scurvy grass, and:

"gave orders that it should be boiled with wheat and portable broth every morning for breakfast, and with peas and broth for dinner, knowing from experience that these vegetables, thus dressed, are extremely beneficial in removing all manner of scorbutic complaints."

Furneaux had prepared to winter in Queen Charlotte's Sound, but Cook thought it too soon to settle down to rest and decided to push on. He was half inclined to go over to Van Diemen's Land and settle the question of its being a part of New Holland, but Furneaux appeared convinced, and the winds were contrary, so he decided on proceeding eastwards, and the Adventure was ordered to refit as rapidly as possible. A boat sent out for timber on 3rd June was chased by a large canoe filled with men, but Cook thought no harm was intended; on a second occasion some natives were on the ship, when a large canoe came up, and those on board requested Cook to fire on it, saying its occupants were enemies. This Cook declined to do, and, instead, invited them to come on board, an invitation that was accepted after a brief ceremonial, and the newcomers behaved themselves quite properly; but soon Cook had to get rid of them all, for he found his men were selling their clothing, which they would shortly require, for things of no value either as curiosities or otherwise. The newcomers went off to Motuara, and Cook followed them up. He had some little conversation with them, but did not remember having seen any of them at his previous visit, and thought none of them recognised him. They had their cooking utensils with them, and he concluded they intended to settle down, at any rate for a time.

Gardens had been started by Furneaux on his arrival, and Cook tried to interest the Maoris in them; he showed them the potatoes, carrots, and parsnips, which they seemed to understand and appreciate, and they promised to look after them. He remarks that the intercourse between the Maoris and the whites did not tend to improve the morals of the former, whom he had hitherto looked upon as superior in that respect to the other South Sea Islanders he had come across.

## THE WATCH MACHINE

On 7th June the two ships put to sea, and on the 8th some accident happened to Arnold's timepiece on board the Resolution, and they were unable to wind it up. So far it had been working very well, but not quite so accurately as Kendal's. On the return of the ship to England, Arnold was informed that either by carelessness or wilfully Mr. Wales had caused this difficulty. Wales attributed this rumour to the Forsters, to whom he wrote on the subject, and it is very evident from their replies that though they did not admit having circulated the report, they were not ignorant that Arnold had been so informed. There does not appear to be any ground for the accusation, but it does appear very probable it originated with the Forsters.

Throughout the rest of June they experienced very rough weather, and it was not till 18th July that they reached 133 degrees West, having seen no signs of land on their way. Cook therefore turned northwards so as to cross the space between his track north and return south in 1769. This course would practically settle one view about the supposed Southern Continent, for it had been laid down by some of the theorists that it must be in the middle latitudes of the South Pacific. New Zealand had been said to be the western side of this continent (already disproved by Cook in his previous voyage), and what Forster calls "the pretended discoveries near America," the eastern side. The proposed course would take the ships through the centre of the part of the ocean in dispute.

On 29th July, Cook sent a boat to the Adventure, as he had heard her crew were very sickly, and found that about twenty of her men were down with scurvy, and the cook had died of the disease. Orders were given that the utmost precautions were to be taken, and wort, carrot marmalade, and rob of lemon were to be freely served out. On the Resolution, at the same time, three men were on the sick list, only one of whom had scurvy, but some of the others were showing symptoms, so similar precautions were taken, with good results.

## DANGEROUS WATERS

Cook was so anxious about the Adventure's crew that he would not look for Pitcairn Island, discovered by Carteret, although he believed he was in its neighbourhood on 1st August (he was about fifteen leagues to the west), but a day or so after was able to have Furneaux on board to dinner, who reported a great improvement. He had some cider on board, which he had served out with gratifying results. Two islands were sighted on the 11th, which Cook named Resolution and Doubtful Islands; he believed them to have been discovered by De Bougainville. The following morning at daylight they found themselves almost on the top of what Cook calls "a half drowned island, or rather large coral shoal of about 20 leagues in circuit." In the lagoon which it surrounded they saw a large canoe under sail. The island was named after Furneaux. As they were now in such a dangerous neighbourhood, Cook ordered that at night the cutter with an officer and seven men should keep in advance of the ships until they arrived in sight of Maitea (Osnaburg Island) on 15th July, when, being in waters he knew, its services were discontinued. He steered for the south side of Otaheite in order to get fresh vegetables as soon as possible, and on the 16th at daybreak they found themselves about two miles from the reef. The wind dropped, and the set of the current was taking them on to the reef, so the boats were ordered out to tow, but getting near an opening through which the tide was rushing with great force, they were unable to keep the ships off. The anchors were let go, and the Adventure, finding holding ground, was brought up; but the Resolution was not so fortunate, and was carried on to the reef and struck two or three times, fortunately without doing any serious damage. A land breeze springing up and the tide slackening enabled them to get in safely, with the loss of three anchors, a cable, and a couple of hawsers; the bower anchor was recovered by Mr. Gilbert the next day. Cook says that though he thought they had a remarkably narrow escape, the natives who saw them did not seem to appreciate that they had been in any danger.

They remained at this anchorage for a week, and obtained plenty of coconuts and bananas; but though they saw hogs, they were unable to purchase any, as the people declared they all belonged to their chief; so, hearing he was in the neighbourhood, Cook landed to call on him, and at once recognised him as Tearee, whom he had seen in 1769. The chief also remembered him, and enquired after several of the Endeavour people. He tried to get Cook to make a longer stay, promising supplies of fresh meat as an inducement, but as such promises had so often been broken before, Cook replied he should leave the next day. Whilst here one of the marines, who had been ailing more or less all the voyage, and had become dropsical, died, and the one man who was suffering from scurvy still remained on the sick list. On the other hand, the Adventure's crew had greatly improved in health with the change to fresh vegetables. One of the natives was found to have picked up coconuts from which the sailors had drunk the milk, and having carefully sealed up the holes, resold them, and did not seem disconcerted when his trick was found out.

Before the ships reached their anchorage at Matavai Bay they were crowded with natives, many of whom Cook recognised, and almost all of whom knew him. Otoo, the king, at once recognised Cook, and enquired after Banks, Solander, and others of the Endeavour; yet Forster gravely asserts that he never saw them at the former visit.

The old fort on Point Venus was reoccupied, tents pitched, and the observatory set up, and the camp was placed under the command of Lieutenant Edgecombe of the Marines.

## SPANIARDS HANGED

The king gave a theatrical entertainment in honour of their arrival, at which his sister was the only female performer. It had some reference to the coming of the ships, but they were not able to follow the thread of the story. Cook could see that Otoo was nervous and uncomfortable, and felt dissatisfied with his reception, so determined to cut short his stay. No one could understand the reason of the unsatisfactory feeling, but Forster suggests that it was owing to the advice of a Spanish deserter, who had left his ship about March 1773. This vessel was commanded by Don Juan de Langara y Huarto, and was from Callao; her voyage has not been published, but the natives gave Forster to understand that four of her sailors had been hanged on her arrival. Cook refers to the presence of a white man, who, when he thought he had been observed, disappeared and was not seen again. Young Forster made an attempt to explore the interior, but finding the climbing more difficult than he expected, soon returned. In the gardens which had been planted at the Endeavour's visit, pumpkins seemed to be the only things which had done well, and for these the natives did not care, "which is not to be wondered at," says Cook. Further enquiries as to the religious ceremonies were made, but nothing very definite was ascertained; it appeared that on very rare occasions special criminals, selected by the high priest, were sacrificed at the Moris. Cook also formed the opinion that the standard of morality amongst the women was much higher than had previously been admitted.

Sailing with a favourable wind on 1st September for Huaheine, the Adventure ran ashore going through the reef, but with the assistance of the Resolution's boats, she was soon towed off without serious damage. Forster, as usual, tries to cause trouble by declaring that Cook would not send assistance till the Resolution was safely anchored, and thus added to the danger of his consort. As the boats were in the water before the accident occurred, in order to render immediate assistance if required, Mr. Forster's story is too thin.

On arrival Cook was informed his old friend Oree was coming to see him, so he went ashore to meet him. The boat was hauled up close to the chief's house, and then five young plantain trees, as emblems of peace, were carried on board one by one, the first three being each accompanied by a young pig with his ears ornamented with coconut fibre; the fourth was accompanied by a dog; and the fifth by the bag which Cook had given Oree in 1769, containing the pewter plate with the inscription relating to the Endeavour's visit, and the beads, and imitation coins. On the advice of his guide, Cook decorated three of the plantains with nails, medals, beads, etc., and he, Furneaux, and Forster, landed with them in their hands. They were requested to sit down, and the trees were taken from them and placed before Oree, the first for God, the second for the king, and the third for Friendship. The chief then came forward and greeted Cook in a most affectionate manner, the tears trickling down his cheeks. Further presents were then exchanged, and the ceremony was over.

## SPARRMAN'S MISADVENTURE

Here they were able to purchase a plentiful supply of everything, pigs, fowls, and fruit, and Cook says if he had been able to stay longer he might have bought as much more as everything seemed abundant. The only disagreeable thing that happened was to Mr. Sparrman, who, out by himself botanising, was set upon and stripped of everything but his trousers—Besant substitutes spectacles for trousers. He made his way towards the boats, and was befriended by a native, who gave him some cloth to put over his shoulders and escorted him to the others. When Oree heard of the affair he placed himself in Cook's hands, and did his best to find out the culprits, and after a time Sparrman's hanger and the greater part of his things were recovered. It seems probable that some native law had been unwittingly broken and Sparrman's treatment was meant as a punishment, for every one else had been particularly well treated. Before leaving Cook added to Oree's treasures a copper plate on which was inscribed, "Anchored here, His Britannic Majesty's Ships Resolution and Adventure, September 1773." Some medals were also given him, and he was requested to show them to any visitors that came.

At Ulietea they were received at a heava or dramatic performance, one portion of which illustrated robbery by two men, and Cook says it was acted "in such a masterly manner as sufficiently displayed the genius of the people in this vice." Fruit and vegetables being rather scarce, Mr. Pickersgill was despatched with a boat from each ship to an island Cook calls O'Taha, where they were said to be plentiful, and he was able to purchase as much as they had means to pay for, at a very reasonable rate; but during negotiations the bag containing the trade was stolen. Pickersgill at once seized everything of value he could lay his hands on, signifying at the same time that all should be returned when the bag and its contents were produced. In the evening a chief, who had been friendly all day, went off and soon after came back with the bag and about half its contents. Eventually all was recovered, and the boats left with good loads in a perfectly friendly manner. When the boats went from Ulietea the crews of the two vessels were again entertained, but during the night all the natives disappeared, to the surprise and annoyance of Cook, who thought something serious had happened to offend them. It turned out that, seeing the boats did not return, the natives thought it was a case of desertion, and were afraid they might be held responsible.

## BAGPIPES APPRECIATED

Leaving here, the course was to the south of west so as to clear the tracks of other explorers, and then to call at Middleburg and Amsterdam. Each night the ships lay to in order that they might not overlook any unknown island, and on 23rd September Harvey's Islands were sighted and named. On 1st October Middleburg was reached, but no good anchorage being found, they went on to Amsterdam. Before they got clear away, however, two canoes came out, and the coast opening up in a more promising manner, they ran in again and found ground in twenty-five fathoms. Plenty of the natives, quite unarmed, came off to the ships, some, amongst whom was a chief named Tioony, were invited on board; the traders were so anxious to do business, that those who could not get near enough to hand their goods into the boats, pitched them over the heads of their friends. Some of the party accompanied Tioony to his house, which was delightfully situated, and were entertained with refreshments, in the shape of coconuts, bananas, and a few shaddocks, called by Forster pumplemoses, and music; and in return the ship's bagpipes played, to the great enjoyment of the natives. Turnbull, who visited the Pacific during the years 1800 to 1804, says that these instruments were remembered, and in Otaheite were specially asked for. The musical contribution of the natives commenced with a song by three girls, who sang rather nicely, and were duly rewarded with presents, whereon all the women began singing in a manner which Cook describes as "both musical and harmonious." A short walk disclosed plantations "well laid out and kept," but as eatables seemed scarce, a departure was made the next day for Amsterdam, the waves breaking high upon the rocks as they followed the coast.

Off the southern point of Amsterdam several canoes came out, and their occupants came aboard without hesitation, presenting cava root as a peace-offering. The ships anchored in eighteen fathoms, and were soon crowded with visitors. Nothing but cloth was offered for sale, so Cook, finding the sailors were parting with clothing they would soon be wanting, issued an order that no curiosities were to be purchased, with the result that next morning hogs, fowls, coconuts, and bananas were forthcoming. Cook, Forster, and some of the others went ashore and found a chief, Attago, who had attached himself to Cook, very useful in their trading. Mr. Hodges painted a picture of this landing, but, as Mr. Forster very justly points out, the attire of the natives is far too classical. It was noticed that many of the natives had lost the top joint of the little finger of one, and in some cases, of both hands. This was understood to be a mark of mourning for the loss of parents.

The fowls here were remarkably good, and the sailors purchased some for the purpose of cock-fighting, but they proved much more successful in the pot. The island is described as well cultivated, not an inch of ground being wasted in roads or fences. Forster reported having seen a large casuarina tree loaded with crows, but they proved to be that pest of the fruit grower—flying foxes. He also states that the Resolution anchored in the same spot as Tasman when he discovered the island.

The natives proved as adept at thieving as the majority of the South Sea Islanders. One man, who had stolen some books from the Master's cabin, got off in his canoe, and being chased, took to the water, and diving under his pursuers' boat, unshipped the rudder, and got clear away. Mr. Wales, in going ashore, took off his shoes and stockings to save them from the wet, when they were at once snatched up by a native, who ran off with them over the coral rocks, leaving poor Wales in what Cook calls "an unpleasant but laughable position," unable to follow over the sharp stone; however, Attago soon afterwards recovered them.

The language was closely allied to that used in the Society Group, many words being identical; and Cook concluded they had some form of religious worship, as he noted enclosed pieces of ground in which one or two particular men were accustomed to repeat speeches apparently of a set nature.

## NEW ZEALAND ONCE MORE

On 7th October, sailing for New Zealand, they were delayed by contrary winds, and did not sight the neighbourhood of Table Cape till the 21st. They stood in to Tolago and Poverty Bays with the intention of presenting any chiefs who came off, with pigs, fowls, and garden seeds in hopes of making a commencement in stocking the island, but none were seen till Cape Kidnappers was reached, when two made their appearance, and were duly given two boars and two sows, and four hens and two cocks, first obtaining a promise that they should not be killed; to these were added a supply of seeds, such as peas, beans, cabbage, turnips, etc. Standing on through a series of heavy squalls, in one of which the Resolution lost her fore topgallant mast, they ran into a violent gale which lasted for a week, and, after a slight moderation, came on with increased fury, and the two vessels parted company.

On 3rd November the Resolution reached her old anchorage in Ship Cove, Queen Charlotte's Sound; but the Adventure was seen no more during the voyage. Forster was much upset by the stormy weather, "the dreadful energy of the language" of the sailors, the absence of their consort which "doubled every danger," the shortness of the table supplies and his own dislike to a further trip to southern latitudes. Hoping the Adventure might yet come in, Cook pushed on with his refit, and thoroughly overhauled his stores. About 4000 pounds weight of ship's bread was found unfit for food, and another 3000 pounds nearly as bad; they were very fortunate, therefore, in getting a plentiful supply of scurvy grass and wild celery, and a small quantity of vegetables from the gardens they had previously laid out.

Any doubts that may have been felt about the cannibalism of the New Zealanders was set at rest by some of the officers who surprised a party engaged in a feast. A human head was purchased from the feasters and taken on board, and a piece of the flesh being offered to a Maori, it was greedily devoured. A South Sea Islander, Odidie, was intensely horrified, and refused to touch the knife with which it had been cut, nor would he be in any way friendly with the eater. Cook firmly believed that only enemies killed in battle were eaten, and did not think the custom arose from any shortness of food.

Enclosing in a bottle, which was buried under a marked tree in the garden, a memorandum giving the dates of his arrival and depar-

ture, the direction he intended to steer, and other information he thought might be useful to Furneaux, Cook sailed on 25th November, and as they passed through the straits, guns were continually fired, and a sharp lookout kept for signs of the Adventure; but nothing was seen, and as no other rendezvous had been appointed, Cook gave up all hope of her rejoining him. The Resolution, when clear, bore up for the south-east, but had the course at the first been north of east, the two ships might possibly have met, for the Adventure was then on her way from Tolago Bay and arrived in Ship Cove four days after the departure of her consort. Cook says his crew were in good spirits, and in no way dejected, "or thought the dangers we had yet to go through were in the least increased by being alone." They were quite ready to go, "wherever I might think proper to lead them." Even Mr. Forster had to admit at a little later date, that:
"notwithstanding the constant perils to which our course exposed us, in this unexplored ocean, our ship's company were far from being so uneasy as might have been expected."

## ARMOUR OF ICE

On 6th December, at 8.30 A.M., they reckoned they were "at the Antipodes to our friends in London, consequently as far removed from them as possible." Here a swell coming from the south-west showed there was no great body of land in that direction, except at a considerable distance. The first ice was seen on 12th December in 62 degrees 10 minutes South, and on the 15th, in 66 degrees South, they were obliged to edge away north as they were surrounded by large quantities of loose ice, and it was very foggy. Working up to between 64 and 65 degrees, they again headed east still hampered by ice and fog, but in a few days the weather improved a little, and they recovered the Antarctic Circle, and reached 67 degrees 31 minutes South on the 23rd, the highest south latitude hitherto attained. The rigging was so coated with ice that it was difficult to work the ship, and Cook altered his course to the north-east. Marra says, under 18th December:
"Icicles frequently hung to the noses of the men, more than an inch long...the men, cased in frozen snow, as if clad in armour, where the running rigging has been so enlarged by frozen sleet as hardly to be grasped by the largest hand...yet, under all these hardships, the men cheerful over their grog, and not a man sick, but of old scars."

Cook says that some of the men suffered from fever brought on by the unavoidable exposure to cold and wet, but it was slight, and "happily yielded to the simplest remedies." The ship was so surrounded by masses of ice as to cause some apprehension, but by taking advantage of every breath of air the danger was averted. Christmas Day was passed in constant watchfulness.

"We were fortunate in having continual daylight, and clear weather, for had it been foggy as on some of the preceding days, nothing less than a miracle could have saved us from being dashed to pieces."

On 7th January 1774, five very successful observations gave the mean longitude as 123 degrees 21 minutes West, the watch gave it 123 degrees 44 minutes, and the dead reckoning as 123 degrees 39 minutes. Cook signifies his keen appreciation of the watch machine, and says: "I must here take notice that our longitude can never be erroneous while we have so good a guide as Mr. Kendal's watch."

## OBEDIENT AND ALERT

A further attempt to the south was made, and on 30th January the high latitude of 71 degrees 10 minutes South was reached, in longitude 106 degrees 54 minutes West, further progress being stopped by a large and solid field of ice. This record was not beaten till 1823, by Weddell, and until recent years very few of the attempts on Antarctic discovery had proved as successful. Satisfied that there was no continent existing within the Arctic Circle except so far south as to be practically inaccessible on account of ice, he acknowledged he did not regret he found it impossible to go further, and, thinking that in the unexplored parts of the South Pacific there was room for many large islands, and also that discoveries already made had been imperfectly laid down on the charts, he decided that it was his duty, as he had a well-found ship and a healthy crew, to remain in these waters and add what he could to the knowledge of geography. He therefore planned to find the land discovered by Juan Fernandez in 38 degrees South, and, if unsuccessful, to proceed to Easter Island and fix its position, as it was very uncertain, then to proceed to Otaheite, where he had a faint hope he might hear of the Adventure, and, proceeding further west, settle the position of Tierra Austral del Espiritu Santo of de Quiros. Afterwards to turn south-east, and, reaching Cape Horn in November, he would have the best part of the summer for exploration in the South Atlantic. He says:

"Great as this design appears to be, I however thought it possible to be executed; and when I came to communicate it to the officers, I had the satisfaction to find they all heartily concurred in it. I should not do these gentlemen justice if I did not take some opportunity to declare that they always showed the utmost readiness to carry into execution in the most effectual manner, every measure I thought proper to take. Under such circumstances it is hardly necessary to say, that the seamen were always obedient and alert; and on this occasion they were so far from wishing the voyage at an end, that they rejoiced at the prospect of its being prolonged another year and of soon enjoying the benefits of a milder climate."

Mr. Forster does not agree with this account, for he says:

"The long continuance in these cold climates began now to hang heavily on our crew, especially as it banished all hope of returning home this year, which had hitherto supported their spirits. At first a painful despondence owing to the dreary prospect of another year's cruise to the south seemed painted in every countenance; till by degrees they resigned themselves to their fate with a kind of sullen indifference. It must be owned, however, that nothing could be more dejecting than the entire ignorance of our future destination which, without any apparent reason was constantly kept a secret to every person in the ship."

It is evident that Cook and his officers did not think it necessary to consult Mr. Forster as to the movements of the ship, or, what is more probable, he was in one of his irritable moods and must say something nasty about someone.

The decision to turn northwards was taken none too soon, for on 6th February a furious storm came on, playing havoc with the sails and running rigging, and though it abated somewhat next morning, it blew very strong till the 12th, and would have been highly dangerous if it had caught them amongst the ice. On the 17th Cook judged he had crossed his outward track of 1769, and on the 20th he notes the thermometer rising to 66 degrees, the only real summer day they had experienced since leaving New Zealand. Having arrived at the position laid down for the land supposed to have been seen by Juan Fernandez, he cruised about but found no signs, so on the 25th stood away for Easter Island.

Cook was now taken seriously ill and was confined to his bed for several days by what he calls the bilious cholic, during which time "Mr. Patten, the surgeon, was to me, not only a skilful physician, but an affectionate nurse." He recovered very slowly, and the want of fresh food told against him when it came to the question of gathering strength. The only fresh meat on board was a dog belonging to Mr. Forster, which was duly sacrificed and made into soup: "Thus I received nourishment and strength from food which would have made most people in Europe sick." Marra's Journal says, under 23rd February:

"This day the Captain was taken ill, to the grief of all the ship's company." 28th February: "The Captain this day much better, which each might read in the countenance of the other, from the highest officer to the meanest boy on board the ship." 4th March: "The Captain perfectly recovered from his illness, to the great joy of the ship's company."

## EASTER ISLAND

At 8 A.M., on 11th March, Easter Island was sighted from the masthead, and shortly after noon some of the gigantic statues mentioned in Roggewin's Voyages were clearly distinguished through the glasses. The position of the ship at noon had been fixed as 27 degrees 3 minutes South, 109 degrees 46 minutes West. Standing on and off till next morning, fair anchorage was found in thirty-six fathoms, but it proved too near the edge of a bank, and they were driven off it in the night. One or two canoes came out to meet them as they were working back, from which plantains were purchased, and Cook proceeded ashore, where he was immediately surrounded by natives; indeed, some even swam out to meet him. Many of them possessed European hats, jackets, handkerchiefs, etc., which they were said to have obtained from the Spaniards in 1770. Their language was very similar to that of Otaheite, and Odidie was able to understand them fairly well. There were no trees exceeding ten feet in height, and the land is described as extremely parched and dreary, though a few plantations were seen. Some remarkable pieces of stonework were noticed, enclosing small areas of ground, in some of which were the statues already mentioned. These were not looked upon by the natives as objects of worship, although they did not like the pavements by which they were surrounded being walked over, or the statues being closely examined. Mr. Forster regarded the enclosures as burial grounds, and the statues (portions of some of them are at the British Museum) as monuments to chiefs.

The water supply being found very bad, though Gonzales is said to have found good springs, and the fresh food for sale but scanty, the stay was cut short, and on 16th March sail was made for the Marquesas, discovered by Mendana in 1595. The next day, according to Marra, the fresh provisions obtained were served out to the crew at the Captain's expense:

"namely, two pounds of potatoes a man, and a bunch of bananas to each mess; and this without reducing their ordinary allowance; an act of generosity which produced its effect; it preserved the crew in health, and encouraged them to undergo cheerfully the hardships that must unavoidably happen in the course of so long a voyage."

## MARKET SPOILT

The Marquesas were reached on 7th April, and after a narrow escape from running on the rocks, satisfactory anchorage was obtained, and they were visited by some of the natives, from whom breadfruit and fish were purchased. The next day further trading was done, nails being the chief medium of exchange, but the natives were inclined to be smart in their dealings, and on several occasions obtained payment without delivery. Cook here suffered from a relapse, but was able to get about, and after warning the officer on watch to keep a smart look-out, or something of importance would be stolen, took his seat in a boat to go in search of a better anchorage. He was then informed that a stanchion had been stolen from the gangway, and the thief had got away to his canoe on the other side of the ship. He ordered a shot to be fired over the canoes, but no one was to be hurt, and he would pull round and secure the thief. The order was apparently misunderstood, for the thief was killed, and the rest of the natives hurried ashore. Soon after trading recommenced, and the lesson appeared forgotten, for an attempt was made to steal the kedge anchor by which the ship was being warped nearer the shore. Cook landed, and the trading went on as if nothing out of the common had occurred, and some pigs (so small that it required forty or fifty to provide one meal for the crew!) and fruit were purchased; but in the afternoon, when the boats went in for water, all the natives had disappeared. This Cook attributed to his not being with them, for the next morning, when he landed, trading was resumed. A short trip was made in the boats along the coast, and when they returned it was found the market was closed. It seems one of the young gentlemen had given a small handful of red feathers he had obtained at Tonga for a small pig, and now nothing else would be accepted, so they sailed for Otaheite on the 11th. Cook was very much annoyed at the ill success in obtaining fresh provisions, for though none of the crew were ill, he thought they stood in need of a change of food. He describes the inhabitants as the finest race he had seen in the South Seas, almost as fair as Europeans, and their language very similar to that of Otaheite. Their arms consisted of clubs, spears, and slings, the two former very neatly made, and with the latter they threw stones a considerable distance but without accuracy. Mr. Forster managed to secure a quantity of small birds with very beautiful plumage.

On the 17th April they sighted the George Islands, discovered by Byron (native name, Tiookea), but, after sending the Master to report on the lagoon, Cook decided it was too dangerous to enter, and Mr. Cooper went off with two boats to see if it were possible to trade. He obtained a few dogs and coconuts, but the attitude of the natives was so uncertain he would not land, and returned to the ship. One of the sailors exchanged a plantain for a dog, so it was concluded the fruit was unknown. On the 19th four more islands were discovered, and named Pallisser Islands, and on rounding one a strong swell rolling in from the south was encountered, "a sure sign that we were clear of these low islands." On the 21st, land a little to the east of Point Venus was sighted, and next morning they anchored in Matavai Bay, being immediately visited by the natives, who seemed greatly pleased to see them again. The old camp was reoccupied, the observatory set up for Mr. Wales, and Cook had again the pleasure to record he had no one on the sick list.

The king, Otoo, came to visit the camp, bringing as his present a dozen pigs and some fruit, and then with some of his friends went on board ship to dinner, and to receive the return present. It was then found that the red feathers were greatly valued, a very fortunate thing as articles of trade were running short. Cook, after the disappointment in securing supplies at the last visit, intended to make a very short stay, but the place now appeared to be very thriving, houses and canoes were being built in all directions, and there was every sign of prosperity, so he decided to remain and refit. On 25th April they had a thunderstorm lasting three hours, such as no one on board had experienced before.

## THE OTAHEITAN FLEET

Going to visit Otoo on the next day, Cook was surprised to see a large number of fully-manned canoes ranged along the coast, and a large body of armed men on the land near them. On landing, he was surrounded by people, and seized by two chiefs, one of whom wanted to carry him off to see the king, and the other to see the fleet, and between the two, "I was like to be pulled to pieces," the crowd making way with cries of "Tiya no Tootee." He was gradually drawn towards the fleet, but refused to go on board, and after a time was allowed to return to his own boats, when he found his companions had been subject to similar treatment. They put out from shore in order to have a good look at the fleet, and counted one hundred and sixty large double canoes, all well equipped and fully manned. The chiefs were swathed in vast quantities of cloth, so that to the Englishmen it seemed almost a miracle they were able to move. The vessels were decorated with flags and streamers, and made a very fine appearance. These were the first line, and, in addition, there were one hundred and seventy smaller double canoes, each having a small house or castle on it, which were thought to be transports and store ships, as the larger ones, as far as could be seen, carried no supplies on board. The number of men on board was estimated to be no less than 7,500, and it was ascertained this armada was intended for the subjugation of Eimeo which had lately rebelled against Otaheite.

Cook was informed Otoo was waiting at the camp for him, but on going there he found he had not been there, and on looking for him again in the afternoon he was still invisible. The fleet had also gone away; and then it was discovered that some of Cook's clothes had been stolen from the wash, and the king and Admiral were both in dread of his anger. However, Cook sent word he should take no steps to recover the stolen articles, and things resumed a friendly aspect, the Admiral, Towha, sending Cook a present of two large pigs and some fruit, giving orders to the bearers that they were to receive nothing in exchange. He soon after paid a visit to the ship, and as it was his first, he examined everything with great curiosity, and appeared greatly impressed with what he saw. One of the natives having been caught making off with a small water cask, Cook determined he should be punished, and made a ceremonial affair of it. The culprit was first sent on board and put in irons, the natives and the crew mustered, and then the thief was taken on shore and triced up. Cook then made a short speech in which he pointed out that when his men were caught stealing from the natives they were always punished, but the natives were always stealing from the ship and crew and getting away unpunished, he therefore ordered the man to be given two dozen lashes. These were duly administered, and Towha made a speech in which he was understood to admit the justice of Cook's action. The marines were then put through their drill, and fired a few volleys with ball, and the proceedings terminated; but Cook declares he did not know whether the natives were pleased or frightened by the ceremony. The king's brother then took some of the officers out to see a part of their fleet at exercise, and they were just in time to see the conclusion and the landing of the men. Cook says the canoes were handled very smartly, and "five minutes after putting ashore you could not tell anything of the kind had been going forward."

The sea stores were again overhauled, and although the greatest care had been taken with the packing, large quantities of the bread were found to be uneatable, rendering the purchase of fresh food at every opportunity of the greatest importance.

A state visit was paid on board by Otoo's father and some other members of the royal family, who presented Cook with:

"a complete mourning dress, a curiosity we most valued. In return I gave him whatever he desired, which was not a little, and having distributed red feathers to all the others, conducted them ashore in my boat."

## MUSKET STOLEN

On 7th May the king expressed a wish to see Cook, so the latter went ashore, but found his Majesty and many of his leading men had disappeared, and the sergeant of marines reported that one of his men had had his musket stolen whilst on duty. Cook gave orders that if the musket was returned nothing further was to be said, and returned to his ship. Suspicion was attracted to six canoes laden with fruit and baggage, so Cook gave chase in his own boat. One of the canoes then made for the ship, and the occupants, women whom he recognised, informed him they were taking some things to the Resolution, and that the king was at Point Venus. Cook went to the camp, to find this was only a story to put him off, and he once again gave chase, ordering another boat to follow. A few shots were fired over the canoes, and five out of the six surrendered, the one he had spoken with getting away. He was now told that the gun had been stolen by a native of Tiarabou, and therefore Otoo was unable to get it back, so after a little discussion he decided to put up with the loss, and sent word to the king that he would say no more about it. In the evening, however, the musket and some articles that had not been missed were returned, and the men who brought them were duly rewarded. Cook says it was remarkable how many had been actively engaged in their recovery. One man in particular described most vividly how he had followed up, attacked and killed the thief of the musket, but at the same time every one was well aware that this hero had never been away from his own house throughout the day. A state call was made on Otoo, and with the usual exchange of presents the old footing was re-established. On the return from this visit a stop was made "at the dockyards, for such they deserve to be called," and the canoes in construction were inspected, two of them being the largest the Englishmen had yet seen.

The king soon after returned the visit, and requested that the big guns should be fired, but Cook thinks it was very doubtful if the experience was enjoyed. A display of fireworks in the evening was much more to the native taste. Referring to the numerous robberies that had been committed, Cook says he found it far the best to deal mildly with the delinquents, and the regulations he made were, as a rule, well kept by the natives. He was now better pleased with his reception, and concluded that the island was in a more prosperous condition than at his last visit. When the ship was ready to resume her voyage, several young natives volunteered to accompany her, and Mr. Forster was most anxious to take one as a servant, but as Cook could see no prospect of returning them to their homes, he would not permit one to go.

## MARRA DESERTS

When the anchor was weighed on 14th May, Marra, the gunner's mate, whose Journal has been quoted, quietly slipped into the water, and endeavoured to reach a canoe which was hanging about to pick him up, but he was seen and taken on board again. In his notes he expresses his regret that the scientific world thus lost the chance of having the experiences of a prolonged residence amongst these people placed before it. At the time of leaving there was great talk of the expedition against Eimeo, and Cook would have liked to have watched the proceedings, but he soon saw that nothing would be done whilst he remained in the vicinity.

On their arrival at Huaheine on the 15th the ship was immediately boarded by Cook's old friend Oree with the usual present, and he and his friends were invited to dine on board. He was asked what he would like for the return present, and named axes and nails, which were given him with the request that he would distribute them amongst his people; this he at once did, to the apparent satisfaction of all. The thieving propensities of the natives were still as bad as ever; a shooting party was robbed of its stock of trade goods, and the day after three officers were seized and stripped, so Cook took an armed party ashore, captured two of the leading chiefs and a large house, and said he should keep them till the things stolen were returned. This had the desired effect, and everything was soon brought back.

On 23rd May they sailed for Ulietea, and on their arrival the next day were well received, though it was evident provisions were rather scarce. They were informed here that two ships had arrived at Huaheine, one commanded by Banks, and the other by Furneaux, and their informant describes both Captains so well that it was some time before Cook ventured to reject the tale as too improbable. It is possible that there was some foundation for the story that ships had been seen, for it afterwards became known that M. St. Dennis had been in the South Pacific about this time with two vessels.

Notwithstanding pressing invitations from the natives to stay, Cook sailed for Lord Howe's Island, discovered by Wallis, reaching it on the 6th June, but as it seemed uninhabited it offered no inducement for any stay. On the 16th a chain of sand-banks and islets surrounding a lagoon into which no practicable entrance could be seen, was named Palmerston's Islands; and on the 20th a landing was effected on Savage Island, but as the natives were very threatening, and the country enabled them to approach closely without exposing themselves, the party retired to the boats. A few spears were thrown, and Marra says that one would have struck Cook had he not seen it coming and stooped in time to avoid it, and then aimed with his gun loaded with small shot at the thrower, but it missed fire; a short time afterwards he again tried it, aiming in the air, and it was discharged. Forster attributes the constant misfires to the bad quality of the flints supplied by the Government, and says that English flints had a very unsatisfactory reputation on the Continent.

MORE THIEVING

The course was now set for Rotterdam, where they arrived on 26th June, and were fairly well received by the natives, who brought supplies of fruit before the anchorage had been reached; but they soon began to play the old game of trying to annex anything that took their fancy. One seized the lead which was in use, whilst a second tried to cut the line with a stone, and was only persuaded to desist by a charge of small shot fired at his legs. A small party of sailors went ashore for water, and a quantity was obtained; but again the natives became too pressing in their attentions. The doctor's musket was stolen, then Mr. Clerke's, then some other things and a cooper's adze; and Cook, though at first inclined to take no notice, felt compelled to seize two canoes, and himself wounded a man, who had rendered himself conspicuous by his disorderly conduct, with a charge of small shot, and it was at first rumoured he was killed. This Cook would not believe as he had been very careful not to fire at a vital spot. After a time the muskets and some of the other things were given up, so the canoes were returned to their owners, and the adze was demanded. Instead of the adze, however, the reported corpse was brought on board, and proved, on examination by the doctor, to be very little the worse for his experience, having a slight wound on the thigh and a second one on the wrist. He was soon on his feet, and the adze was then produced. The next day the people were very civil, and the crew were able to water without interruption.

On 16th July they sighted Aurora Island, discovered by Bougainville, but it came on to blow hard, so they did not attempt to anchor. The natives came down fully armed as if to oppose a landing, and the ship passed on to Whitsunday Island. Off Malicolo good anchorage was found, and the natives came on board, and were so pleased with their reception they returned next day in greater numbers, and whilst Cook was in his cabin with some who appeared to be chiefs, a great noise arose on deck. A boat keeper had declined to allow a native to get into his boat, and the islander was fitting an arrow to his bow as Cook came on deck, with the intention of shooting the sailor. Cook shouted at him, and he at once diverted his aim to the Captain, but the latter was too quick, and peppered him with small shot, spoiling his aim. He was not much hurt, and proceeded to fit another arrow to his bow, when Cook gave him the second barrel and induced him to retire. Some of the others also discharged a few arrows, so a musket was fired over them, without any effect. A four-pound gun was tried, and the effect was truly marvellous; the natives in the rigging and on deck threw themselves into the water, whilst those in the cabin jumped from the ports, and the ship was left in peace. Cook was not favourably impressed by these islanders, and describes them as "in general, the most ugly ill-proportioned people I ever saw." Forster, however, thought they were very intelligent. They were judged to be a different race from the Society or Friendly Islanders, and spoke a different language.

### POISONOUS FISH

After leaving, many of those on board were very ill for a week or ten days from having eaten of a fish which Forster calls a red sea bream, and Cook believed to be the same as those which poisoned de Quiros's people, and in his account says that:

"The fish had eaten of poisonous plants, all parts of the flesh became empoisoned. The ship appeared like the Hospital of a city which had the plague; there was none who could stand on their feet."

Owing to the care of the surgeons, however "all were recovered."

The next land seen was a small group of islands, named Shepherd's Islands, "in honour of my worthy friend, the Plumian Professor of Astronomy at Cambridge"; and Mr. Forster complains that Cook's "rashness and reliance on good fortune become the principal roads to fame, by being crowned with great and undeserved success." This was very out of place at the time, for Cook was exercising the very greatest precautions, as he fully recognised the dangers by which they were surrounded. He always stood off and on during the night, and only proceeded through unknown waters by day. Several of these islets were of a peculiar formation, and one high columnar rock was named the Monument; Forster gives its height as 140 yards, the other accounts are satisfied with feet. Many of the group were inhabited, but no favourable opportunity for landing occurred.

On 1st August a fire broke out on board, and Forster writes:

"Confusion and horror appeared in all our faces at the bare mention of it, and it was some time before proper measures were taken to stop its progress, for in these moments of danger few are able to collect their faculties and act with cool deliberation."

After about half a page of this, on fires in general, he observes:

"Providentially the fire of this day was very trifling and extinguished in a few moments."

Then a few days after a marine, who had fallen overboard, was smartly picked up, and being well looked after by his comrades, was soon showing no ill effects of his accident, thus giving Mr. Forster an opportunity to write of it as an example of "the result of an esprit du corps to which sailors, at present, are utter strangers." An utterly unwarranted sneer.

At Erromango, on 4th August, Cook went in with the boats, and the natives tried to induce them to come on shore, but something roused suspicion after he and one man had got into the water, so, making signs that he would come back later, he stepped back. The natives then rushed the boats, trying to drag them onto the beach, and succeeded in stealing two oars, at the same time wounding several of the boats' crews, amongst them Mr. Gilbert, the Master, with a shower of stones, spears, and arrows. Cook attempted to give one of the chiefs a charge of small shot, but his gun missed fire, and he was obliged, very reluctantly, to order the marines to fire, with the result that several of the natives were wounded. Under the circumstances it was not considered worth while remaining, so the ship left for Tanna, some twelve leagues to the south. A bright light had been noticed in that direction the night before, which proved to have been caused by a volcanic eruption.

A good anchorage was found at Tanna, and the ship warped close in. Several natives coming on board to trade soon developed the usual propensity to carry off anything that took their fancy — on this occasion the anchor buoys were the special attraction. Muskets were fired over their head to no purpose, so a four-pounder was discharged, which for a time had a good result; but soon they were as bad as ever, so two or three musquetoons were fired close to them, and though none were hurt, the crew were able to get their dinner in peace.

## HOT SPRINGS

An old man, called by Cook Paowang, appeared to be inclined to be friendly, so Cook landed with a strong party to look for water under his guidance, and met with some of the elders, exchanging presents with them. The next day the ship was warped in, and three boats went ashore, but the natives were very threatening, and after some futile attempts to put things on a peaceable footing a signal was given to the ship and several guns were fired, when all the natives ran away except Paowang, who was suitably rewarded for his confidence. After a time permission was obtained to get wood, water, and ballast, and whilst trying to lift a stone out of a pool below high-water mark, one of the crew scalded his hand badly. The pool proved to be one of a series of springs running down a spur of the volcano into the sea. Several were tested with the thermometer, and as much as 202 degrees Fahrenheit was attained. Forster found a number of cracks on the ridge from which sulphurous vapour and smoke issued, and one of the crew who had been suffering severely from rheumatism received great temporary benefit from bathing in one of the springs.

Many good plantations of yams, sugar-cane, and plantains were seen, but they could purchase very little as their articles of trade were not appreciated. The natives did not understand the use of iron, and did not require cloth as they went almost entirely naked. Though no direct signs of cannibalism had been found, Cook was convinced that the practice was not unknown.

After leaving Tanna, the western coasts of the different islands were followed up till De Bougainville's Passage was reached, when the course was set for Espiritu Santo. In passing Malicolo canoes put off for the ship, but the wind being favourable, Cook would not delay, and gave Forster the opportunity to remark that the main object of the voyage, i.e. the obtaining a knowledge of the natural history of the islands, was made subservient to the production of a new track on the chart of the Southern Hemisphere.

## CARDINAL MORAN'S GEOGRAPHY

On 25th August they entered the bay which Cook believed to be that discovered by De Quiros, and named by him the Bay of St. Philip and St. Iago in the Tierra Austral del Espiritu Santo, now known as the New Hebrides. In this conclusion Cook has the support of Dalrymple and modern geographers, but Forster, for some reason which is not quite clear, felt compelled to differ. Cardinal Moran, the Catholic Archbishop of Sydney, also believes Cook to have been mistaken, for in his History of the Catholic Church in Australia, he places De Quiros's discovery in Port Curtis, Queensland, where he claims that the first Catholic service ever celebrated in Australia was held. He puts aside the fact that the latitude of Port Curtis, 24 degrees South, does not agree with that given by De Quiros, 15 degrees 20 minutes South, by saying that the positions of newly discovered places were, in those days, "often purposely concealed lest other navigators might appropriate to themselves and their respective countries, the results of the discovery." He quotes details given in De Quiros's petitions to the King of Spain, and says: "All these details fit in admirably with Port Curtis on the Queensland coast." Now De Quiros says the country he discovered was thickly inhabited by a people who were armed with bows and arrows, possessed vessels of earthenware, lived in houses of wood, roofed with palm leaves, were amply supplied with oranges, limes, pears, almonds larger than those of Spain, hogs, fowls, goats, capons, etc. That in the bay where he anchored there was no sandy barren ground, no mangroves, no ants, no mosquitoes, and that his anchorage lay between two considerable rivers. How these details fit in with Port Curtis may be evident to his Eminence, but is not apparent to less distinguished mortals. The district of Port Curtis when discovered was very thinly populated, and shows no signs of ever having been otherwise. Bows and arrows and earthenware vessels were absolutely unknown throughout Australia; houses did not exist, except in the form of temporary shelters of branches, leaves, and bark; the fruits and animals mentioned were unknown; and sandy barren country with mangroves, ants, and mosquitoes does exist in considerable quantity. The anchorage, had De Quiros ever been there, might have been between two rivers, the Boyne and Calliope (both of small size), but Cardinal Moran, to make this detail "fit in admirably", has recourse to the bold measure of moving the mouth of the Burnett River from Wide Bay to Port Curtis—some 2 1/2 degrees to the north of its real position.

On the other hand, Cook's description of the New Hebrides fits in with much greater accuracy. The latitude was found to be 15 degrees 5 minutes South, and Mr. Cooper, who went ashore with the boats, reported that he landed near a fine stream of fresh water, "probably one of those mentioned by De Quiros; and if we were not deceived, we saw the other." The country was described by Cook thus:

"an uncommonly luxuriant vegetation was everywhere to be seen; the sides of the hills were chequered with plantations; and every valley watered by a stream; of all the productions of nature this country was adorned with, the coconut trees were the most conspicuous."

A few canoes ventured near enough to have some presents thrown to them, but here the intercourse ended, for Cook felt that, notwithstanding the inviting appearance of the place, he had no time to spare from the great object of the expedition, namely, the exploration of the Southern Ocean, and, as the wind was favourable, sailed for New Zealand for a refit.

# 1774 TO 1775
# SECOND VOYAGE CONCLUDED

On 4th September Midshipman Colnett sighted a large island, which was named New Caledonia, the point first seen being called Cape Colnett. An opening in the surrounding reef having been found by the boats, the Resolution worked up to an anchorage and was quickly surrounded by canoes whose occupants were totally unarmed. At first they were shy of coming near, but at length one canoe was persuaded to receive some small presents, and in return gave some fish which "stunk intolerably," but for all that it was received in hopes more satisfactory trading might result. To some who came on board dinner was offered, but they would touch nothing but yams. They appeared to know nothing of dogs, goats, or hogs, but greatly appreciated both red cloth and nails. Cook landed and was well received, and water was pointed out, but it was too inconvenient of access; the land near a village was well cultivated and irrigated, the products being chiefly yams, plantains, and coconuts, the latter were not bearing much fruit.

On 6th September Mr. Wales secured a moderately satisfactory observation of an eclipse of the sun, and was able to fix their position as 20 degrees 17 minutes 39 seconds South, 164 degrees 41 minutes 21 seconds East. On the same day the ship's butcher, Monk, "a man much esteemed in the ship," fell down the forehatch, and died the following day from the injury received. Whilst some of the crew were engaged in watering, a small party went up the hills to view the surrounding country, but as all the natives they met turned back to follow them, Cook remarks, "at last our train was numerous." They were able to see right across the island, and estimated the width to be not more than ten leagues. On returning it was found the clerk had purchased a fish, something like a sun-fish; and as the artist was engaged in drawing and describing it, the cook took the liver and roe for supper in the cabin, with the result that Cook and the Forsters were nearly poisoned, and were only cured by the most careful attention of the surgeon. When the natives saw the fish the next morning they immediately signified it was unfit to eat, but Cook says nothing of the kind had been intimated when it was purchased.

NORFOLK ISLAND

The natives were described as robust and well made, "and not in the least addicted to pilfering, which is more than can be said of any other nation in this sea." The only tame animals they had were large fowls with very bright plumage. The country was said to consist of rocky hills, and the trees identical with those seen in New South Wales. Leaving a sow and boar behind, in hopes of their being allowed to breed, and marking a tree with the name of the ship and the date, they left for the Isle of Pines, where they arrived on the 19th. Here they were in very dangerous waters, and Cook says the safety of the ship was owing to the splendid way in which the watch was kept, and the brisk manner in which she was handled by the crew. Forster noted "innumerable columnar forms of a considerable height which we distinguished by the help of our glasses"; he put them very proudly down as of basaltic formation, and afforded considerable amusement to Cook when he was able to prove they were only trees of the Pine family; in fact, some were afterwards cut down on Botany Island and used for spars. They were unable to effect a landing on the Isle of Pines owing to the rocky nature of the shore, but by some unknown means Mr. Hodges painted a view of the interior of the island, published under that title in Cook's Voyages. Norfolk Island was discovered on 10th October, and a landing was effected, but no sign of inhabitants was seen, though a welcome supply of fish, birds, and cabbage palm was obtained. The vegetation bore a resemblance to that of New Zealand.

On 17th October Mount Egmont was sighted, and anchoring in Queen Charlotte's Sound an immediate search was made for a bottle containing letters which had been left for the Adventure. It was not to be found, nor was there anything to show by whom it had been taken, but the next day they saw where an observatory had been set up, and trees cut down with axes, and so came to the conclusion their consort had been there. The natives, who were at first very shy, but when they recognised Cook "went jumping and skipping about like madmen," informed them that the Adventure came in soon after they had left, and remained two or three weeks. A story also was told that a ship had been lost on the north side of the straits shortly before Cook arrived, and some of the people having had their clothes stolen by the natives, fired on them, but when their ammunition was exhausted were all killed. This story, evidently a distorted account of what happened to some of the Adventure's crew, was disbelieved by

Cook, who thought there had been some misunderstanding. Cook, from fresh observations, found that he had placed the South Island on his chart some 40 minutes too far to the east, and had made the distance between Queen Charlotte's Sound and Cape Pallisser 10 minutes nearer to each other than they should have been. In this connection he speaks in the highest terms of the desire of Mr. Wales to have everything as accurate as possible.

On 11th November the Resolution left the Sound at daybreak to cross the South Pacific between latitudes 54 and 55 degrees, and the course convinced Cook there was no possibility of there being any large piece of land in that portion of the ocean. He therefore stood for the western entrance of Magellan's Straits, sighting Cape Descada on 17th December, following the coast round to Christmas Sound, which they reached on the 20th, the country passed being described as "the most desolate and barren I ever saw." At Christmas Sound they were more fortunate, for wood, water, wild celery, and a large number of geese provided them with a welcome banquet for Christmas Day. They were visited by some of the natives, described as "a little, ugly, half-starved, beardless race; I saw not a tall person amongst them." The scent of dirt and train oil they carried with them was "enough to spoil the appetite of any European," consequently none were invited to join the festivities. They had European knives, cloth, handkerchiefs, etc., showing they had been in communication with white men; and Forster notes they had canoes which could not have been made in the neighbourhood, for there was no timber of sufficient size.

## CAPE HORN CORRECTED

Cape Horn was passed on 29th December, and Cook made his longitude 68 degrees 13 minutes West, a little too far to the westward; it should be 67 degrees 16 minutes West. This is absolutely correct, according to Wharton. On 1st January 1775 they landed on a small island off Staten Island, and then put in to a fine sheltered harbour on the main island, which consequently was named New Year Harbour. The weather proved unfavourable for surveying, but enough was ascertained to convince them that the Tierra del Fuego and Staten Island coasts were not so dangerous to navigation as they had been represented.

On 3rd January they left to look for Dalrymple's Gulf of Sebastian, which Cook thought was non-existent, and on the 6th they reached the position given on the chart, but could find no signs of any land. Bearing up to the north, Georgia Island was seen on the 14th, and was found to be entirely covered with snow, creating surprise as it was now the height of summer. The ship ran in between Georgia and Willis Islands, and possession was formally taken of the group, though Cook did not think that "any one would ever be benefited by the discovery." Working as far south as 60 degrees, he turned to the east, being "tired of these high southern latitudes where nothing was to be found but ice and thick fogs," and a long hollow swell coming from the westward convinced him that he was correct in his assumption that the Gulf of Sebastian and a large body of land did not exist. On the 30th two large islands were seen, and then three rocky islets to the north; the largest was named Freezeland Peak, after the sailor who sighted it, S. Freesland; and behind these was an elevated coast which received the name of Southern Thule, as being the most southerly land then discovered. The position of the ship was given as 59 degrees 13 minutes 30 seconds South, 27 degrees 45 minutes West.

During the early part of February they ran down east between 58 and 59 degrees South, frequently having to throw the ship up into the wind to shake the snow out of her sails, for the weather was very bad. After another unsuccessful attempt to find Cape Circumcision, the ship's head was turned towards the Cape of Good Hope on 23rd February, and Cook had the satisfaction of feeling he had solved the problem of the non-existence of any southern continent except in close proximity to the Pole. He firmly believed from his observations of the icefields that such a continent in the far south did exist, but he asserted that further exploration in that direction would be of little service to navigation, and would be hardly worth the cost and danger that must be incurred.

On 16th March two Dutch ships were seen steering to the west, and a boat was sent off to the nearest, which proved to be the Bownkirke Polder, from Bengal. They were offered any supplies the Dutchman had, notwithstanding the latter was rather short, owing to his being some time out from port. Some English sailors on board told of the Adventure having been at the Cape of Good Hope some twelve months previously, and that she had reported the massacre of a boat's crew in New Zealand. At the same time three more sail came up, one, an English ship, did not intend to call at the Cape, so Cook forwarded by her a letter to the Admiralty and received some provisions, and, most valuable gift, a packet of old newspapers. On the 22nd the Resolution anchored in Table Bay, saluting the Dutch flag with thirteen guns, and the next morning Cook waited on the Governor, who did everything he could to assist him and render his stay agreeable.

## THREE ON THE SICK LIST

Cook was greatly pleased to be able to report three men only on the sick list, and the remainder were granted as much leave as the refitting of the ship would permit. The rigging, of course, had suffered severely, and had to be replaced at an exorbitant cost from the Government Stores; but Cook calls attention to the state of the masts, which he considered, after sailing some 20,000 leagues, bore testimony to the care and ability of his officers and men, and also to the high qualities of his ship.

M. de Crozet put in on his way to Pondicherry, and was impressed with Cook's courtesy and qualifications as an explorer. He was able to give the first information of M. de Surville's voyage, and that he had cleared away a mistake Cook had made in assuming that the New Caledonia reefs extended to the Great Barrier Reef on the east of Australia. Forster says that Cook pointedly avoided having any intercourse with any of the Spaniards who were there, but gives no reason for it. He also bought a quantity of wild animals and birds, many of which died before reaching England, and he roundly but unjustly accused the crew of having killed them.

Touching at St. Helena, where Kendal's watch was found to differ by about two miles from the observations of Mason and Dixon at the Cape and those of Maskelyne at St. Helena, he proceeded to Ascension, where he obtained a good supply of fresh turtle, and then to Fernando de Noronho, fixing the position as 3 degrees 50 minutes South, 32 degrees 34 minutes West, and crossed the line on 11th June. Calling in at the Azores, land was sighted near Plymouth on the 29th, and next day they anchored at Spithead; and Cook, Wales, Hodges, and the two Forsters immediately started for London, having been away from England three years and eighteen days. During this time they had lost four men, three from accident and one from disease—a record unprecedented in the annals of British Naval history.

The war with the American colonies was naturally occupying the attention of the public, but the newspapers found space to publish more or less authentic information as to their arrival and proceedings on the voyage. One paper gravely said that:

"Captain Cooke will be appointed Admiral of the Blue, and command a fleet which is preparing to go out in the spring, as a reward for the discoveries he has made in his last voyage in the South Seas."

On 9th August Cook was summoned to St. James's Palace and had a long audience with the King, presenting several charts and maps and submitting several drawings, some of which were ordered to be engraved for the private museum. In return the King presented him with his commission as Post-Captain and his appointment to H.M.S. Kent. The commission, signed by Sandwich, Penton, and Pallisser, bears date 9th August. Furneaux was made Captain. He sailed for America in October, and was present at the attack on New Orleans in 1777; he died at the age of forty-six, some four years later. Kempe, Cooper, and Clerke were promoted to Commanders; and Isaac Smith, Lieutenant. Mr. Wales was appointed Mathematical Master at Christ's Hospital, and Charles Lamb mentions him as having been a severe man but:

"a perpetual fund of humour, a constant glee about him, heightened by an inveterate provincialism of North Country dialect, absolutely took away the sting from his severities."

Mr. Forster was received by the King at Kew, and was afterwards presented to the Queen, to whom he gave some of the birds bought at the Cape. He also attracted attention from another quarter, for Lloyd's Evening Post reports that on 6th August, his house at Paddington "was broke open and robbed of effects of considerable value." Again the Morning Post, 23rd August, reports:

"Monday night, as Mr. John Reynold Forster was returning from Chelsea in a post chaise, he was attacked by three highwaymen, near Bloody Bridge, who robbed him of three guineas and a watch set with diamonds."

## GREENWICH HOSPITAL

Acting on advice from the Admiralty, Cook, on 12th August, applied for the position of one of the Captains of Greenwich Hospital, vacant through the death of Captain Clements, stipulating that if occasion arose in which his services would be of use elsewhere, he might be permitted to resign. This application was immediately granted, and his appointment is dated on the same day as his application. The salary was 200 pounds per year, with a residence and certain small allowances such as fire and light, and one shilling and twopence per day table money. It is apparent from his letters that though he may have taken over some of the duties (but that is improbable, owing to his time being fully occupied preparing his Journal for the press and then making arrangements for his final voyage), he never entered upon residence but remained at Mile End. He, however, found time to write two letters to Mr. Walker of Whitby, in the first of which he speaks rather despondingly of being "confined within the limits of Greenwich Hospital, which are far too small for an active mind like mine"; and in the second he gives a rapid sketch of the voyage, which, by its clear conciseness, proves the worthlessness of Mr. Forster's sneer, repeated by later writers, that the public account of the voyage owed more to the editing of Canon Douglas than to the writing of Cook.

Soon after Cook's arrival in London, Furneaux handed him his Journal of the proceedings of the Adventure from the time of their separation off the coast of New Zealand. They were blown off the land near Table Cape in the beginning of November 1773, again sighting it near Cape Pallisser, only to be blown off again, their sails and rigging suffering severely. They put into Tolago Bay for temporary repairs and water, and left again on the 13th, but had to put back till the 16th, and even then the weather was so bad that they did not reach Queen Charlotte's Sound till the 30th, when the bottle left by Cook was at once found, telling they were six days too late. They pushed on as rapidly as possible with the refit, and then were further delayed by finding a large quantity of the bread required rebaking, but they were ready to sail by 17th December. Mr. Rowe was sent out with a boat to get a supply of vegetables, and the ship was to have sailed the following day, but the boat did not return. Burney was then sent off with a party of marines in search, and after a time discovered the missing men had been all killed and some of them eaten by the Maoris. Portions of the bodies were found and identified—Rowe's hand, by an old scar, Thomas Hill's hand, had been tattooed in Otaheite; Captain Furneaux's servant's hand; and midshipman Woodhouse's shoes were found, and a portion of the boat. The natives who had these remains were fired on, but Burney could take no further steps, for he estimated there were fifteen hundred of the natives near the place. Furneaux believed that the attack was unpremeditated as the Maoris had been quite friendly, and both he and Cook had been at the place during their previous visit. He concluded that some sudden quarrel had arisen and the boat's crew had been incautious.

## MASSACRE

On his next voyage Cook obtained an account of the affair from the natives, when they said that the crew was at dinner and some of the Maoris attempted to steal some bread and fish, whilst one tried to get something from the boat which had been left in charge of the Captain's black servant. The thieves were given a thrashing, and a quarrel arose, during which two muskets were discharged and two natives were shot. The Maoris then closed in and killed all the sailors immediately. The Yorkshire Gazette of 4th June 1887 states that it was reported that a midshipman escaped the massacre, and after many wanderings reached England in 1777. If this improbable story is true he must have been Mr. Woodhouse, whose shoes were found, for he was the only midshipman in the boat.

On 23rd December the Adventure sailed, but owing to contrary winds did not get away from the coast for some days. She stood south-east till 56 degrees South was reached, and then the cold being extreme and the sea high, her course was set for the Horn, reaching as high as 61 degrees South with a favourable wind. Stores were running short, so after an unsuccessful search for Cape Circumcision she sailed for Table Bay, and having refitted, again left on 16th April for England, and dropped her anchor at Spithead on 14th July 1774.

Mr. Forster states that this second voyage of Cook cost 25,000 pounds, but does not give the source of his information.

# 1775 TO 1776
# ENGLAND

After his return Cook was busily engaged preparing his Journal and charts for publication, which had been sanctioned by the Admiralty, and was considerably annoyed and delayed by the conduct of Mr. Forster, who immediately on his return complained that the 4,000 pounds granted him to cover the whole of his expenses had proved totally inadequate. He claimed that Lord Sandwich had promised, verbally, that he was to have the exclusive duty of writing the History of the Voyage, was to receive the whole of the profits thereof, and to be provided with permanent employment for the remainder of his life. This promise was totally denied by Lord Sandwich, and it certainly does not appear to have been a reasonable one to make on behalf of the Admiralty.

After a protracted discussion, it was agreed that Cook should write the account of the voyage and the countries visited; whilst Forster was to write a second volume containing his observations as a scientist; the Admiralty was to pay the expenses of engraving the charts, pictures, etc., and, on completion of the work, the plates were to be equally divided between Cook and Forster. Cook was to proceed with his part at once and submit it to Forster for revision, and Forster was to draw up a plan of the method he intended to pursue and forward it to Lord Sandwich for approval.

Cook proceeded to carry out his share, and furnished Forster with a large amount of manuscript; but the latter proved obstinately insistent in having his own way in everything, with the result that, after submitting two schemes to Lord Sandwich, both extremely unsatisfactory, he was forbidden to write at all, and it was decided that Cook should complete the whole work, and it should be revised by the Reverend John Douglas, Canon of Windsor, afterwards Bishop of Carlisle.

## FORSTER'S YARNS

Notwithstanding the prohibition against Forster, a book was published under his son's name, and the latter claims that he started on the voyage with the intention of writing, took copious notes, and, excepting that he utilised those taken by his father, the work was entirely his own. He forgets, however, to say that a quantity of

Cook's manuscripts had been in his father's hands, and does not explain how so much of his book corresponds with curious exactitude with that of Cook (in many cases word for word), and how, when the papers of Cook failed to provide him with further facts, he was obliged to rely on would-be philosophical dissertations which it is to be hoped were not obtained from his father's notebooks. Young Forster says that the appointment was first of all given to his father in a spirit of pique on the part of Lord Sandwich, and then the order forbidding him to write was made because the father had refused to give Miss Ray, Lord Sandwich's mistress, who had admired them when on board the ship, some birds brought home from the Cape of Good Hope as a present to the Queen. In the end the Forsters forestalled Cook's book by about six weeks, and as this was after Cook had left England on his last voyage, Mr. Wales undertook the defence of the absent against the sneers and insinuations that were plentifully given out all round. The Forsters infer that Cook was unreliable because he suppresses mention of the bombardment of the Loo fort at Madeira, an event which never happened; and because he places Valparaiso (where he had never been) in the position given on the Admiralty chart supplied to him, which proved to be some 10 degrees out. The Master who had refused to give up his cabin was, of course, never forgiven; and as for Mr. Wales, who had observed the Transit of Venus at Hudson's Bay in 1769, for the Royal Society, he, poor man, had neither knowledge nor experience in astronomical science. The crews of the two ships also, carefully selected men though they were, some of whom had been the previous voyage, were morally and physically bad, and utterly incapable of performing their duty in a proper and seamanlike manner. A little allowance must be made for the two authors, for the father suffered severely from rheumatism, the son was of a scorbutic tendency, and both were unaccustomed to sea life, and doubtless the hardships inseparable from such a voyage pressed heavily upon them.

A second Journal was published by F. Newbery about the same time, and Cook hearing of it, sent Anderson, the gunner, to find out the author. With little difficulty he was found to be Marra, the gunner's mate who tried to desert at Otaheite, and the publication was stayed till after the authorised version was out.

A volume of Cook's letters to Dr. Douglas relating to the preparation of his Journal for the press is preserved at the British Museum, and it shows how Cook to the very last endeavoured to serve Mr. Forster's interests, and to smooth matters over so that they could work together. The last one Dr. Douglas received before Cook's departure was dated from Mile End, 23rd June 1776, the day before he joined his ship at the Nore.

*Dear Sir, It is now settled that I am to publish without Mr. Forster, and I have taken my measures accordingly. When Captain Campbell has looked over the manuscript it will be put into the hands of Mr. Strahan and Mr. Stuart to be printed, and I shall hope for the continuation of your assistance in correcting the press. I know not how to recompense you for the trouble you have had and will have in the work. I can only beg you will accept of as many copies after it is published as will serve yourself and friends, and I have given directions for you to be furnished with them. When you have done with the Introduction, please send it to Mr. Strahan or bring it with you when you come to Town, for there needs be no hurry about it. Tomorrow morning I set out to join my ship at the Nore, and with her proceed to Plymouth where my stay will be but short. Permit me to assure you that I shall always have a due sense of the favour you have done me, and that I am with great esteem and regard, Dear Sir, your obliged and very humble servant,*
*James Cook.*

Notwithstanding the Forsters' endeavour to discount its success by forestalling the publication by some weeks, Cook's work was well received by the public, and Mrs. Cook, to whom the whole of the profits were given, reaped considerable benefit from its sale.

## FELLOW OF ROYAL SOCIETY

On 29th February 1776, Captain James Cook was unanimously elected a Fellow of the Royal Society, and his certificate of election was signed by no less than twenty-six of the Fellows. He was formally admitted on 17th March, on which date a paper written by him, on the means he had used for the prevention and cure of scurvy, was read. That he valued his success in dealing with this disease, which, at that time, even in voyages of very moderate length was the most terrible danger to be encountered, is plainly set forth in his Journal of the voyage. He says:

"But whatever may be the public judgment about other matters, it is with real satisfaction and without claiming any merit but that of attention to my duty, that I can conclude this account with an observation which facts enable me to make, that our having discovered the possibility of preserving health amongst a numerous ship's company, for such a length of time in such varieties of climate and amidst such continued hardships and fatigues, will make this voyage remarkable in opinion of every benevolent person, when the disputes about a Southern Continent shall have ceased to engage the attention and to divide the judgment of philosophers."

During his early days at sea it was no unusual thing for a man-of-war to be short-handed through scurvy after a cruise of a few weeks, and in a voyage across the Atlantic as many as twenty per cent of the crew are known to have perished. To give some of his own experiences in the Navy: On 4th June 1756, H.M.S. Eagle arrived in Plymouth Sound, after cruising for two months in the Channel and off the French coast, and Captain Palliser reported landing 130 sick, buried at sea 22, and since his arrival in port his surgeon and 4 men had died, and both his surgeon's mates were very ill; this out of a complement of 400!

Boscawen, sailing from Halifax for Louisberg in 1758, left several ships behind on account of scurvy, one being the Pembroke, of which Cook was Master; she had lost 29 men crossing the Atlantic, but she was able to rejoin before the others as they were in a worse plight. Wolfe reported to Lord George Sackville that some of the regiments employed at Louisburg had "300 or 400 men eat up with scurvy." Of the Northumberland when at Halifax, Lord Colville wrote that frozen (fresh) beef from Boston kept his men healthy when in port, "but the scurvy never fails to pull us down in great numbers upon our going to sea in spring."

Having had such experiences Cook appears to have made up his mind to fight the dreadful scourge from the very first, and though the popular idea is that he only turned his mind to it during the second voyage, it is very evident that on the Endeavour he fought it successfully, and it is most probable would have laid claim to victory had it not been for the serious losses incurred through the malarial fever and its usual companion, dysentery, contracted at Batavia. In proof of this reference may be made to the report of Mr. Perry, surgeon's mate, and, after Mr. Monkhouse's death, surgeon on board. He states they rounded the Horn with the crew "as free from scurvy as on our sailing from Plymouth," i.e. after five months. He reports FOR THE WHOLE OF THE VOYAGE, FIVE CASES OF SCURVY, "three in Port at New Holland, and two while on the Coast of New Zealand, not a man more suffered any inconvenience from this distemper." He was one of the five cases, but, at the same time, it must not be understood that no others developed symptoms of scurvy, only they were so closely watched and at once subjected to such treatment that the disease was not able to gain the upper hand. Cook wrote to the Secretary to the Admiralty immediately after his arrival at Batavia, saying, "I have not lost one man from sickness." He means here, as elsewhere in his Journals, "sickness" to be taken as scurvy, and at that time he had lost only seven men: two of Mr. Banks's servants from exposure; three men drowned; Mr. Buchan, a fit, probably apoplectic; and one man, alcoholic poisoning. He arrived at home with a total loss of forty-one, including Tupia and his boy; thirty-two of these deaths were from fever and dysentery, and 2, Mr. Hicks and Sutherland, from consumption.

## TREATMENT OF SCURVY

The chief anti-scorbutics used on the Endeavour, according to Mr. Perry's report, were:

"Sour Kraut, Mustard, Vinegar, Wheat (whole), Inspissated Orange and Lemon juice, Saloup, Portable Soup, Sugar, Molasses, Vegetables (at all times when they could possibly be got), were some in constant, others in occasional use."

Saloup was a decoction made from the Orchis mascula root, a common meadow plant, or else from Sassafras, and was at one time sold in the streets as a drink before the introduction of tea and coffee. In the United Service Museum there is a cake of the portable soup which was on board the Endeavour, in appearance like a square of "whitish glue, which in effect it is," says Sir John Pringle, President of the Royal Society.

Mr. Perry continues: "Cold bathing was encouraged and enforced by example. The allowance of Salt Beef and Pork was abridged from nearly the beginning of the voyage, and the usual custom of the sailors mixing the Salt Beef fat with the flour was strictly forbidden. Salt Butter and Cheese was stopped on leaving England, and throughout the voyage Raisins were issued in place of the Salt Suet; in addition to the Malt, wild Celery was collected in Tierra del Fuego, and, every morning, breakfast was made from this herb, ground wheat and portable soup."

Of the personal cleanliness of the crew, which Cook looked upon as of the first importance, Marra says (when writing of the Resolution's voyage) he was very particular:

"never suffering any to appear dirty before him, in so much that when other Commanders came on board, they could not help declaring they thought EVERY DAY Sunday on board of Captain Cook."

He inspected the men at least once a week, and saw they had changed their clothing and were dry; the bedding was dried and aired when occasion offered, and the whole ship was stove-dried; special attention being paid to the well, into which an iron pot containing a fire was lowered.

Fresh water was obtained when possible, for Cook remarks, "nothing contributes more to the health of seamen than having plenty of water." He was provided with a condenser, but it was too small and unsatisfactory, and he looked upon it as "a useful invention, but only calculated to provide enough to preserve life without health." He attributed the losses on the Adventure to Furneaux's desire to save his men labour, and neglecting to avail himself of every opportunity of obtaining fresh water. Cook throughout the voyage was never short of water; Furneaux was on two or three occasions.

Dr. McBride advised the use of fresh wort made from malt as an anti-scorbutic, and the Endeavour was ordered to give it a thorough trial. Fresh ground malt was treated with boiling water and allowed to stand, then the liquid was boiled with dried fruit or biscuit into a panada, and the patient had one or two meals with a quart or more of the liquid per diem. This treatment was favourably reported on, but, at the same time, so many other precautions were taken that it was not possible to say which was the most successful. Banks, who was threatened, tried the wort, but thinking it affected his throat, substituted a weak punch of lemon juice and brandy, which had satisfactory results. After a time the malt, though dry and sweet, had lost much strength, so as strong a wort was made as possible, and ground wheat boiled with it for breakfast, "a very pleasant mess which the people were very fond of," and Cook "had great reason to think that the people received much benefit from it."

## SOUR KRAUTE

Cook set great store on the Sour Kraute, and says:

"The men at first would not eat it, until I put it in practice—a method I never once knew to fail with seamen—and this was to have some of it dressed every day for the Cabin Table, and permitted all the officers, without exception, to make use of it, and left it to the option of the men to take as much as they pleased, or none at all; but this practice was not continued above a week before I found necessary to put every one on board to an allowance, for such are the Tempers and Disposition of seamen in general, that whatever you give them out of the common way, although it be ever so much for their good, it will not go down, and you will hear nothing but murmurings against the man that first invented it, but the moment they see their superiors set a value upon it, it becomes the finest stuff in the world, and the inventor is an honest fellow."

A pound of this was served to each man, twice a week, at sea, or oftener if thought necessary.

Portable soup, at the rate of an ounce per man, was boiled with the pease thrice a week, and when vegetables could be obtained it was boiled with them, and wheat or oatmeal for breakfast, and with pease and vegetables for dinner, and "was the means of making the people eat a greater quantity of vegetables than they would otherwise have done." The Rob of Lemon and Orange was a doubtful quantity, for though Cook had no great confidence in its efficacy, Furneaux reported very favourably on its use, but it was expensive. Of vinegar, Cook was of opinion that it was of little service, and preferred smoking the ship with wood-fires to washing with vinegar, which had been strongly advised. He substituted sugar for oil, as he esteemed it "a very good anti-scorbutic, whereas oil (such as the navy is usually supplied with) I am of opinion has the contrary effect."

Cook says that the introduction of the most salutary articles would prove unsuccessful unless accompanied by strict regulations so the crew were divided into three watches except on some extraordinary occasion, in order that they might not be so exposed to the weather, and had a better chance to get into dry clothes if they happened to get wet. Hammocks, bedding, clothes, and ship were kept as clean and dry as possible, and when the ship could not be "cured with fires," once or twice a week she was smoked with gunpowder, mixed with vinegar or water:

"to cleanliness, as well in the ship as amongst the people, too great attention cannot be paid: the least neglect occasions a putrid and disagreeable smell below which nothing but fires will remove."

He finishes his paper read before the Royal Society as follows:

"We came to few places where either the art of man or the bounty of nature had not provided some sort of refreshment or other, either in the animal or vegetable way. It was my first care to procure whatever of any kind could be met with, by every means in my power, and to oblige our people to make use thereof, both by my example and authority; but the benefits arising from refreshments of any kind soon became so obvious that I had little occasion to recommend the one or exert the other."

## COPLEY GOLD MEDAL

On the 30th November 1776 Sir John Pringle, President of the Royal Society, in his address to the Fellows, announced that the Copley Gold Medal had been conferred on Captain Cook for his paper on the Treatment of Scurvy, and gave some corroborative facts which had come under his own observation, concluding his speech as follows:

"If Rome decreed the Civic Crown to him who saved the life of a single citizen, what wreaths are due to that man, who, having himself saved many, perpetuates in your Transactions the means by which Britain may now, on the most distant voyages, preserve numbers of her intrepid sons, her mariners; who, braving every danger, have so liberally contributed to the fame, to the opulence, and to the Maritime Empire of this country."

Before Cook left England on his last voyage he had been informed that the medal had been conferred on him, but he never received it, and it was presented to Mrs. Cook, and is now in the British Museum.

During May 1776 Cook sat for his portrait, now in the Painted Hall, Greenwich, to Sir Nathaniel Dance. There are several portraits of him in existence; three by Webber, one being in the National Portrait Gallery; one by Hodges; and one or two others by unknown artists. Mr. Samwell, surgeon on the third voyage, says of an engraving by Sherwin, from the portrait by Dance, that it "is a most excellent likeness of Captain Cook; and more to be valued, as it is the only one I have seen that bears any resemblance to him." This portrait of Dance's represents Cook dressed in his Captain's uniform, seated at a table on which is a chart. The figure is evidently that of a tall man — he was over six feet in height — with brown unpowdered hair, neatly tied back from the face; the clear complexion shows little effect of exposure to the sea breezes, the pleasant brown eyes look from under rather prominent brows, the nose rather long, and a good firm mouth. The whole face gives a very pleasant impression of the man, and conveys the idea that it was a good likeness.

## COOK VOLUNTEERS

Omai, a native of Otaheite, was brought to England by Furneaux, was introduced to the King, made much of in Society, was painted by Reynolds, Dance, and Hodges, and seems to have conducted himself fairly well. He was to be sent back to his own country; and from the orders given to the Resolution, when she returned, it was evident she was to be the ship to take him. There was some difficulty as to the man to take command of the new expedition, as the Admiralty felt they could not send out Cook again so soon after his return. However, early in February 1776, he was invited to dine with Lord Sandwich, to meet Sir Hugh Pallisser and Mr. Stephens, the Secretary, when the proposed expedition was discussed and the difficulty of finding a commander was brought forward. It is said that after some conversation Cook jumped up and declared he would go, and as the result of this resolve he called at the Admiralty Office on 10th February, and made formal application for the command, which was accepted on the same day, and he there and then went to Deptford and hoisted his pendant on the Resolution. Her complement was the same as the previous voyage, i.e. 112 men, including 20 marines; and the Quarter Bill, preserved in the Records Office, shows the stations and duties of each of the crew, and the positions of the civilians who in cases of necessity were expected to take their places as small arms men.

The companion ship, the Discovery, was built by Langborne of Whitby, and was purchased for 2,450 pounds from W. Herbert of Scarborough. According to the Records she was 229 tons burthen, but Cook puts her down as 300 tons; and Burney says the two ships were splendid sailing company, any advantage there might be resting with the Discovery. The command was given to Charles Clerke, who had been both the previous voyages.

The Resolution hauled out of dock, 10th March, completed her rigging and took in stores and provisions, "which was as much as we could stow and the best of every kind that could be got." On the 6th May the pilot went on board to take her down to Longreach for her guns and powder, but owing to contrary winds she did not reach there till the 30th. On 8th June she was visited by Lord Sandwich, Sir Hugh Pallisser, and others from the Admiralty, "to see that everything was compleated to their desire and to the satisfaction of all who were to embark in the voyage." A bull, two cows and their calves, with some sheep, were embarked as a present from King

George to the Otahietans in hopes to start stocking the island. A good supply of trade was shipped, and extra warm clothing for the crew was supplied by the Admiralty:

"and nothing was wanting that was thought conducive to either conveniency or health, such was the extraordinary care taken by those at the head of the Naval Departments."

Cook and King were to take observations on the Resolution, and Bailey, who was with the Adventure the previous voyage, was appointed as astronomer to the Discovery; the necessary instruments being supplied by the Board of Longitude. The chronometer, made by Kendal, which had given such satisfaction last voyage, was again on board the Resolution. It was afterwards with Bligh in the Bounty, sold by Adams after the Mutiny to an American, who sold it again in Chili. It was then purchased for 52 pounds 10 shillings, repaired, and rated, and after keeping fair time for some years was presented by Admiral Sir Thomas Herbert to the United Service Museum, and is still in working order.

## CLERKE IN THE FLEET

On 15th June the two ships sailed for the Nore; there the Resolution waited for her Captain, whilst the Discovery, under the command of Burney, went on to Plymouth, but, meeting with damage in a gale, had to put into Portland for temporary repairs. Captain Clerke was detained in London, "in the Rules of the Bench," as he had become financially responsible for a friend who left him in the lurch. He wrote to Banks, saying, "the Jews are exasperated and determined to spare no pains to arrest me." It appears that he contracted the illness which led to his death at this period.

# 1776 TO 1777
# THIRD VOYAGE

On 24th June Cook and Omai joined the Ship at the Nore, leaving next day for Plymouth, arriving there on 30th, three days after the Discovery. On 8th July the final orders, which Cook had helped to draw up, were received. They were to the effect that he was to proceed by the Cape of Good Hope; to look for some islands said to have been seen by the French in latitude 48 degrees, about the longitude of Mauritius; to touch at New Zealand, if he thought proper; and then to proceed to Otaheite and leave Omai there, or at the Society Islands, as the latter might wish. Leaving Otaheite about February he was to strike the North American coast in about 45 degrees latitude, avoiding, if possible, touching at any of the Spanish dominions, and proceeding northwards to explore any rivers or inlets that seemed likely to lead to Hudson's or Baffin's Bay. For the winter he was to proceed to the Port of St. Peter and St. Paul in Kamtschatka, or other suitable place, and in the ensuing spring he was again to try and find a passage either to the east or west; failing that, the ships were then to return to England. A reward of 20,000 pounds had been offered to any British merchant ship that discovered a passage between Hudson's Bay and the Pacific; and now this offer was thrown open to any ship flying the British flag, and the passage might be to the east or west so long as it was north of latitude 52 degrees.

On 9th July the marines, who had been carefully selected, embarked under the command of Lieutenant Molesworth Phillips, and the following day officers and men were paid up to 30th June, and petty officers and seamen received in addition two months' advance.

## THE RESOLUTION SAILS

The Resolution sailed on 12th July, the crew looking on it as a lucky day, being the anniversary of the day they had sailed on the last voyage; but as Clerke had not yet arrived, the Discovery remained behind. Putting in to Teneriffe, Cook purchased a supply of wine, which he did not think as good as that of Madeira, but remarks that the best Teneriffe wine was "12 pounds a pipe, whereas the best Madeira is seldom under 27 pounds." Here they met "Captain Baurdat" (the Chevalier de Borda), who was making observations in order to time two watch machines, and were afforded an opportunity of comparing them with their own. Looking into Port Praya in hopes to find the Discovery they crossed the line on 1st September in longitude 27 degrees 38 minutes West, and sighted the Cape of Good Hope on 17th October, anchoring in Table Bay the next day. The ship was found to be very leaky in her upper works, as the great heat had opened up her seams which had been badly caulked at first. "Hardly a man that could lie dry in his bed; the officers in the gun-room were all driven out of their cabin by the water that came in through the sides." The sails were damaged, some being quite ruined before they could be dried.

The reception accorded by the Dutch was all that could be desired, and all the resources of the place were at Cook's disposal. Letters were sent to England and one invalid, Cook wishing afterwards that he had sent one or two more, but he had at the time hopes of their complete recovery. On 31st October they were unable to communicate with the shore owing to a heavy south-easterly gale which did not blow itself out for three days, and the Resolution was the only ship in the bay that rode through it without dragging her anchors. On the 10th November the Discovery arrived, having left Plymouth on 1st August. She sighted land above twenty-five leagues north of Table Bay, but had been blown off the coast in the storm.

It may be noted here that the French, Spanish, and United States Governments issued instructions to their naval officers that Captain Cook and his ships were to be treated with every respect, and as belonging to a neutral and allied power. An honour to Cook, and also to the nations who conferred it on him.

When her consort arrived Cook was almost ready for sea, so the refit of the Discovery was pushed on as quickly as possible, but some delay arose in the delivery of bread ordered. Cook says he believes the bakers would not put it in hand till they saw the Discovery safely at anchor. However, on 30th November Clerke was handed his instructions, and the two Captains went on board their respective ships to find them fully supplied for a voyage which was expected to last at least two years. Live stock had been purchased at the Cape, and one journalist says that on leaving, the Resolution reminded him of Noah's Ark.

They did not get clear of the coast till 3rd December owing to light winds, and then on the 6th "a sudden heavy squall" cost the Resolution her mizzen topmast; not a very serious loss, for they had a spare stick, and the broken one "had often complained," but Burney says that owing to the weather it took them three days to complete the repairs. The cold, rough weather also had a bad effect on the live stock, several of them perishing.

### DENSE FOG

On 12th December the islands discovered by Marion du Fresne and Crozet in 1772 were sighted, and as they were unnamed in the map, dated 1775, given by Crozet to Cook, he called them Prince Edward's Islands, and a small group further to the east was named Marion and Crozet Islands. Then sailing south through fog so dense that, Burney says, they were often for hours together unable to see twice the length of the ship, and, though it was the height of summer, the cold was so intense that the warm clothing had to be resorted to, they sighted Kerguelen's Land on 24th December. The Chevalier de Borda had given Cook 48 degrees 26 minutes South, 64 degrees 57 minutes East of Paris as the position of Rendezvous Island; this Cook took to be an isolated rock they only just weathered in the fog, to which he gave the name of Bligh's Cap, for he said: "I know nothing that can Rendezvous at it but fowls of the air, for it is certainly inaccessible to every other animal." Cook, unaware that Kerguelen had paid two visits to the place, found some difficulty in recognising the places described. The country was very desolate, the coarse grass hardly worth cutting for the animals; no wood, but a good supply of water was obtained; and here the Christmas Day was spent on the 27th, as the 25th and 26th had been full of hard work. A bottle was found by one of the crew containing a parchment record of the visit of the French in 1772; on the back Cook noted the names of his ships and the year of their visit, and adding a silver twopenny piece of 1772, replaced it in the bottle which was sealed with lead and hidden in a pile of stones in such a position that it could not escape the notice of any one visiting the spot. Running along the coast to the south-east they encountered very blowy weather, and finding the land even more desolate than that at Christmas Harbour, they left on the 31st for New Zealand. Anderson, the surgeon, on whom Cook relied for his notes on Natural History, says: "Perhaps no place hitherto discovered in either hemisphere under the same parallel of latitude affords so scanty a field for the naturalist as this barren spot."

The whole catalogue of plants, including lichens, did not exceed sixteen or eighteen.

A SOUTHERLY BUSTER

The first part of January 1777 was foggy, and Cook says they "ran above 300 leagues in the dark." On the 19th a squall carried away the fore topmast and main topgallant mast, and it took the whole day to replace the first, but they had nothing suitable for the top gallant mast. On 26th January they put into Adventure Bay, Van Diemen's Land, and obtained a spar; Cook spoke of the timber as being good but too heavy. A few natives were seen, but did not create a favourable impression, still Cook landed a couple of pigs in hopes to establish the breed, a hope doomed to be unsatisfied. The Marquis de Beauvoir relates that in 1866 he saw in Adventure Bay a tree on which was cut with a knife: Cook, 26th Jan. 1777, and he was informed it had been cut by the man himself. They seem to have seen nothing to raise a doubt about Furneaux's conclusion that Van Diemen's Land formed a part of Australia, so no attempt was made to settle the question, and they sailed for New Zealand on the 30th, meeting with a "perfect storm" from the south; the thermometer rose:

"almost in an instant from about 70 degrees to near 90 degrees, but fell again when the wind commenced, in fact the change was so rapid that there were some on board who did not notice it."

These storms are of frequent occurrence, and are locally known as Southerly Busters.

On 10th February Rocks Point, near Cape Farewell, was sighted, and on the 12th they anchored near their old berth in Queen Charlotte's Sound, and a camp was immediately established. Here they were visited by a few of the natives, some of whom remembered Cook and were recognised by him. At first they thought he had come to avenge the Adventure's losses, but after a time were persuaded to put aside their distrust, and they flocked down to the shore, every available piece of ground being quickly occupied by their huts. Cook describes how one party worked. The ground was selected, the men tearing up the grass and plants, and erected the huts, whilst the women looked after the canoes, properties, and provisions, and collected firewood; and he kept the children and some of the oldest of the party out of mischief by scrambling the contents of his pockets amongst them. At the same time he noticed that however busy the men might be, they took care to be within easy reach of their weapons; and he on his side had a strong party of marines on duty, and any party working at a distance from the ship was always armed and under the command of an officer experienced in dealing with the natives. Cook was pleased to notice his men were not inclined to associate with the Maoris, and he always tried to discourage familiarity between his crew and the natives of the islands he visited. It is worthy of remark that two of the Resolution were on the sick list, whilst the Discovery had a clean bill of health.

One of their constant visitors was a man Cook calls Kahoura, who was pointed out as having been the leader at the massacre of the Adventure's men, and it was a matter of surprise to the natives that having him in his power Cook did not kill him; but after the fullest possible enquiry Cook believed it was best to let matters rest, as the attack had evidently arisen out of a sudden quarrel, and was totally unpremeditated. Burney thinks the Maoris felt a certain contempt for the English, either because they were too generous in their dealings, or else because the murders were unavenged.

The gardens that had been made at the last visit had in some respects prospered; in particular the potatoes from the Cape had improved in quality, but as they had been appreciated by the natives, there were few to be got. Burney, on the other hand, declares that nothing could be heard of the pigs and fowls that had been left. Omai was anxious to take a New Zealander away with him, and soon found one to volunteer. It was explained that he must make up his mind that he would not be able to return, and as he seemed satisfied he and a boy were taken. When they were seasick they deeply and loudly lamented leaving their home, but on recovery they soon became "as firmly attached to us as if they had been born amongst us."

## THE WEEKLY PAPER

Sailing on 25th February, they crossed the tropic on 27th March, some 9 degrees further west than Cook wished to have done, and had seen nothing of importance. It is interesting to note that Burney says each ship published a weekly paper, and on signal being made a boat was sent to exchange when possible. He says Cook was a "Constant Reader," but not a "Contributor." It is to be regretted that no copies exist of this, probably the first oceanic weekly.

On 29th March, a small island Cook calls Manganouia was discovered in 21 degrees 57 minutes South, 201 degrees 53 minutes East (Burney gives 21 degrees 54 minutes South, 202 degrees 6 minutes East.) but the landing-places were too dangerous on account of the surf. A native came on board who was able to converse with Omai, and said they had plenty of plantains and taro, but neither yams, hogs, nor dogs. He unfortunately fell over a goat, which he took to be a large bird, and was so frightened he had to be put ashore. The next day another island was seen, and as they were very short of fodder for the animals, Gore was sent to see if trade could be opened up with the inhabitants. In this he was fairly successful, and obtained a quantity of plantain stems, which were found to be a satisfactory substitute for grass; but the trading was not brisk, for the people wished to receive dogs in return, and it was evident that though they had none, they knew what they were. They were afraid of the horses and cattle, and took the sheep and goats for some kind of large birds. A party went ashore and were treated fairly well, but when they wished to return to their boats all sorts of difficulties were raised, and Cook credits Omai with their safe return; for it seems he gave judiciously boastful replies to the many questions that were asked him, and at the psychological moment exploded a handful of powder, with the result that opposition to their departure was withdrawn. Burney says Omai was most useful on a landing party, as he was a good sportsman and cook, and was never idle. After this experience Cook would not run further risks, so made for a small uninhabited island where some vegetables were obtained and branches of trees, which, cut into short lengths, were eagerly eaten by the cattle, and Cook says: "It might be said, without impropriety, that we fed our cattle on billet wood." Payment for what had been taken was left in a deserted village.

On 6th April they reached Hervey's Island, and were somewhat surprised to be visited by several canoes, as on Cook's previous visit no signs of inhabitants had been noticed. Omai gathered from one or two natives who came on board to sell a few fish, that the Resolution and Adventure had been seen in 1776 when passing the island. King was sent to look for a landing-place, but, seeing that the women were quietly bringing down arms to their menfolk on the beach, he thought it better to return to the ship, and sail was made for the Friendly Islands, the Discovery being sent on about a league ahead, as she was better able "to claw off a lee shore than mine." At this time Cook was getting rather short of water, so he set the still to work, and obtained from "13 to 16 gallons of fresh water" between 6 A.M. and 4 P.M. "There has lately been made some IMPROVEMENT, as they are pleased to call it, to this machine, which in my opinion is much for the worse." Falling in with repeated thunderstorms in which they caught more water in an hour "than by the still in a month, I laid it a side as a thing attended with more trouble than profit."

At one of the Palmerston Group they found, amongst other things drifted over the reef, some planks, one of which was very thick, with trunnell holes in it, and a piece of moulding from some ship's upper works, painted yellow, with nail holes showing signs of iron rust: probably the remains of some wrecked European ship. At Comango, where they anchored on 28th April, Cook notes:

"It was remarkable that during the whole day the Indians would hardly part with any one thing to anybody but me; Captain Clerke did not get above one or two hogs."

A supply of water was obtained and wood was cut, but most of the trees were what Cook calls Manchineel, the sap from which produced blisters on the men's skin, and Burney says some of them were blind for a fortnight, having rubbed their faces with their juice-stained hands. One of the carpenters had a bad fall and broke his leg, but for the rest, says Burney, they were "in good health; thank God, no appearance of scurvy."

## FLOGGING NO GOOD

Cook again complains of the thefts committed so continually, and says that no punishment they could devise was effectual, for "flogging made no more impression than it would have done upon the mainmast." The chiefs would advise him to kill those caught, but as he would not proceed to such a length the culprits generally escaped unpunished. Here the Discovery lost her best bower anchor, the cable having been chafed by the coral and parted when weighing; Burney describes how by pouring oil on the water they were able to see and recover it from a depth of seventeen fathoms. Landing on Happi they were very well received, and obtained plentiful supplies of fresh food, which was most opportune. An entertainment of boxing, wrestling, and combats with clubs made from green coconut boughs was held in their honour; and Cook says that they were carried on with the greatest good-humour in the presence of some three thousand spectators, "though some, women as well as men, have received blows they must feel some time after." When this was over the chief, Feenough, presented Cook with supplies that required four boats to take to the ships; it "far exceeded any present I had ever before received from an Indian Prince." The donor was invited on board to receive his return present, which proved so satisfactory that on his return to the shore he forwarded still more in addition to his first gift, and was amused by a drill of the marines and a display of fireworks, which, though some were spoilt, were the cause of astonishment and pleasure to the wondering natives. During one of his walks on shore Cook saw a woman just completing a surgical operation on a child's eyes. She was removing a film growing over the eyeballs, and the instruments used are described as slender wooden probes. He was not able to say if the operation were successful.

The chief, Feenough, went off to an island about two days' sail away, in order to obtain some of the feather caps which were held in high estimation; and Cook promised to wait for his return, but finding the fresh supplies were running short, he sailed along the south of the reef and put in to a bay in Lefooga. On the way the Discovery ran on a shoal, but managed to back off without damage. Although he was not short of water, Cook went ashore to inspect some well which he had been informed contained water of a very superior quality, but he found it very bad, and says: "This will not be the only time I shall have to remark that these people do not know what good water is." Near these wells was a large artificial mound about forty feet high, and fifty feet diameter on the top, on which large trees were growing. At the foot was a hewn block of coral, four feet broad, two and a half feet thick, and fourteen feet high, but the natives present said that there was only one half of it above ground. It was supposed to have been erected to the memory of a great chief, but how many years ago it was impossible to guess.

## KING POLAHO

Whilst anchored here, a large sailing canoe arrived, having on board a chief who was treated by the natives with the utmost respect, and the visitors were given to understand that Tattafee Polaho was the king of all the islands. He was invited on board, and brought with him as a present:

"two good fat hogs, though not so fat as himself, for he was the most corporate, plump fellow we had met with. I found him to be a sedate, sensible man; he viewed the ship and the several new objects with uncommon attention, and asked several pertinent questions."

In return Cook was invited ashore, and when they were seated, the natives who had been trading submitted the articles they had received for Polaho's inspection, who enquired what each one had sold, and seemed pleased with the bargains made. Everything was returned to its owner, excepting a red glass bowl to which the king had taken a great fancy. According to Mr. Basil Thomson, who was for some years in the Pacific Islands, a red glass bowl was given by the King of Tonga to the notorious Mr. Shirley Baker, as a relic of Captain Cook, but was unfortunately broken in New Zealand. It was most probably the one in question. Before leaving, Polaho presented Cook with one of the red feather caps made from the tail feathers of the bird the Sandwich Islanders call Iiwi (Vestiaria coicinea), which were evidently considered of extreme value. At the same time he gave Cook, Clerke, and Omai some of the red feathers of paraquets which, though much in demand, were not to be purchased.

On 29th May they sailed for Tongatabu, but, the wind failing, they nearly ran ashore on the 31st on a low sandy island on which the sea was breaking very heavily. Fortunately all hands had just been engaged in putting the ship about, "so that the necessary movements were not only executed with judgment but with alertness, and this alone saved the ship." Cook confesses that he was tired of beating about in these dangerous waters, and felt relieved to get back to his old anchorage off Annamooka. Feenough here rejoined the ship, and his behaviour before Polaho was sufficient evidence as to the high position held by the latter, for he made a deep reverence to him, and afterwards would not eat or drink in his presence, but left the cabin as soon as dinner was announced.

## AN ENTERTAINMENT

On 6th June they sailed for Tongatabu again, accompanied by some sailing canoes which could all easily outdistance the two ships. A good anchorage was found, and Cook's old friends, Otago and Toobough, were soon on board to greet them. As it was proposed to make a short stay, the cattle were landed, the observatory set up, and the sail-makers set to work to overhaul the sails, for much-required repairs. Cook speaks very highly of the orderly behaviour of the natives, many of whom had never seen a white man before. Hearing much of an important chief named Mariwaggee, Cook persuaded the king to escort a party to his residence, which was found to be pleasantly situated on an inlet where most of the chiefs resided, surrounded by neatly fenced plantations; but they were informed that Mariwaggee had gone to see the ships. This was found to be untrue, but the next day he appeared, accompanied by a large number of both sexes, and Cook at once landed with some presents for him, only to find he was accompanied by another chief, to whom something had to be given as well. Fortunately the two were easily satisfied, and the present was divided between them. Mariwaggee was found to be the father of Feenough, and the father-in-law of the king. He gave a grand entertainment of singing and dancing in honour of the strangers, which commenced about eleven in the morning and lasted till between three and four in the afternoon, and wound up with a presentation of a large number of yams, each pair of the roots being tied to a stick about six feet long, and decorated with fish. Cook says it was hard to say which was the most valuable, the yams for food or the sticks for firewood; but, as for the fish, "it might serve to please the sight, but was very offensive to the smell, as some of it had been kept two or three days for this occasion." More singing and dancing then took place, and then the English gave a display of fireworks, which "astonished and highly entertained" the natives.

Being afraid that some of his live stock might be stolen, Cook tried to interest some of the chiefs in them by presenting the king with a bull and cow and some goats; to Feenough a horse and mare, and to Mariwaggee a ram and two ewes. Some one, however, was not satisfied, and a kid and two turkey cocks were stolen; and as thefts had been frequent and very daring, including an attempt to steal one of the anchors of the Discovery, which would have been successful had not one of the flukes of the anchor got fixed in one of the chain plates, Cook determined to put his foot down. He seized three canoes, and, hearing Feenough and some other chiefs were in a house together, he placed a guard over them and informed them they would be detained till the stolen goods were returned. They took the matter coolly, and said that everything should be returned. Some of the things being produced, Cook invited his prisoners on board ship to dine, and when they came back the kid and a turkey were brought, so the prisoners and canoes were released. At one time a small hostile demonstration was made by the natives, but the landing of a few marines and an order from the king put an end to it.

## SMART WORKMEN

The following day Cook was invited on shore and found some natives busy erecting two sets of poles, one on each side of the place set apart for the guests. Each set consisted of four placed in a square about two feet apart, secured from spreading by cross pieces, and carried up to a height of about thirty feet, the intervening space being filled with yams. On the top of one structure were two baked pigs, and on the other alive one, with a second tied by its legs about half way up. Cook was particularly struck by the way the men raised these two towers, and says if he had ordered his sailors to do such a thing, they would have wanted carpenters and tools and at least a hundredweight of nails, and would have taken as many days as it did these people hours. When the erections were completed, piles of bread-fruit and yams were heaped on either side, and a turtle and some excellent fish were added, and then the whole was presented to Cook.

A party of officers from both ships went off to an island without leave, and returned two days after without their muskets, ammunition, and other articles which had been stolen. They persuaded Omai to make a private complaint to the king, which resulted in the chiefs leaving the neighbourhood. Their disappearance annoyed Cook, and when the affair was explained to him he severely reprimanded Omai for speaking on the matter without orders. This put Omai on his mettle, and he managed to persuade Feenough to return, and informed the king that no serious consequences should ensue. Matters were then easily smoothed over; most of the stolen goods, including the missing turkey, were returned, and the king said he ought not to have been held responsible, for, if he had known that any one wished to see the island, he would have sent a chief who would have ensured their safety.

An eclipse of the sun was to occur on 5th July, and Cook decided to remain so as to secure observations, and meanwhile employed himself in exploring the neighbourhood and studying the customs of the natives. On one occasion, thinking to see an interesting ceremony, he accompanied Polaho, who was going to do state mourning for a son who had been dead some time. The result was disappointing, and the chief impression left with Cook seems to have been that over their clothing of native cloth, those present wore old and ragged mats; those of the king being the raggedest, and "might have served his great-grandfather on some such like occasion."

July 5th proved dark and cloudy, with heavy showers of rain, and the observations were unsatisfactory, especially as the clouds came up thickly in the middle of the eclipse, and the sun was seen no more for the rest of the day. This failure was not of great importance, for the longitude had already been satisfactorily ascertained by several very good lunar observations, so as soon as the eclipse was over everything was sent on board the ships, including the sheep which had been presented to Mariwaggee. No one had taken any notice of them since they were landed, and Cook felt sure they would be killed by the dogs as soon as the ships left.

## A NATIVE CEREMONY

As the wind proved contrary, and it was understood that the king's son was to be initiated into the estate of manhood, eating with his father for the first time, Cook determined to remain a few days longer. A party of the officers went over to the island of Moa, where the ceremony was to be held, and found the king in a very dirty enclosure, drinking kava; and as the method of preparing this beverage was uninviting to Europeans, they went for a walk till about ten o'clock. Finding large numbers of people assembling in an open space near a large building they rejoined the king, taking off their hats and untying their hair, "that we might appear the more decent" in the eyes of the natives. The proceedings consisted of marching of men laden with yams tied on to sticks, of considerable speech-making, and various performances of which the signification could not be understood, and then the prince made his appearance. He seated himself with a few of his friends on the ground, and some women wound a long piece of cloth round them, and after some more speech-making and mysterious pantomime with sticks representing yams, the proceedings ended for the day. As there were signs that so many white onlookers was not altogether acceptable to the natives, some of the party returned to the ships; but Cook resolved to see it out, and joined the king at supper, and the latter enjoyed some brandy and water so much that Cook says "he went to bed quite grogish. "

After breakfast Cook paid a visit to the prince and presented him was enough English cloth to make a suit, receiving native cloth in return. After dinner the people mustered for the remains of the ceremony, and Cook determined to join the principal party, so he seated himself with it, and would not understand when requested to leave. He was then requested to bare his shoulders as a mark of respect, and immediately did so, and was then no further molested. A somewhat similar performance was gone through as the day before, but the significance of which could not be ascertained, and then suddenly all the people turned their backs on king and prince, who, Cook was afterwards informed, had had pieces of roast yam given them to eat. An exhibition of boxing and wrestling was then given, and after a speech or two the proceedings terminated. Cook was informed that in about three months a much greater affair would take place at which ten men would be sacrificed.

On 10th July the ships sailed through a very difficult passage, arriving off Middleburg on the 12th, where they were visited by their old friend Taoofa. The country appeared flourishing, and they obtained some turnips raised from seed sown at Cook's last visit. An exhibition of boxing was given, and was to have been repeated the following night, but unfortunately some of the natives fell upon a sailor and stripped him of his clothes. Cook thereupon seized two canoes and a pig, demanding that the culprits should be given up. A man who had the shirt and trousers was brought, and so the canoes were returned and the pig paid for, and next day the thief was liberated. The remainder of the sailor's clothes were afterwards found, but so much torn as to be worthless.

They left the Friendly Islands on the 17th, after a stay of more than two months, during which time they had been living almost entirely on food they had purchased from the natives, with whom they had been on fairly good terms. The 29th brought them into a very heavy squall which cost the Resolution a couple of staysails and her consort a main topmast and main topgallant yard, springing the head of her main-mast so badly that the rigging of a jury-mast was attended with some danger, but it was at length accomplished, a spare jib-boom being furnished for the purpose by the Resolution. Otaheite was reached on 12th August, and amongst the first visitors on board were Omai's brother-in-law and others who knew him before he went away; they treated him as if he was an Englishman and a stranger, but when he took his brother-in-law to his cabin and gave him some of the valuable red feathers a change came over them all, and they expressed the greatest interest in him. Cook says Omai "would take no advice, but permitted himself to be made the dupe of every designing knave." Of these red feathers Cook says they were of such value that "not more than might be got from a tomtit, would purchase a hog of 40 or 50 pounds weight." Nails and beads were not looked at, although they had previously been very acceptable.

### SPANISH SHIPS

Two ships from Lima were found to have visited the island twice since Cook's last call, and the first time the Spaniards built a house with material they had with them. They left four men in charge, and were away for about ten months. At the second visit their Commodore died, and was buried near the house which was left at their departure, and the natives built a shade over it to protect it from the weather. It consisted of two rooms, furnished with table, bed, bench, and a few other trifles, and the timbers were found to have been carefully marked to facilitate erection. Near by was a cross having the following inscription cut on it:

CHRISTUS VINCIT, CAROLUS III. IMPERAT, 1774.

Cook caused to be cut on the back:

GEORGIUS TERTIUS REX. ANNIS 1767, 69, 73, 74, ET 78.

At the end of their first visit the Spaniards took away four natives to Lima; one died, one remained at Lima, and the other two returned with the ships; but Cook thinks they were not improved by their experience, and had not added to their respectability in the eyes of their countrymen.

In view of the cold climate to be faced in the near future, Cook was desirous to save his stock of spirits, and mustered the crew of the Resolution in order to explain the position; he pointed out that the supply of coconuts was abundant, and the benefit of the spirits would be appreciated amongst the cold winds and ice of the north, but left the decision to them. He was gratified to find the crew was willing to accept his suggestion, and ordered Clerke to put the matter before the crew of the Discovery, when it was again well received. An order was accordingly issued to stop:

"serving grog except on Saturday nights, when they had full allowance to drink to their female friends in England, lest amongst the pretty girls of Otaheite, they should be wholly forgotten."

During a state visit paid by the chief of the district, at which Omai attended "dressed in a strange medley of all he was possessed of," Cook was informed that the Spaniards laid claim to the country, and had given instructions that Cook was not to be allowed to land if he returned. However, the chief executed a formal surrender of his province to Cook, and presents were exchanged, the whole ceremony ending with a display of fireworks which "both pleased and astonished" the natives. Some of the civilians reported that they had discovered a Roman Catholic chapel in their walks; but on inspection it proved to be what Cook at once suspected, the grave of a chief decorated with different coloured cloths and mats, and a piece of scarlet broadcloth which had been given by the Spaniards.

## RED FEATHERS

On the 23rd August the two ships arrived in Matavai Bay, where they were well received by Otoo, who was gratified by a present of a fine linen suit, a hat with a gold band, some tools, a feather helmet from the Friendly Islands, and, what he seemed to value most, a large bunch of the celebrated red feathers. In return he sent on board the ships enough food to have lasted both crews for a week, if it had only been possible to keep it good for that length of time. The royal family dined on board the Resolution; and after dinner Cook and Omai called on Oparee, taking with them a peacock and peahen sent to the island by Lord Bessborough, a turkey cock and hen, a gander and three geese, a drake and four ducks to make a start in stocking the island. A gander was seen, which the natives said had been left by Wallis ten years previously; several goats and a bull left by the Spaniards were also seen, so Cook landed three cows as company for the last. The horses and sheep were also landed, and Cook remarks that getting rid of all these animals lightened him: "of a very heavy burden; the trouble and vexation that attended the bringing these animals thus far is hardly to be conceived. But the satisfaction I felt in having been so fortunate as to fulfil His Majesty's design in sending such useful animals to two worthy nations sufficiently recompensed me for the many anxious hours I had on their account."

Whilst here, the two ships were thoroughly overhauled and everywhere put into as good a state of repair as the appliances available would permit. The stores were found to be in a better state than had been expected, and very little of the bread was damaged. Gardens were laid out and planted with potatoes, melons, pineapples, etc.; but Cook was not very sanguine of their success, for he had seen how a vine planted by the Spaniards had been spitefully trampled down, as the natives, tasting the grapes before they were ripe, had concluded it was poisonous. It was carefully pruned into proper shape again, and Omai was instructed to set forth its merits and how it should be cultivated.

Towards the end of the month a man reported that the two Spanish ships had returned, and showed a piece of cloth he said he had obtained from them, so Cook, not knowing if England and Spain were on friendly terms, prepared for the worst, and the two ships made ready for defence if necessary. Lieutenant Williamson was despatched in a boat for news, but could see no ships, nor signs of any having been on the coast since the English left their last port of call.

## A HUMAN SACRIFICE

At their last visit an expedition was being prepared against the revolted island of Eimeo, but it did not seem to have been very successful in its object, for there were still disturbances going on between the two nations, and on 30th August news came that the Otaheitans had been driven up into the hills. A grand meeting was held to discuss matters, and great efforts were made to enlist the services of Cook; but he would not assist in any way, as he did not understand the cause of the quarrel, and he had always found the inhabitants of Eimeo friendly towards him. Having heard that a chief named Towha had killed a man as a sacrifice to their God, Cook obtained permission to witness the remaining ceremonies as he thought it offered an opportunity to learn something of the religion of this people. He therefore started with Dr. Anderson, Mr. Webber, and the chief Potatow in a boat, accompanied by Omai in a canoe, for the scene of action. On their arrival the sailors were instructed to remain in the boat, and the gentlemen were requested to remove their hats as soon as they reached the Morai where the ceremonial was to take place. When they got there the body of the victim was seen in a small canoe in front of the Morai and just in the wash of the sea, in charge of four priests and their attendants, the king and his party some twenty or thirty paces away, and the rest of the spectators a little further still. Two priests came forward to Otoo, one placing a young plantain tree in front of him, and the other touching his foot with a bunch of red feathers, and then rejoining the others, who immediately went off to a smaller Morai near, and, seating themselves facing the sea, one commenced reciting a long prayer, occasionally sending one of his attendants to place a young plantain on the body. Whilst this recitation was going on an attendant stood near holding two small bundles "seemingly of cloth; in one, as we afterwards found, was the Royal Maro, and the other, if I may be allowed the expression, was the ark of the Eatua" [God].

This prayer being ended, the priests returned to the beach, and more prayers were said, the plantains being moved, one by one, from the body and placed in front of the priests. Then the body, wrapped in leaves, was put on the beach, with the feet to the sea, and the priests gathered round, some sitting, some standing, the prayers still going on. The leaves were then stripped off the body, and it was turned sideways on to the sea, and one priest standing at the feet repeated another long prayer in which he was occasionally joined by the others. Each priest at this time held in his hand a bunch of the red feathers. Some hair was now pulled from the head of the corpse, and an eye taken out, wrapped in leaves and presented to Otoo, who did not touch them, but sent them back with a bunch of feathers, soon after sending a second bunch he had asked Cook to put in his pocket for him when starting. At this time a king-fisher made a noise in some trees near, and Otoo remarked, "That is the Eatua," evidently looking on it as a good omen.

The body was now moved away to the foot of one of the small Morais, the two bundles of cloth being placed on the Morai at its head and the tufts of feathers at its feet, the priests surrounding the body and the people gathering in closer. More speeches were made, and a second lock of hair plucked from the head and placed on the Morai. Then the red feathers were placed on the cloth bundles, which were carried over to the great Morai and laid against a pile of stones, to which the body was also brought, and the attendants proceeded to dig a grave, whilst the priests continued their recitations. The body was then buried, and a dog Towha had sent over (a very poor one, says Cook) was partially cooked and presented to the priests, who called on Eatua to come and see what was prepared for him, at the same time putting it on a small altar on which were the remains of two dogs and three pigs, which smelt so intolerably that the white men were compelled to move further away than they wished. This ended the ceremony for the day.

## THE KING'S MARO

Next morning they all returned to the Morai; a pig was sacrificed and placed on the same altar, and about eight o'clock the priests, Otoo, and a great number of people assembled. The two bundles were still in the same place as on the previous night, but two drums were now standing in front of them between which Otoo and Cook seated themselves. The priests, placing a plantain tree in front of the king, resumed their praying, each having his bunch of feathers in his hand. They then moved off to a place between the Morai and the king and placed the feathers bunch by bunch on the bundles, the prayers still going on. Four pigs were then produced, one immediately killed, and the others put in a sty for future use. The bundle containing the king's Maro was now untied and spread carefully on the ground before the priests. The Maro was about five yards long by fifteen inches broad, composed of red and yellow feathers, chiefly yellow. At one end was a border of eight pieces about the size and shape of horse-shoes fringed with black pigeon's feathers; the other end was forked, the ends being of unequal length. The feathers were arranged in two rows and had a very good effect. They were fastened on a piece of native cloth, and then sewn to the English pendant which Wallis left flying when he sailed from Matavai Bay. After the priests had repeated another prayer, the emblem of royalty was carefully folded up and replaced on the Morai, and then one end of what Cook called the Ark of the Eatua was opened, but the visitors were not permitted to see what it contained. The entrails of the pig were then prayed over, and one of the priests stirred them gently with a stick, evidently trying to draw a favourable omen from their movements. They were then thrown on the fire, the partly-cooked pig was deposited on the altar, and when the bunches of feathers that had been used had been placed in the Ark, the ceremony was over.

The meanings of all this could not be discovered, but it was found that when a victim was wanted, a chief picked him out and sent his servants to kill him. This was done without any warning to the man who was to suffer, usually by a blow with a stone on the head, and it appeared that at the subsequent ceremony the presence of the king was absolutely indispensable. Chiefs of an enemy's tribe who were killed in battle were buried with some state in the Morais, the common men at the foot.

On the way back to the ship Cook called on Towha, who had supplied the victim. He was anxious to ascertain Cook's opinion of the affair, and was not pleased to learn that Cook thought such a proceeding was more likely to offend the Deity than to please him. He then enquired if the English ever practised such ceremonies, and was very angry when he was informed that if the greatest chief in England killed one of his men he would be hanged; and Cook says they left him "with as great a contempt for our customs as we could possibly have for theirs." The servants evidently listened to Omai with great interest and a different opinion on the subject than that of their master.

They went to inspect the body of a chief who had been embalmed; they were not allowed to examine it very closely, but it was so well done that they were unable to perceive the slightest unpleasant smell, though the man had been dead some months. All chiefs who died a natural death were preserved in this manner, and from time to time were exposed to public view, the intervals between the exposures gradually extending till at length they were hardly ever seen. The method of preservation was not ascertained, and was probably a secret of the priests.

## EQUESTRIAN EXERCISE

Cook and Clerke astonished the natives by riding the horses that had been brought out; their progress through the country was always watched with great interest, and Cook thought that this use of the animals impressed the people more than anything else done by the whites. Omai tried his powers on several occasions, but as he was always thrown before he got securely into the saddle, his efforts only produced entertainment for the spectators. It is curious to note that forty years afterwards the people had so thoroughly lost even the tradition of such use of the horse that Mr. Ellis relates how, when one was landed for the use of Pomare, the natives assisted to get it ashore, but when once landed they ran away and hid in fear of the "man-carrying pig." About this time Cook suffered from a bad attack of rheumatism in the legs, and was successfully treated by Otoo's mother, three sisters, and eight other women. The process he underwent, called Romy, consisted of squeezing and kneading from head to foot, more especially about the parts affected. Cook says he was glad to escape from their ministrations after about a quarter of an hour, but he felt relief, and, after submitting to four operations of the kind he was completely cured.

Otoo was very desirous to send a present of a canoe to King George, and Cook was very willing to take it, but when he found it was a large double canoe he was obliged to decline from want of space. As the desire to send it was quite spontaneous on Otoo's part, and as the canoe was a very fine specimen of native work, the refusal was given with great regret.

In a journal published by Newbery, the anonymous writer says that two officers fought a duel whilst the ships were at Otaheite. He does not give the cause, but says three shots were exchanged, resulting in one hat being spoiled, and then the antagonists shook hands and were better friends afterwards. The story is not confirmed by any of the other journals.

On 29th September, after giving Otoo a short run out to sea and back, the two ships sailed for the north side of Eimeo, arriving the next day, and were greeted by a chief, Maheine, who was bald-headed. Of this defect he seemed much ashamed, and always appeared with his head covered with a sort of turban. Cook thinks perhaps this shame rose from the fact that natives caught stealing on the ships were often punished by having their heads shaved, and adds that "one or two of the gentlemen whose heads were not overburdened with hair, lay under violent suspicions of being titos (thieves)."

One of the few remaining goats was stolen, but after threats of serious reprisals was given up, together with the thief, who was eventually discharged with a caution; but on a second one disappearing and not being found after careful search, Cook felt that he must make an example, or nothing would be safe, so he ordered one or two houses and canoes to be destroyed, and sent word to Maheine that he would not leave a canoe on the island if the goat was not returned. The goat was recovered, and the next day the people were as friendly as if nothing had occurred. Cook was particularly annoyed, for he had sent a present of red feathers to Otoo, and requested him to send in return a couple of goats to Eimeo.

## OMAI SETTLED

On 11th October the ships sailed for Huaheine, and when they arrived Cook was so ill he had to be landed from the ship, but he makes no mention of it in his Journal. He thought this island would be more suitable for Omai than Otaheite, and as Omai was agreeable a piece of ground was obtained from the chief and a small house erected and a garden laid out and planted. The interest of the different chiefs of the neighbourhood was sought on Omai's behalf, and as it was seen that some of the natives were inclined to take advantage of his good nature, Cook let it be understood that if, should he return and find Omai in an satisfactory condition, some one would feel the weight of his displeasure. Then the most serious thing that can be brought against Cook's treatment of the natives occurred. In extenuation it must be remembered that he admits that he was inclined to be hot-tempered, though it did not last; he had been constantly irritated by repeated losses, and he was at the time really seriously ill, and also when all was over he sincerely regretted he had taken such strong measures. Mr. Bayley's sextant was stolen from the observatory: Cook at once demanded from the chiefs that it should be returned, but they paid no attention. The thief, however, was pointed out, seized, and taken on board ship; the sextant was recovered, but Cook says, finding the thief to be "a hardened scoundrel, I punished him with greater severity than I have ever done any one before, and then dismissed him." He is said to have had his head shaved and his ears cut off, but Gilbert (midshipman on the Discovery) says this was not done till he had been rearrested for damaging Omai's garden, trying to set fire to the house, and threatening to kill Omai as soon as the ships left. Cook had intended to remove him from the island, but, being in irons, he stole the keys from a sleeping guard and made his escape. Omai found that many of the articles which were practically useless to him, would be appreciated on the ships, so he very wisely changed them for hatchets and other useful articles. A notice of the visit with the names of the ships was cut on the end of Omai's house, and, after firing a salute of five guns, the ships sailed on 2nd November. Omai accompanied them for a short way, and Mr. King says that when he parted from Cook he completely broke down and cried all the way ashore. Cook speaks well of him, saying he seldom had to find fault with him, that he had many good qualities, but, like the rest of his race, he lacked powers of observation, application, and perseverance.

## DESERTIONS

On the 3rd they were off Ulietea, and as they were able to run in close to the shore a staging was erected, and the ballast ports were opened so as to give the rats, which had become very troublesome, a chance of going ashore. One of the marines also took the opportunity to desert, taking his musket with him, but after a little trouble was arrested; and having previously borne a very good character, he was let off with a short imprisonment. A second desertion occurred from the Discovery, Mr. Mouat, midshipman, and a seaman getting away. Cook says the affair gave him more trouble than both men were worth, but he insisted on getting them back to prevent others following their example, and "to save the son of a brother officer from being lost to the world." They were found to have gone off in a canoe to another island, and Cook ordered Clerke to detain the chief, his son, daughter, and son-in-law on the Discovery, where they had gone to dine, and to inform them they would be kept as hostages till the runaways were returned. Three days afterwards the deserters were brought back, and the hostages were at once released. It was afterwards found out that there had been a plot to seize Cook in retaliation, when he went for his usual bath in the evening, but, as it happened, he was so much worried that he put it off and so escaped. Burney notes that Cook could not swim. Before leaving they received a message from Omai, saying he was all right, but asking for another goat as one of his was dead. Clerke was able to oblige him with two kids, one of each sex.

# 1777 TO 1779
# THIRD VOYAGE CONTINUED

In case of separation, Clerke was ordered to cruise for five days near where his consort had been last seen, and then to steer for New Albion (so-called by Sir Francis Drake), endeavouring to fall in with it about latitude 45 degrees North, and there cruise for ten days; then, if his consort was not picked up, to proceed north to the first suitable port and recruit his men, keeping a good look-out for his companion. Then he was to sail on 1st April to 56 degrees North, and again cruise about fifteen leagues from the coast till 10th May, when he was to proceed north and endeavour to find a passage to the Atlantic, according to the Admiralty instructions already in his hands. If unsuccessful he was to winter in some suitable port of Kamtschatka, leaving word with the commandant of St. Peter and St. Paul Harbour, where he was to be found, and to be at the last-named place not later than 10th May of the following year. Then, if he had no news of the Resolution, he was to follow out the Admiralty instructions to the best of his ability.

The two ships left for Bolabola on 7th December to get an anchor left by De Bougainville, in order to make hatchets for exchange, as the demand had been so great their stock was running short. They had no difficulty in purchasing it, and it was good enough for their purpose, though not so heavy as they expected.

They crossed the line on the 23rd in longitude 203 degrees 15 minutes East without having seen land since leaving Bolabola. Two days after they picked up a low island and managed to get some turtle, and also a rather unsatisfactory observation of an eclipse of the sun, the clouds interfering with the view of the commencement. Their position had been settled by other observations, so the ill-luck was unimportant. About three hundred turtle were obtained, averaging from 90 to 100 pounds each, and as much fish as they could consume during their stay was caught. Coconuts, yams, and melons were planted, and the island received the name of Christmas Island.

## SANDWICH ISLANDS

Leaving on 2nd January they did not sight land till the Sandwich Islands were reached, in latitude 21 degrees 12 minutes 30 seconds North. At the second one seen, called Atoui by the natives, they were quickly surrounded by canoes; the occupants, very like the Otaheitans in appearance and language, were armed with stones, which they threw overboard as soon as they found they were not likely to be wanted, and though none could be persuaded to come on board the ships, they freely parted with fish for anything they could get in exchange. As the ships sailed on, more canoes came out bringing further supplies, and Cook rejoiced at arriving at a land of plenty, for his stock of turtle was just finished, and he was anxious to save his sea stores. At length some were tempted on board, and were greatly astonished at what they saw, but their wonder did not last long, and stealing soon broke out as usual. When they came to an anchor Cook landed and found a favourable place for watering, so a party was set to work the next day, and found no difficulty in getting assistance from the islanders, whilst at the same time a brisk trade was carried on in pigs and potatoes. Cook says: "No people could trade with more honesty than these people, never once attempting to cheat us, either ashore or alongside the ship." They seem to have dropped their thieving very quickly. At night a nasty sea got up, and as Cook did not like the position of his ship he weighed to run a little further out, but the wind suddenly dropping round to the east, he had to set all sail to clear the shore. For a day or two no very satisfactory anchorage could be found, and the weather was rather unsettled, so, making one of the chiefs a present of an English sow and boar, and a male and two female goats, the ship bore away to the northwards.

According to Baron von Humboldt these islands were discovered by a Spaniard, Gaetano, sailing from Manilla to Acapulco in 1542, and it was one of the few discoveries made by the Spaniards during this passage, for they were strictly forbidden to deviate from the track laid down on their charts. The name La Mesa (the table) down on the chart Cook had with him, describes the island, says Burney, but the longitude is several degrees out. It is undoubtedly a fact that Europeans had been at the islands previously to Cook's visit, for at least two pieces of iron were found, one being a portion of a broadsword and the other a piece of hoop-iron.

## NEW ALBION

On 7th March, New Albion was sighted at a distance of ten or twelve leagues, and the position of the ship at noon was 44 degrees 33 minutes North, 236 degrees 30 minutes East; Cook's orders were to make the coast "about 45 degrees North," so they may be said to have been carried out with fair exactness. Cook says that on the charts he had, a large entrance or strait was represented, and in the account of Martin d'Aguilar's voyage in 1603 mention is made of a large river, near where he struck the coast, but he did not see any signs of either. Proceeding up the coast the progress was very slow as the weather was very stormy. On 22nd March they passed the position of the strait of Juan de Fuch, but again no sign of its existence was seen. On the 29th the style of the coast changed, and high snowy mountains with well-wooded valleys running down to the sea came into view, and at length Hope Bay opened out. Here they came in contact with the first natives they had seen, who put off in their canoes to the ships, showing signs neither of fear nor distrust. At first they appeared mild and inoffensive, and would trade anything they had with them; but when they got used to the ships it turned out that they were adepts at thieving; no piece of iron, brass, or copper was safe. Fish-hooks were cut from the lines and boats were stripped of their fittings. They sold bladders of oil for the lamps, and it was found that they were often partly filled with water, but this was winked at in order to get on a thoroughly friendly footing. This being a favourable opportunity to put the two vessels in order and to give the crews a spell of rest ashore, a good anchorage was sought out, and the observatory set up. On 4th April, whilst wood and water was being got in, the natives, who had given no trouble beyond their stealing, were observed to be arming, and precautions were taken, but the Indians explained that their preparations were made against some of their own countrymen who were on their way to fight them. After a time some canoes made their appearance, and on a deputation going out to meet them a discussion took place, and some sort of an agreement was made between the two parties, but the newcomers were not allowed to approach the ships nor to join in the trading.

    The stay here was longer than was intended, for the Resolution's fore and mizzen masts were found to be very defective, and her rigging had got into a very bad state. The fore-mast was repaired and the mizzen replaced with a new stick, and when a great deal of work had been done this proved faulty, and a second one had to be cut. New standing rigging was fitted to the main-mast, and a set made from the best of the old, for the fore-mast. When the heaviest part of this work was completed Cook visited the country about King George's Sound, and was courteously received at a village by the natives, to most of whom he was known. Here he found the women employed making dresses out of bark in much the same way as that employed by the New Zealanders. Sending some sailors to cut grass for the sheep and goats he had left, the natives made a claim which was at once satisfied; but when the men were ordered to go on cutting, fresh claimants sprung up, till Cook says he thought each blade of grass had a separate owner. When at last the natives found that they could get no more, the cutting was allowed to go on without the slightest further objection.

## PUNCH AND THE DEVIL

The people are described as being short, with broad flat faces, high cheek-bones, swarthy complexions, and no pretensions to good looks. Burney says that it was only after much cleaning that their skins were found to be "like our people in England." Cook says they were docile, courteous, and good-natured, but liable to fits of passion.

"I have often seen a man rave and scold for more than half an hour without any one taking the least notice of it, nor could any one of us tell who it was he was abusing."

Burney describes their language as harsh, and when in a warm discussion, apparently insufficient, and then they had to eke it out with such nods and jumps as reminded one of "Punch and the Devil." Their clothing was chiefly made of skins, and a kind of cloth made from fibre or wool and hair, or a mixture of both. "In these clothes and a coarse mat and straw hat they would sit in their canoes in the heaviest rain as unconcernedly as if they were in perfect shelter." Their houses of logs and boards made by splitting large trees, were some as much as 150 feet long by 20 to 30 feet wide, and 7 or 8 feet high; they were divided into two compartments, each apparently the property of one family. The roof was of loose planks, which they moved about so as to let the light fall where it was wanted. Cook judged these were only summer residences, and that they had better houses inland. The furniture consisted of a few boxes, some wooden vessels for their food, and a few mat bags. Their cooking was fairly good, but excessively dirty, and their persons and houses "filthy as hogs' sties." They often had two wooden figures in their houses resembling human figures, of which they spoke mysteriously; but as they could have been purchased in every case for a small quantity of old iron or brass, they could not have been much venerated. Their arms were bows and arrows, slings, spears, and a small club of wood or stone, something like the New Zealander's patoo, and a stone tomahawk, the handle fashioned like a human head, the stone cutting-part being a large tongue, and they were decorated with human hair. The defensive armour was a double cloak of hide, usually moose, serviceable against arrows or spears, but they were greatly surprised to see a bullet fired through a cloak folded four times. The only vegetables obtained were a few nettles and wild garlic, but Burney says that at the back of the village was a plantation of cherry trees, gooseberries and currants, raspberries and strawberries, "but unluckily for us none of them in season." On 20th April a man who had been allowed to go into Cook's cabin, made off with his watch, and got away from the ship. Fortunately his canoe was seen alongside the Discovery, and notice being given a search was made, and the watch found in a box unharmed. Such a loss would have been serious. Two old-fashioned silver table-spoons, supposed to be Spanish, and a pewter wash-basin were purchased from the Indians.

## RESOLUTION LEAKS

On 26th April a start was made, and before leaving, an Indian, who had specially attached himself to Cook, gave him a valuable beaver skin, and was so pleased with the return present he received that he insisted on Cook taking from him a beaver cloak upon which he had always set great store. In return "he was made as happy as a prince by a gift of a new broadsword with a brass hilt." The next day, when well clear of the land, a perfect hurricane arose, and the ships lay to, heading to the south-east. The Resolution sprang a leak, and the water could be seen and heard rushing in, but after some little anxiety one pump was found to be sufficient to keep the upper hand. The gale lasted two days, but on the second they were able to get an observation which gave the position of the ship as 50 degrees 1 minute North, 229 degrees 26 minutes East, about opposite to where the Straits of de Fonte were marked on his chart. They were now able to run along the coast and see and name the most salient points, but time was too valuable to make any halts by the way. The land appeared to be of considerable height, the hills covered with snow, but near the sea, well wooded. Mount St. Elias was sighted 4th May, at a distance of forty leagues, and on the 6th they arrived in the bay in which Behring had anchored, so his name was given to it on the chart. Here the land trended away to the west; the wind was westerly and light, and consequently their progress was very slow. Landing on an island to try to get a view of the other side from the top of a hill, it was found so steep and thickly wooded he had to give up the attempt. He therefore left a bottle containing some coins given him by his friend, Dr. Kaye, and named the island after him. Here they found currant and strawberry plants, but the season was too early for fruit.

Near Cape Hinchinbroke Gore went off to an island to shoot, but seeing two large canoes containing about twenty Indians, he thought it wiser to return to the ship. He was followed up, but none of the natives would come on board, and after a time intimating they would return next day, retired. Two men in small canoes did return during the night, but finding that every one on board was not asleep, beat a hurried retreat. The next day the ships got into a better position, and more Indians turned up, with whom they had little difficulty in entering into trading relations; but as they desired pieces of iron about ten inches long by three wide, and it was rather a scarce article on board, very little, chiefly skins, was purchased. At first only one man came on board, and as he saw only two or three people on the Discovery, he went to the Resolution and brought over some of his friends, who rushed the deck with their knives drawn. However, the crew quickly ran up with their cutlasses ready, so the natives retired, remarking that the white men's knives were longer than theirs. At the Resolution they broke every glass scuttle they could reach with their paddles, says Burney. Cook points out that they must have been quite ignorant of the use of firearms, and concludes by saying:

"However, after all these tricks, we had the good fortune to leave them as ignorant as we found them, for they neither heard nor saw a musket fired unless at birds."

The leak on the Resolution was attended to, and in places the oakum caulking was found to have disappeared completely; one writer says it was caused by rats, and that the ship was saved by rubbish having choked up the leak.

## TWO SETS OF TEETH

Bad weather detaining them, Cook had an opportunity of studying the inhabitants. He had with him a description of the Esquimaux, by Crantz, and found these men to be very similar in appearance, dress, and appliances. They all had the bottom lip slit horizontally, giving them the appearance of having two mouths. In these slits pieces of bone were fixed to which were tied other pieces, forming a great impediment to their speech, and in some cases giving the idea that the wearer had two sets of teeth. Some also had pieces of bone, cord, or beads run through the cartilage of the nose, and all had their faces plentifully smeared with black and red paint.

After examining an inlet, which received the name of Sandwich Sound, they got away, steering to the south-west past Cape Elizabeth, sighted on that Princess's birthday, which they hoped would prove the western extremity of the coast, but on getting round, land was reported further on to the west-south-west, and a gale sprang up, forcing them off their course. In two days they worked back again, discovering more land behind what they had seen already. This Cook believed to be Cape Saint Hermogenes mentioned by Behring, but his chart was so inaccurate he could not positively identify it, or any other place mentioned on it. Cape Douglas, after the Dean of Windsor, was named, and placed in 58 degrees 56 minutes North, 206 degrees 10 minutes East; and the next day a high point in a range was called Mount St. Augustine, after the saint whose day it happened to be. They then worked into an estuary formed by the rivers (one being afterwards named Cook's River, by orders of Lord Sandwich), in order to satisfy some of the officers who thought there might be a possible communication with Hudson's Bay. A good supply of very fine salmon was obtained from natives in the neighbourhood, and Cook formed the opinion that a paying fur trade might be opened up as the skins offered were of considerable value.

Working slowly up the coast they passed through the islands off Quelpart on the 18th, when the Discovery signalled to speak; a boat was sent, and returned with a small box curiously tied up with neatly-made twine. It had been delivered on board by an Indian, who first attracted attention by displaying a pair of old plush breeches and a black cloth waistcoat, and when he came on board, took off his cap and bowed like a European. The box was found to contain a paper written in Russian, but unfortunately the only things that could be understood were the two dates, 1776 and 1778. It was supposed to have been written by a Russian trader, and given to the Indian to place it on board the first ship he met with.

On the 20th, in 54 degrees 18 minutes North, 195 degrees 45 minutes East, a volcano throwing out dense smoke was observed; and in the afternoon they received a visit from a man who had evidently been in contact with Europeans, for he was wearing green cloth breeches and a stuff jacket. He took off his cap and bowed as the visitor to the Discovery had done, but unfortunately they were unable to understand his language.

On 26th June they had a narrow escape during a thick fog, when it was not possible to see anything a hundred yards away. Breakers were heard, so the anchors were let go and fortunately held. An hour or so after the fog lifted, and they found themselves about three-quarters of a mile from a rocky island, having passed between two elevated rocks, a place through with, Cook says, "I should have ventured on a clear day," for all that they found themselves in "such an anchoring place that I could not have chosen a better."

## ANDERSON DIES

On 27th June they were off the island of Onalaschka, and came across a party of natives who were towing two whales they had killed; they were somewhat shy, but had evidently seen ships before, and were more polite than those previously met with. One was upset from his canoe, and Cook took him down into the cabin and provided him with dry clothes; "he dressed himself with as much ease as I could have done." His clothes were of birds' skins, the feathers inside, and patched in places with silk, and over all he wore a sort of shirt of whale's intestine, which, secured round the edge of the hole in which he sat in his canoe, rendered him practically waterproof. Whilst in this neighbourhood they received a second letter in Russian, but having no one on board who could translate, it was returned with some presents to the bearer, who retired bowing his thanks. After some detention from fogs and adverse winds they got away once more and pushed slowly northwards. On 3rd August Mr. Anderson the surgeon, who had been ill for some months, died, and Cook, having named an island, sighted soon after his death, Anderson's Island, "to perpetuate the memory of the deceased, for whom I had a very great regard," appointed Mr. Law to the Resolution and Mr. Samwell to the Discovery as surgeons.

On 9th August, Cape Prince of Wales, 65 degrees 46 minutes North, 191 degrees 45 minutes East, was sighted, and they believed it to be the most westerly point of North America. They landed on what, from Heydinger's Chart, was the eastern end of the island of Alaska, but it afterwards was found to be the eastern extremity of Asia. This chart, says Burney, was found "not only to be incorrect but almost unintelligible." The country was very desolate, neither tree nor shrub to be seen, and the inhabitants seemed afraid of their visitors, though not absolutely unfriendly. They were taller and stouter than those on the American side, and their clothing very superior.

The ships fell in with the ice blink on the 17th, in 70 degrees 33 minutes North, 197 degrees 41 minutes East, rather earlier than had been expected, and soon afterwards with the ice itself in the shape of a large field extending as far as the eye could reach from west to east. Here they got a supply of fresh meat in the shape of sea-horse, of which animal they killed a good many. The flesh was fishy and indifferent eating, but Cook says anything was preferable to salt meat.

They still slowly but steadily pushed north along the American shore, but, being hampered by fog and ice, they crossed over to the west side with no better fortune, for on the 26th they found themselves embayed in the field with large quantities of heavy loose ice along the edges. Having sighted Cape North on 29th August, Cook decided the season was too far advanced, and that it would be better to proceed to winter quarters, and accordingly ran down the Asiatic coast in search of wood and water, of which he stood in need; but was disappointed, and making over to the other side was fortunate to find a considerable quantity of driftwood which served his purpose. Before leaving the straits, Cook remarks:

"In justice to Behring's memory, I must say he delineated this coast very well, and fixed the latitude and longitude of the points better than could be expected from the methods he had to go by."

## SALMON PIE

Anchoring in Norton Sound, Cook sent away the boats to explore, and set to work to determine between the correctness of the chart drawn by Stocklin and his own observations, and after a series of no less than seventy-seven sets of observations he was able to show that Stocklin was wrong. It was at this place that he decided to winter in the Sandwich Islands, as a port in Kamtschatka would oblige his crews to remain idle for nearly six months before further exploration to the north could be undertaken. The course was now set for Samgoonoodha Harbour, but they did not arrive there till 3rd October, having met with very heavy weather, in which the Resolution again began to leak badly. On 8th September an Indian brought a singular present in the form of a pie made like a loaf, containing some highly seasoned salmon, accompanied by a letter in Russian. In return Corporal Ledyard of the Marines, "an intelligent man," was sent with a few bottles of rum, wine, and porter, to obtain further information, and with orders, if he met with any Russians, he was to "make them understand that we were English, Friends, and Allies." On the 10th Ledyard returned, bringing three Russian sailors, but as there was no interpreter there was difficulty in understanding anything thoroughly. One of the newcomers was understood to say he had been out with Behring, but Cook thought he was too young. They appeared to have great respect for that officer, and Ledyard said he had seen a sloop which he understood was his ship. They stayed on the Resolution all night, and promised to return with a chart of the islands that lay between that place and Kamtschatka. It was understood that there were several settlements in the immediate neighbourhood employing altogether about four hundred Russians.

## LETTERS TO LONDON

On the 14th Cook and Webber were at an Indian village a short distance from the ships, when they saw a canoe arrive containing three men and accompanied by some twenty or thirty single canoes. A tent was rigged up for one of the first three, a Russian named Ismyloff (Ismailoff) the chief trader of the district, whilst the others made shelters of their canoes and grass, and so all were independent of the Indians. Ismailoff invited Cook to join him at his meal, which consisted of dried salmon and berries, and some sort of conversation was carried on by means of signs and figures. Ismailoff proved to be well acquainted with the geography of the district, and pointed out several errors in the modern maps. He said he had been with Lieutenant Lindo's expedition as far north as Tchukotskoi Nos, and saw Clerke's Island; but when he could or would not say what else they had done during the two years the expedition was out, Cook began to have doubts. He also said the Russians had several times tried to gain a footing on the American shore, but the Indians had driven them off with the loss of two or three of their leaders. He also spoke of a sledge expedition in 1773 to three islands opposite the Kolyma River, which Cook thought might be the one mentioned by Muller, he related that he had sailed, in 1771, from a Russian settlement called Bolscheretski, in the Kurile Islands, to Japan, but the ship was ordered away because they were Christians, so they went to Canton and sailed on a French ship to France, and from thence he went to Petersburg, and was then sent out again. He was quite clear as to his dates, and put them on paper; but as he was perfectly ignorant of any French, "not even the names of the commonest articles," though he had been such a long time amongst French people, Cook was again inclined to be sceptical. He stayed all night, dining with Clerke, and returned again on the 19th, with charts, which he permitted to be copied, and some manuscripts. One chart showed the Asiatic coast as far as 41 degrees North, with the Kurile Islands and Kamtschatka, and the second, the more interesting to the English, showed the discoveries made by the Russians to the east of Kamtschatka, exclusive of the voyages of Behring and Tcherikoff. Cook found the longitudes in places were very different from those on the Russian maps, and was afraid the mistake might be carried through, but the latitudes were fairly correct. As far as he could ascertain, the instrument used for the survey had been the theodolite. Before leaving, Ismailoff gave Cook letters for the Governor of Kamtschatka and the Commandant of Petropaulowsk; and Cook, finding "he was tolerably well versed in astronomy," gave him a Hadley's octant, and though it was the first one he had seen, he soon made himself acquainted with its uses. A letter to the English Admiralty was also entrusted to him to be forwarded via Petersburg, as opportunity might offer. This letter and a chart of the northern coasts was delivered in London the following year. On 26th October the two ships got away, and, in case of separation, Clerke was given his rendezvous, first, the Sandwich Islands, and second, Petropaulowsk in the middle of May. On 28th the discovery met with a nasty accident during a gale; the fore and main tacks carried away, killing one man, and seriously injuring the boatswain and two others. On 25th November the islands were sighted, and the customary orders as to the officers appointed to trade with the natives were issued, and no curiosities were to be purchased before the ships had received satisfactory supplies. They first called in at Mowee, where the natives soon came out and appeared friendly, and traded with less suspicion than any of the South Sea Islanders they had met with before.

Having procured a quantity of sugar-cane, Cook ordered it to be used in brewing, as he found a strong decoction of the juice produced a wholesome and palatable beer, and would enable him to save the spirits for the colder climates. However, the crews would have none of it, so Cook and his officers made use of it whenever cane was procurable, and gave himself:

"no trouble either to oblige or persuade them to drink it, knowing there was no danger of scurvy so long as we had plenty of other vegetables, but that I might not be disappointed in my views, I gave orders that no grog should be served in either ship." He then goes on to say: "Every innovation whatever, tho' ever so much to their advantage, is sure to meet with the highest disapprobation from seaman. Portable soup and sour kraut were at first both condemned by them as stuff not fit for human beings to eat. Few men have introduced into their ships more novelties in the way of victuals and drink than I have done; indeed, few men have had the same opportunity or been driven to the same necessity. It has, however, in a great measure been owing to such little innovations that I have always kept my people, generally speaking, free from that dreadful distemper, the Scurvy."

This extract shows how bitterly Cook felt the stupid ingratitude of his men for the constant care he took of them, and is one of the very few passages in his Journals in which he speaks in their disfavour. This, curiously, was erased by some unknown hand; King asserts it must have been done by Gore, as he is certain it was not by either Cook or Clerke, who took command after Cook's death.

## FAULTY SAILS

In trying to weather the south-east end of Mowee in heavy weather, the leach ropes of the main topsail and two topgallant sails gave way, and the sails were blown to pieces. Cook says, "neither the cordage, canvas, nor indeed hardly any other stores used in the Navy, are equal in quality to those in general use in the merchant service"; and he relates how such failures have constantly resulted in "infinite trouble, vexation, and loss." He illustrates his complaint by the fact that rigging, blocks, and sails that were purchased with his ship, although they had been fourteen months in use, wore longer than any of the things of the same kind put on board new from the king's stores.

On 24th December they succeeded in getting to windward of the island, but the signal to the Discovery to tack having been omitted she stood on, and it was some days before she rejoined company. January 1779 was ushered in with heavy rain, but clearing away before noon they were able to approach to about five miles from the shore, where they lay to and traded with the natives. The next three days were spent working slowly down the coast and keeping a good look-out for their consort, occasionally stopping to do a little trading with the islanders, some of whom came as much as fifteen miles out to them. The chief article of commerce was salt, which was of very good quality. On the 5th January the southern point of Owhyhee was rounded, and they lay off a large village, where they were quickly surrounded by canoes laden "with hogs and women": the latter are not held up as patterns of all the virtues. Vegetables seemed to be scarce, and Cook concluded that either the land could not produce them, or the crops had been destroyed by volcanic action, very recent traces of which were to be seen.

"Wednesday 6th January 1779. The next morning the people visited us again, bringing with them the same articles as before. Being near the shore I sent Mr. Bligh, the Master, in a boat to sound the coast, with orders to land and look for fresh water. On his return he reported that at two cable lengths from the shore he had no soundings with a 160 fathoms of line; that when he landed he found no fresh water, but rain water lying in holes in the rocks, and that brackish with the spray of the sea, and that the surface of the country was wholly composed of large slags and ashes, here and there partly covered with plants. Between 10 and 11 o'clock we saw the Discovery coming round the south point of the Island and at 1 P.M. she joined us, when Captain Clerke came on board and informed me that he had cruised four or five days where we were separated and then plyed round the last part of the Island, but meeting with unfavourable winds, was carried some distance from the coast. He had one of the islanders on board all the time; it was his own choice, nor did not leave them the first opportunity that offered."

This is the last entry made by Cook in the Journal he was preparing for publication, and is a fair sample of the manner in which the entire Journal was written, and certainly does not justify the sneers that have been uttered about bad grammar and spelling, the double negative notwithstanding. In handwriting, spelling, and grammar he can compare well with his press either in the Navy or civil life; and many of the examples of bad spelling given have been abbreviations common in the Navy, which his critics did not understand.

## KARAKAKOA BAY

On 17th January they anchored in Karakakoa Bay, where large numbers of canoes laden with provisions for sale came out; Cook estimates that at one time there were no less than a thousand round the ship, their occupants entirely unarmed. They soon proved to be adepts at thieving; one man stole the rudder of a boat, so Cook ordered a shot or two to be fired over the escaping thief, but "as it was not intended that any of the shot should take effect, the Indians seemed rather more surprised than frightened," and the man got away. The lids of the Resolution's coppers were stolen, and the discovery had her rigging much cut about for the sake of the iron. The decks were so crowded with the natives that Burney says it kept a quarter of the crew hard at work to make room for the working of the ship.

## AN INSECURE POSITION

The last entry made by Cook in his Ship's Journal, and probably the last words he ever wrote, runs as follows:

"Sunday 17. Fine pleasant weather and variable faint breezes of wind. In the evening Mr. Bligh returned and reported that he had found a bay in which was good anchorage and fresh water, tolerable easy to come at. Into this bay I resolved to go to refit the ships and take in water. As the night approached, the Indians retired to the shore, a good [many] however desired to sleep on board, curiosity was not their only motive, at least not with some of them, for the next morning several things were missing, which determined me not to entertain so many another night. At 11 A.M. anchored in the bay which is called by the natives [a blank, filled in by another hand, Karakakoa] in 13 fathoms of water over a sandy bottom, and a quarter of a mile from the North-East shore. In this situation the South point of the bay bore South 1/4 West, and the North point West 1/4 South. Moored with the stream anchor to the Northward. Unbent the sails and struck yards and topmasts. The ships very much crowded with Indians and surrounded by a multitude of canoes. I have nowhere in this sea seen such a number of people assembled at one place, besides those in the canoes, all the shore of the bay was covered with people and hundreds were swimming about the ships like shoals of fish. We should have found it difficult to have kept them in order had not a chief or servant of Terreeoboo's, named Parea, now and then [shown] his authority by turning or rather driving them all out of the ship.

"Among our numerous visitors was a man named Touahah, who we soon found belonged to the church; he introduced himself with much ceremony, in the course of which he presented me with a small pig, two coconuts and a piece of red cloth which he wrapped round me. In this manner all or most of the chiefs introduced themselves, but this man went further, he brought with him a large hog and a quantity of fruits and roots, all of which he included in the present.

In the afternoon I went ashore to view the place accompanied by Touahah, Parea, Mr. King and others; as soon as we landed Touahah took me by the hand and conducted me to a large Morai, the other gentlemen with Parea, and four or five more of the natives followed."

Mr. King describes this Morai as being about forty yards long by twenty broad, and about fourteen feet high, the top flat, well paved, and surrounded by a wooden railing. An old building stood in the centre from which a stone wall ran to the fence dividing the top into two parts. On the landward side were five poles upwards of twenty feet high, supporting an irregular kind of scaffold, and on the seaside half were two small houses with a covered communication between. On their arrival Cook was presented with two ugly images wrapped with red cloth, and a sort of hymn was sung. Then they were marched to the scaffolding, where was a table on which lay fruits and vegetables surmounted by a very much decomposed pig, and in a semicircle round one end of this table were twelve images. Placing Cook near the scaffolding, Koah, as King and others call Touahah, took up the pig and holding it towards him made a long speech. Then, dropping the offensive porker, he made signs that the two were to climb on to the uncertain scaffolding. This being done, a procession came forward bearing a live hog and a piece of red cloth. This last article was handed up to Koah, who proceeded to wrap it round Cook, who was clinging to his elevated but not very safe position. The pig was then offered to Cook and a long address chanted. The two principal performers then descended and returned to the table, Koah snapping his fingers at the figures and making what appeared to be sarcastic remarks, till he came to the centre one, when he prostrated himself and kissed it, requesting Cook to do the same. The party then proceeded to the other part of the Morai, and Cook was seated between two images with his arms stretched out, one upheld by Koah, the other by King. A cooked pig and other food was then presented with much ceremony, the meat cut up and kava prepared; whilst Koah's assistant chewed some coconut, wrapped it in cloth, and then rubbed it over Cook's face, head, shoulders, and arms. Koah and Parea then pulled pieces of the pig and put them into the mouths of the two officers. King says that Parea was a particularly cleanly person, so he did not so much mind this feeding, but Cook, remembering how Koah had handled the putrid hog, was unable to swallow a mouthful, "and his reluctance, as may be supposed, was not diminished, when the old man, according to his own mode of civility, had chewed it for him." Cook then put an end to further proceedings by distributing some presents to the attendants and returning to the ship.

Though the meaning of this ceremony could only be a matter of conjecture, it was very evident that it was intended as a mark of high respect to the person of Captain Cook. The title of Orono given to him, and often quoted as evidence that he had permitted himself to be looked upon as a god by the natives was also given to one, if not more, of their own chiefs; and Burney says that the marks of honour conferred on him were exactly the same as those conferred on any one of their own superior chieftains. The grotesque description given by some of the missionary writers of the whole population crawling after him on hands and knees as a mark of adoration is utterly untrue, for Mr. King, who was ashore almost the whole time of the ship's stay, and was continually with Cook, distinctly says:

"The crowd which had collected on the shore, retired at our approach; and not a person was to be seen, except a few lying prostrate on the ground, near the huts of the adjoining village."

None of those who were on the voyage and have left any record behind them, suggest that Cook was treated in any respect otherwise than as a great chief and a man.

A small potato field was placed under tabu, near the Morai, for the purpose of the observatory, and a camp under the command of King was established there. This camp was daily supplied with meat and vegetables, even more than could be consumed, and several canoe-loads were sent off to the ships. After enquiry it was found that the whole expense of this food was borne by Koah, and no return whatever was demanded.

## A ROYAL VISIT

A tabu was placed on the whole of the bay on the 24th, and trading came to a complete standstill, the reason given being the coming of the king, Terreeoboo. He arrived the next day, and commerce at once revived. He paid a private visit, with his wife and children, to the Resolution, remaining on board some time, and proved to be the same chief they had seen at the Island of Mowee. The next day he, accompanied by several important chiefs, all dressed in rich feather cloaks and armed with long spears and daggers, paid a state visit. Koah was also present in a canoe with other priests and two large basket-work idols, whose distorted faces were adorned with pearl-shell eyes and dog's teeth; he was attended by two other canoes, one filled with pigs and vegetables, and these paddled round the ships, the priests singing "in most solemn fashion," and returned to the shore. Cook followed; King turned out the guard and saluted Terreeoboo, and then conducted him to the tent, where, after seating himself for a few moments, he took off his helmet and cloak and placed them on Cook, at the same time ordering five or six more, of great value, to be placed at his feet. Hogs, bread-fruit, etc., were then brought in. Cook and Terreeoboo exchanged names as a peculiar mark of friendship, and the ceremony ended by the presentation of the two boat-loads of provisions by a deputation of the priests. One of those present was a nephew of the king, called by the English Maiha-Maiha, afterwards known to the world as Kamehameha I.

As many of the chiefs as the Resolution's pinnace would hold were taken off with the king to the ship, and the latter was duly invested with a white linen shirt and Cook's own sword. During the whole of this performance no canoes excepting those actually engaged were to be seen in the bay, and all the natives remained lying on the ground or in their houses. Clerke, who had been too ill to share in these ceremonies, landed for the first time on the 28th, and, though quite unexpected, he received a very handsome present of food, and Terreeoboo paid the Discovery a state call, taking with him presents similar to those given to Cook. In the afternoon he paid a second (private) call in a small canoe with three paddles, one of which he wielded himself. On this occasion there were no prostrations, but if any native met his chief he simply got out of the way unless some service was required of him.

The ships were running very short of firewood, and as there was none growing less than a mile and a half off the sea, Mr. King was ordered to try and purchase the fence surrounding the top of the Morai. He hesitated, as he thought that: "even the bare mention of it might be considered by them [the priests] as a piece of shocking impiety. In this, however, I found myself mistaken. Not the smallest surprise was expressed at the application, and the wood was readily given, even without stipulating for anything in return."

He saw the sailors were carrying away the figures as well, and spoke to Koah on the subject, who raised no objection, except with regard to the centre one, which was at once returned. Burney says that two launch-loads for each ship were obtained, "a seasonable supply, as we had been four months since we wooded."

On 31st January Whatman, one of the gunner's crew, and greatly attached to Cook, died and was buried in the Morai. Besant thinks that this had some influence on the minds of the natives, and may have contributed to Cook's death, but as it was done by Terreeoboo's special request it is difficult to see how the idea can be justified.

## A LARGE PRESENT

Enquiries were several times made as to the date of the departure of the ships, and hints were given that supplies were running short; but at the same time they were informed that if they returned the next bread-fruit season, their wants should be again supplied. When the news went forth that they would leave in two days, Terreeoboo issued a proclamation for food to be brought in so that he might make a large present on their departure; and on the appointed day Cook and King were invited to Terreeoboo's residence, where they found all that had been given in exchange to the natives was laid out on the ground, and a short distance away a large quantity of vegetables of all kinds and a herd of pigs, which were handed over on a return present being made. King says that the gift "far exceeded everything of the kind we had seen." The camp ashore was then broken up, and a great effort was made to persuade Cook to permit Mr. King to remain, as he had succeeded in making himself a great favourite with all. A house that had been used by the sailmakers was accidentally set on fire, Burney says by natives looking for a knife lost by one of the sailors; but Besant, who places the fire at a later period, says it was done intentionally in revenge for the sailors having enticed some of the women there, and infers that Gilbert is his authority, but in the extracts he publishes from Gilbert's manuscript there is nothing of the kind, and no one refers to any other fire till after Cook's death.

# 1779 TO 1780
# THIRD VOYAGE CONCLUDED

On 4th February the ships unmoored and sailed from the bay, steering to the north in hopes of finding a better anchorage. The wind was very light, and the progress was so slow that it gave Terreeoboo an opportunity of sending off a further present of food. Soon after a gale sprang up, and the canoes which had accompanied them beat a hasty retreat, leaving a good many, mostly women, on board the ships. About midnight the fore and main topsails were split, but towards morning the wind died away and they were able to bend fresh sails. A second gale came on again at night, putting them under double-reefed topsails, with topgallant yards sent down, and at daybreak the fore-mast was found to be so badly sprung that it was absolutely necessary it should be unstepped for immediate repairs. After considerable hesitation, for he fully recognised that the place must be almost denuded of surplus provisions, Cook decided to return to Karakakoa Bay as no other convenient place was known, and the ships again anchored there on the 11th, starting immediately to unstep and get the mast ashore, when it was found to be rotten at the heel as well as sprung. Wood that had been cut at Eimeo for anchor stocks was used for fishing the head, and the work proceeded rapidly: the priests making the camp tabu, so that there should be no interference with the workmen.

When the ships arrived in the bay, hardly a canoe was to be seen, and none came out to the ships. This, contrasted with their first reception, was the cause of some surprise, and, in view of what happened afterwards, of some suspicion; but Mr. King, who had more intercourse with the natives than any of the other officers, was thoroughly satisfied that "they neither meant nor apprehended any change of conduct." Burney says that Terreeoboo and some of the chiefs visited them on the 12th, and asked many questions about their return, and did not seem well satisfied with the answers received.

## TROUBLE COMMENCES

Everything went smoothly till the afternoon of the 13th, when the officer in charge of the watering party complained to King that the conduct of some of the natives was suspicious, and some of the chiefs were driving away men he had engaged to help in rolling the casks to the boats. King sent a marine with side arms to help to restore order, but shortly after was informed the natives were arming with stones and getting very noisy, so he went down himself, with a marine armed with his musket, and succeeded in setting matters right. Just at this time Cook came ashore, and King reported what had occurred, receiving orders to fire with ball if he received any insolence or stones were thrown. Soon afterwards shots were heard from the Discovery, and a canoe was seen making for the shore, closely pursued by one of the ship's boats. Cook, King, and a marine ran to intercept them, but were too late, as the occupants of the canoe landed before they could reach the spot. Burney says the disturbance commenced by a native stealing a pair of carpenter's tongs, jumping overboard with them, and placing them in a canoe which at once paddled off. The thief was caught, flogged, and put in irons till the tongs were returned from the shore. The same tongs were again stolen in the afternoon, and the thief got away with them, pursued by Edgar, the Master, in the ship's cutter, and joined by the Resolution's pinnace. The thief reaching shore first, put the tongs, the lid of a harness cask, and a chisel in a second canoe which went out, and handed them over to Edgar. Edgar, seeing Cook and King running along the shore, thought it right to detain the second canoe, which unfortunately belonged to Parea, who at the time of the theft was in Clerke's cabin and, promising to obtain the tongs, had immediately left for the shore. He tried to regain possession of his canoe, but was knocked down by a sailor, and then some of the natives, who before this had been quietly looking on, began to throw stones, and so roughly handled the sailors in the pinnace that, being unarmed, they beat a retreat, swimming to some rocks out of reach of the missiles. Edgar and Vancouver remained ashore and fared badly, till Parea, who had recovered from his blow and apparently forgotten it, ordered his countrymen to stay their hands, and managed to save the pinnace from being broken up. He wanted the boats to go back to the ships, but as the oars had been taken away this was impossible. He then started to find them, and as soon as his back was turned the throwing began again. Edgar wished to go to the camp to find Cook, but some of the natives advised him to follow them and they would take him to Parea. He soon met him carrying one oar, followed by a man with a broken one, so they were able to make shift in the boats to the camp, being overtaken on the way by Parea in his canoe bringing Vancouver's cap, which had been lost in the scuffle.

Owing to his pursuit of the thief Cook did not hear of all this trouble till after dark, too late to take any further steps, but King says he appeared very disturbed by the news, and remarked: "I am afraid these people will oblige me to use some violent measures, for they must not be left to imagine that they have gained an advantage over us." He then went on board his ship and ordered all natives ashore, whilst King returned to the camp, and doubling his sentries, gave orders he was to be called if any natives were seen about. At eleven, five were seen hovering near, but when they found they were observed they made off, and later one got close to the observatory, but ran when the sentry fired over his head. When on his way to the ship the next morning for the chronometer, King was informed that the Discovery's cutter had been stolen; it had been moored to the anchor buoy. On board the Resolution he found Cook busy loading his double-barreled gun and a landing party of marines being prepared. Cook said he was going ashore to try to gain possession of some of the principal chiefs in order to keep them prisoners till the boat was returned, and that he had already sent out boats to prevent any one leaving the bay, with the intention of destroying their canoes if he could not recover the cutter by more peaceable means. The Resolution's great cutter was sent after a large sailing canoe that was making off, the small cutter was guarding the western point of the bay, and Cook, with the pinnace and launch, were going to Kowrowa to try and get Terreeoboo on board the ship. He, and in fact every one else, were confident the natives would offer no resistance if they heard the sound of but one musket.

A little before eight o'clock Captain Cook, Lieutenant Phillips, a sergeant, corporal, and seven marines left the ship for Kowrowa, and King returned to his camp after being ordered to try and assure the natives near the observatory that they would not be hurt, to keep his men together, and to be prepared to meet any outbreak. Having seen his men were on the alert, King visited the priests and satisfied them that Terreeoboo would receive neither injury nor insult.

### COOK LANDS

Having picked up the Resolution's launch, under the command of Lieutenant Williamson, on his way, Cook landed the marines, and marched into the village, where he received the usual marks of respect. He asked to see the king and his two young sons. The two boys came forward and conducted him to the hut where their father was, and after a short conversation he felt assured that Terreeoboo knew nothing about the stealing of the boat. He invited the three to accompany him to the Resolution, and the king at once consented and got up to go. However, the boys' mother came up with a few chiefs and tried to persuade him not to go, and then they caught hold of him and forced him to sit down. Meanwhile a large crowd had gathered round, and Phillips, who seems to have acted with coolness and judgment throughout the affair, drew up his men in line on some rocks near the water, about thirty yards away. After trying for some time to persuade the natives to allow their chief to go with him, Cook gave up the attempt, observing to Phillips that it would be impossible to compel them to do so without great risk of bloodshed. Unfortunately, just at this time news arrived that a chief of the first rank had been killed at the other side of the bay. The shots had been heard soon after the landing of Cook's party.

It was now recognised that matters had become very serious; the natives were seen to be donning their war mats, and one man, armed with a stone in one hand and a large iron spike in the other, threatened Cook in a very insulting manner. He was told to keep quiet, but only became more furious, so Cook fired a charge of small shot into him, but his mats saved him from injury. Stones were thrown at the marines, and a chief attempted to stab Phillips, but was promptly knocked down with the butt of the latter's musket. Cook now fired his second barrel loaded with ball and killed one of the natives, but Sergeant Gibson told him it was the wrong man, so he received orders to kill the right one, and did so. The stone-throwing became heavier, and the marines responded with a volley, but before they had time to reload the natives rushed them, killing four out of the seven and wounding the rest, Phillips being stabbed between the shoulders, but, before the blow could be repeated he managed to shoot his assailant.

## COOK'S DEATH

Cook was now close to the water's edge, and had turned round to order the boats' crews to cease firing and pull in. This is believed to have caused his death, for, whilst he faced the natives, none of them, except the one shot by Gibson, had offered him actual violence, but when he turned to give orders he was struck on the head and stabbed in the back, falling with his face in a pool of water. As soon as he fell a great shout arose; he was dragged ashore, and the natives, snatching the dagger from each other, showed savage eagerness to share in his destruction. Phillips and his wounded marines plunged into the water and, covered by musketry fire, gained the boats; their officer, though wounded, jumping out again to the assistance of the last man who, severely injured by a blow on the face, was in great danger of being captured. The boats, seeing there was no possibility of recovering the bodies of the five who were killed, were ordered to return at once to the ships from which they had only been absent an hour. Nine stand of arms, Cook's double-barreled gun and his hanger fell into the hands of the natives. As soon as this was reported, the boats were recalled from the bay, and a strong reinforcement was sent to Mr. King with orders to strike his camp and get the Resolution's foremast off to the ship. The Indians were seen to be assembling to the right of the tents, so the guns were turned on them, and a party was posted on the Morai to cover the place where the mast lay. About one o'clock everything was got away from the shore, only a few stones being thrown by natives who thought their mats were proof against bullets, and only found out their mistake too late.

Notwithstanding what had occurred, one of the priests, whom Burney calls Kerriakair, remained with the English till everything had been removed, and supplied the men with food and water. King, about four o'clock, was sent to try to recover the bodies of the Captain and marines. He was at first received with a volley of stones, which fortunately fell short; he displayed a white flag and pulled inshore, whilst the remaining boats lay off to cover him with their fire if needed, but the stone-throwing was stopped, and the natives also showed the white flag. In answer to King's demand some of the chiefs promised that the bodies should be delivered the next day, and Koah, swimming off to one of the boats, explained that they could not be given up at once as they had already been taken some distance up country. Burney, however, says that they gathered, from signs made by some other Indians, that the bodies had already been cut to pieces, and one man came down into the water flourishing Cook's hanger "with many tokens of exultation and defiance."

### KOAH FRIENDLY

On the 15th Captain Clerke formally took over the command of the Resolution, and appointed Lieutenant Gore to the Discovery. During the day Koah visited the ship several times, and in vain tried to persuade Clerke or King to go ashore, but it was thought inadvisable to run any further risks. In the evening Kerriakair and a friend came off in a small canoe bringing a bundle containing the flesh of Cook's thighs, saying that the body had been burned and the limbs distributed amongst the chiefs. They had brought all they could get unknown to the others, and Kerriakair strongly advised Clerke not to trust too much to Koah; he said that the inhabitants of the island were not inclined for peace except those in the immediate neighbourhood, who would of course, in case of hostilities, be the chief sufferers. He gave the number of natives killed as twenty-six, with a large number of wounded.

On the 17th the ships were warped inshore so as to command the watering place, the launches were sent in for water, with the other boats fully armed, in support. They were received with showers of stones from the houses, and from behind stone walls, notwithstanding guns fired from the ships and musketry from the boats at any of the natives who exposed themselves. Meanwhile Koah again visited the ships, offering a pig as a present, and asking for someone to be sent ashore for the bodies; but he was sent away, and was soon afterwards seen amongst the stone-throwers. In the afternoon the boats went again for water, but as the natives recommenced hostilities they were ordered to keep clear, whilst the ships' guns were worked for a quarter of an hour; then the boats' crews landed and burned all the houses between the watering place and the Morai, killing some six or seven of the natives. In the evening, about five o'clock, some dozen natives bearing white flags and sugar-cane marched down to the beach headed by Kerriakair carrying a small pig. He said he came as an envoy from Terreeoboo to make peace, and was accordingly taken on board the Resolution. It was ascertained from him that the boat had been stolen by some of Parea's people and had been broken up after Cook's death. During the night some canoes came out and did a little trading; and the next morning the bay was seen to be planted with white flags in different directions, and the waterers were allowed to work unmolested, whilst Kerriakair asked permission, at once granted, to make an offering to one of the images on the Morai. Soon after Koah came off with a pig, but was not admitted to either ship; he then went off to the waterers, who sent him away. So he amused himself by throwing stones at a small party of sailors on the Morai, and drew a couple of shots from them, but escaped unhurt. Soon after a party of natives marched down to the beach with bread-fruit, etc., which they left on the beach and was afterwards taken on board. A chief, Eapoo, carried a message on board from Terreeoboo, and next day brought presents of food. On the 20th the foremast of the Resolution was stepped and rigging commenced, and in the middle of the day a large body of natives marched in procession to the watering place, beating drums, yelling, carrying white flags, sugar-cane, etc., with Eapoo at their head bearing a parcel wrapped in cloth containing some of Cook's bones. He went off to the Resolution with Clerke, and soon after a boat was sent ashore for a present of food from Terreeoboo. The next day, with the same ceremonial, Eapoo again appeared with all the remaining bones it was possible to recover, and was this time accompanied by Karowa, Terreeoboo's youngest son.

"The 21st February. At sunset the Resolution fired ten minute guns, with the colours half staff up, when the remains of our late Commander were committed to the deep."

Lieutenant Williamson was severely blamed by his brother officers for not going to the assistance of the pinnace at the time of the attack on his Captain, and it is said that had it not been for Clerke's ill health he would have been tried by court-martial. He was afterwards, when in command of the Agincourt, tried for "disaffection, cowardice, disobedience to signals, and not having done his duty in rendering all assistance possible." He was found guilty on the last two counts only, and was "placed at the bottom of the list of Post-Captains, and rendered incapable of ever serving on board of any of His Majesty's ships."

## COOK'S REMAINS

Ellis, in his Tour through Hawaii, says that King's account of Cook's death, from which the above has been largely drawn, agrees in a remarkable manner with that given by the natives. They in no way blamed their visitors for what occurred, and even after his death appear to have looked upon Cook as a man of a superior race to themselves. His breastbone and ribs were long preserved as relics, and in 1832 Ellis states there were many living who remembered the occasion, and all agreed that Cook's conduct to their countrymen was humane.

Captain Clerke says:

"Upon examining the remains of my late honoured and much lamented friend, I found all his bones, excepting those of the back, jaw, and feet — the two latter articles Earpo brought me in the morning —

the former, he declared, had been reduced to ashes with the trunk of the body. As Carnacare (Kerriakair) had told us, the flesh was taken from all the bones, excepting those of the hands, the skin of which they had cut through in many places, and salted, with the intention, no doubt, of preserving them; Earpo likewise brought with him the two barrels of Captain Cook's gun — the one beat flat with the intention of making a cutting instrument of it; the other a good deal bent and bruised, together with a present of thirteen hogs from Terreaboo."

The hands, as has been mentioned before, were identified by the scar left by the explosion of his powder flask in Newfoundland, which almost severed the thumb from the fingers.

On 22nd February they were able to sail from this unlucky place, and touching at one or two of the islands worked their way northwards to Kamtschatka, the Resolution reaching Owatska Bay on 29th April, followed by the discovery on 1st May. They were very handsomely treated by Major Behm, the Governor of Bolcheretsk, a place about 135 miles from the town of St. Peter and St. Paul in Awatska Bay, notwithstanding Mr. Ismailoff's letters of introduction were on somewhat unsatisfactory lines. Mr. Webber was fortunately able to converse in German, which the Russian officers understood; and he ascertained that Ismailoff had represented the two vessels as very small, and hinted that he believed them to be little better than pirates. The Governor provided the ships with what he could give them, and promised to obtain further stores from Okotsk for them against their return. For these kindnesses the English could make but little return, and even then it was with difficulty that the Russians could be persuaded to receive anything, for they said they were only acting up to the wishes of their Empress, who desired all her allies should be treated with courtesy. One return, however, they were able to make which was of great service. At the time of the visit of the ships a large number of the soldiers and inhabitants were suffering very seriously from scurvy, and Clerke at once put them under the care of his medical officers, who, by the use of sour kraut and sweet wort made from the ship's stock of malt, soon caused "a surprising alteration in the figures of most of them and their speedy recovery was chiefly attributed to the effects of the sweet wort."

They were informed by the Major that on the day of the arrival of the English party at Bolcheretsk he had received a letter from the most northerly outpost on the Sea of Okotsk, stating that the tribe of Tschutski, which had been long at feud with the Russians, had sent in an embassy offering friendship and tribute, giving as a reason that they had been visited by two large vessels in the preceding summer, and had been received on board with great kindness, and had entered into a league of friendship with their visitors: they therefore thought it their duty to ratify this treaty formally. These two ships could have been none other than the Resolution and Discovery, though evidently the Tschutski thought they were Russian.

## DEATH OF CLERKE

Leaving on 13th June, the Asiatic coast was followed up, and 1st July they were off the Gulf of Anadyr, where fogs and ice began seriously to interfere with their progress, so they abandoned the Asiatic for the American side, but with no better luck. They reached the latitude of 70 degrees 33 minutes North, about five leagues short of the point reached the previous year, and at length, realising further efforts were useless and resulting in serious damage to the ships from continual contact with the loose ice, Clerke determined to return to Awatska Bay and refit and then return to England. On 22nd August, the day before they reached the Bay, Captain Clerke, who had long been suffering from serious ill health, died, and was buried under a tree a little to the north of the post of St. Peter and St. Paul; the crews of both ships and the Russian garrison taking part in the funeral ceremony, and the Russian priest reading the service at the grave. Clerke had been all three voyages with Cook, and was only thirty-eight years of age.

Gore now took command of the Resolution, Burney, Rickman, and Lanyon being his lieutenants, whilst King was the new Captain of the Discovery, and Williamson and Hervey his lieutenants; Bayley going with Gore in charge of the astronomical observations. On 9th October they left Awatska and were off Cape Nambu, Japan, on the 26th, but were driven off the coast by bad weather, and anchored in Macao Roads on 1st December. Here, after considerable delay, stores were obtained from Canton, and the seaman managed to dispose of most of the furs they had obtained in the north. King estimates that the two ships received, in money and goods, as much as 2000 pounds for the skins, and says that the men were so anxious to return for more that they were almost in a state of mutiny.

On 11th April the ships reached the Cape, where the officers were cordially received by Governor Plattenberg, who expressed the deepest regret to hear of the loss of Cook, and requested that he should be sent a portrait of the Captain to place in a blank space he pointed out between two portraits of De Ruyter and Van Tromp—a gracious compliment. Sailing from Simon's Bay on 9th May, the trades were picked up on the 14th, and on 13th June the line was crossed in longitude 26 degrees 16 minutes West. The coast of Ireland was sighted on 12th August, and an attempt was made to get into Galway Bay, but strong southerly winds drove them to the north, and at length, rounding the north of Scotland, they put into Stromness, whence Captain King was despatched overland to the Admiralty. The ships arrived off the Nore on 4th October, after an absence of "four years, two months, and twenty-two days."

## KING MEETS KING

On 14th February 1781, the second anniversary of Cook's death, King, accompanied by Mr. Banks, was presented to His Majesty, who was pleased to accept the Journals of the Resolution and Discovery kept during this eventful voyage.

# APPRECIATION AND CHARACTER

Of course as nothing had been heard of the expedition for a considerable time, a certain amount of anxiety was felt, which at length found vent in paragraphs in the public press, and on 11th January 1780 the London Gazette contained the following:

"Captain Clerke of His Majesty's Sloop the Resolution, in a letter to Mr. Stephens, dated the 8th of June 1779, in the harbour of St. Peter and St. Paul, Kampschatka, which was received yesterday, gives the melancholy account of the celebrated Captain Cook, late Commander of that Sloop, with four of his private Marines having been killed on the 14th of February last at the island of Owhyhe, one of a Group of new-discovered Islands in the 22nd degree of North Latitude, in an affray with a numerous and tumultuous Body of the Natives."

"Captain Clerke adds, that he received every friendly supply from the Russian Government; and that as the Companies of the Resolution and her Consort, the Discovery, were in perfect Health, and the two Sloops had twelve months Stores and Provisions on board, he was preparing to make another Attempt to explore a Northern Passage to Europe."

## THE EMPRESS OF RUSSIA

The London Gazette of 8th February says:
"The Empress of Russia expressed a most deep concern at the Loss of Captain Cook. She was the more sensibly affected from her very partial regard to his merits; and when she was informed of the hospitality shown by the Russian Government at Kamschatka to Captain Clerke, she said no Subject in her Dominions could show too much Friendship to the Survivors of Captain Cook."

The letter written by Clerke was sent by express through Petersburg; that is to say, it was written in the extreme east of Asia in June, and was sent overland across Siberia to Petersburg, and thence via Berlin to London, and was there published in under the six months. A wonderful journey when the difficulties of transit are taken into consideration.

In the numerous appreciative notices that appeared in the press relating to Cook and his work, the Morning Chronicle alone strikes a jarring string, which is at once met by a reply; and a day or two after the same paper publishes a long letter signed Colombus (the style suggests the pen of Sir Joseph Banks) in which the character and methods of Cook are most strenuously defended, the writer claiming to have obtained his knowledge of the man "through long intercourse with him."

The Gazetter of 24th January says: "His Majesty, who had always the highest opinion of Captain Cook, shed tears when Lord Sandwich informed him of his death, and immediately ordered a pension of 300 pounds a year for his widow."

The amount really granted to Mrs. Cook was 200 pounds per annum, and the Admiralty in addition gave her half the proceeds of the Journal of the Third Voyage, a share in the Journal of the Second Voyage, and a share of the plates used in illustrating the two publications: a very considerable addition to her income. A Coat of Arms was also granted to the family by order of the King, and Sir W. Besant records his belief that it was the last one ever granted as a direct "recognition of Service." His description of it is:

"Azure, between the two polar stars Or, a sphere on the plane of the meridian, showing the Pacific Ocean, his track thereon marked by red lines. And for a crest, on a wreath of the colours, is an arm bowed, in the uniform of a Captain of the Royal Navy. In the hand is the Union Jack on a staff proper. The arm is encircled by a wreath of palm and laurel. A very noble shield indeed."

The notes of appreciation of his talents and services came from all parts of the world, and none more kindly than from the series of brilliant Frenchmen who followed in his footsteps. De Crozet did not hesitate to throw away his own charts when he recognised the superiority of Cook's; and Dumont d'Urville calls him "the most illustrious navigator of both the past and future ages whose name will for ever remain at the head of the list of sailors of all nations."

### MRS. COOK'S LETTER

The Royal Society was naturally amongst the first to recognise the great worth of its late Fellow, and the loss the Society had suffered from his death. It had already granted him one of its highest honours in the form of the Copley Gold Medal for his successful contest with the scurvy, and it now decided to mark its appreciation by striking a special gold medal in his honour. This was forwarded by Sir Joseph Banks, President of the Royal Society, to Mrs. Cook, and acknowledged by her in the following touching letter:

Mile End,
16th August 1784.
Sir,
I received your exceeding kind letter of the 12th instant, and want words to express in any adequate degree my feelings on the very singular honour which you, Sir, and the honourable and learned Society over which you so worthily preside, have been pleased to confer on my late husband, and through him on me and his children who are left to lament the loss of him, and to be the receivers of those most noble marks of approbations which, if Providence had been pleased to permit him to receive, would have rendered me very happy indeed.

Be assured, Sir, that however unequal I may be to the task of expressing it, I feel as I ought the high honour which the Royal Society has been pleased to do me. My greatest pleasure now remaining is in my sons, who, I hope, will ever strive to copy after so good an example, and, animated by the honours bestowed on their Father's memory, be ambitious of attaining by their own merits your notice and approbation. Let me entreat you to add to the many acts of friendship which I have already received at your hands, that of expressing my gratitude and thanks to that learned body in such a manner as may be acceptable to them.

I am, Sir, etc., etc.,
Elizabeth Cook.

The medal actually presented to Mrs. Cook is now in the British Museum.

## DEATHS OF THE SONS

It is greatly to be regretted that so little can be ascertained about Cook's private life that would be of service in forming an intimate knowledge of his character, but this is accounted for by the fact that after he had joined the Navy his time was so fully occupied by that service that he had but little opportunity to form private friendships such as fall to the lot of most men. The intimacies that he did form were mostly connected very closely with his naval duties, and his opportunities of correspondence were necessarily limited by absence from all ordinary means of communication. For a man of his marked celebrity it is very curious that there should be such a dearth of anecdote that it is difficult to find anything that is unconnected with his profession. Of his own family relations there is also little known, as Mrs. Cook, probably esteeming the few letters she had from him as too sacred to be seen by any other eye than her own, as the late

Canon Bennett suggests, destroyed them before her death. Still some idea of their life together, short as it really was, notwithstanding it lasted, in name, for over sixteen years, may be gained from the manner in which his widow always spoke of him after his death. She always wore a ring containing a lock of his hair, and measured everything by his standard of morality and honour. The greatest disapprobation she could express was "Mr. Cook would never have done so." He was always Mr. Cook to her. She kept four days each year as solemn fasts, remaining in her own room. The days were those on which she lost her husband and three sons, passing them in reading her husband's Bible, prayer and meditation, and during bad weather she could not sleep for thinking of those at sea. For her husband's sake she befriended her nephews and nieces whom she never saw. Of her three sons, two entered the Navy. One, Nathaniel, was lost with his ship, the Thunderer, in a hurricane off Jamaica in 1780. The eldest, James, rose to the rank of Commander, and in January 1794 was appointed to H.M. sloop Spitfire. He was at Poole when he received his orders to join his ship at Portsmouth without delay. Finding an open boat with sailors returning from leave about to start, he joined them. It was blowing rather hard, and nothing was ever heard of the passengers or crew, except that the broken boat and the dead body of the unfortunate young officer, stripped of all money and valuables, with a wound in the head, was found ashore on the Isle of Wight. The third son, Hugh, was entered at Christ's College, Cambridge, in 1793, but contracting scarlet fever he died on 21st December of that year, and was buried in the church of St. Andrew the Great, being joined by his brother James a few weeks afterwards, when the mother was left indeed alone. She survived her husband for the long period of fifty-six years, living at Clapham with her cousin, Admiral Isaac Smith, and at length joined her two sons at Cambridge at the advanced age of ninety-three.

Cook's character as given by those with whom he worked, men who day after day were by his side, was a fine one. His greatest fault seems to have been his hasty temper, which he admitted himself, often most regretfully; but Captain King says it was "disarmed by a disposition the most benevolent and humane," and it never was displayed in such a manner as to cause the loss of respect and affection of his people. He was healthy and vigorous in mind and body, clearheaded and cool in times of danger, broad minded and temperate, and plain and unaffected in manner. His powers of observation were of the first rank, his knowledge of Naval mathematics far surpassed the ordinary level and amounted to genius, but, above all, his devotion to duty was the commanding feature of his character. Nothing was allowed to interfere when he saw his course before him; personal convenience was not allowed to weigh for one moment, but at the same time he never lost sight of the interests of those under him and spared them when possible. He was somewhat silent and reserved in manner, but when questioned on any subject on which he felt he was an authority, his answers were clearly and distinctly given, and his reasons disclosed his powers of observation to the full. He was kindly, generous, and hospitable, and by no means the stern character that has been painted, for even in such a matter-of-fact document as his official Journal, a spirit of fun occasionally gleams out.

Such was the man whose name will ever stand in the very first ranks of the British Empire Builders; honest, kindly, generous, a faithful servant and a noble leader.

www.ingramcontent.com/pod-product-compliance
Lightning Source LLC
Chambersburg PA
CBHW021353300426
44114CB00012B/1209